Lyndon Johnson's War

It hardly seems possible that in a week the Johnson years will be over. I cannot help but think as the end draws near that he was in office at what must have been the most turbulent conjunction of elemental forces since the collisions of the 1850's. How do you judge a President's performance when you cannot begin to understand the currents of change and upheaval that engulfed his era? He tried to act as he thought the crises demanded, at a time when no one really knew what the crises were. Perhaps in time it will be said that a lesser, simpler man might have been crushed in the awful sweep of things we have experienced in the last five years. His would have been perplexing years even in a halcyon era, for as Creon said in Oedipus, 'Natures such as this chiefly torment themselves.'

Personal letter from Bill Moyers to Harry McPherson, January 1969

Lyndon Johnson's War

The Road to Stalemate in Vietnam

LARRY BERMAN

W • W • NORTON & COMPANY • NEW YORK • LONDON

Burgess
DS
558
.B465
1989

The text of this book is composed in Gael with display type set in Craw Modern.
Composition and manufacturing by The Haddon Craftsmen, Inc.

Library of Congress Cataloging-in-Publication Data

Berman, Larry.
  Lyndon Johnson's war: the road to stalemate in Vietnam/Larry Berman.
  p. cm.
  Includes index.
  1. Vietnamese Conflict, 1961–1975—United States. 2. United
States—Politics and government—1963–1969. 3. Johnson, Lyndon B.
(Lyndon Baines), 1908–1973. I. Title.
DS558.B465 1989
959.704'33'73—dc19   88-25360

ISBN 0-393-02636-1

W. W. Norton & Company, Inc. 500 Fifth Avenue, New York, N.Y. 10110
W. W. Norton & Company Ltd., 37 Great Russell Street, London WC1B 3NU

1 2 3 4 5 6 7 8 9 0

For the Vietnam Generation

Contents

VI

VII

VIII

IX

X

Preface

"This is not Johnson's war. This is America's war. If I drop dead tomorrow, this war will still be with you," Lyndon Johnson bellowed to journalist Chalmers Roberts from the White House Oval Office on October 13, 1967. But LBJ was wrong, and as it became evident that the war had become a sinkhole, the more Vietnam became Johnson's war. Three weeks later LBJ confided to his principal advisors, "I am like the steering wheel of a car without any control."[1]

Lyndon Johnson's War focuses on the repercussions from President Johnson's failure to address the fundamental incompatibility between his political objectives at home and his military objectives in Vietnam. A Rip van Winkle who had gone to sleep in November 1963, when Johnson had taken over the presidency, and awoke in March 1968, when he announced he would not seek a second term, would look with bewilderment at the paths chosen by such an experienced political man as Lyndon Johnson. In retrospect, Lyndon Johnson's political decisions were poorly conceived, frequently contradictory, and ultimately self-defeating.

In a previous volume, *Planning a Tragedy,* I focused on Lyndon Johnson's decision of July 1965 that Americanized the war. Johnson had believed that losing Vietnam in the summer of 1965 would have wrecked his plans for a Great Society. The president then had used his legislative talents to forge a marginal political and military consensus; in order to avoid a divisive national debate on the American commitment to Vietnam, the president had decided not to mobilize the Reserves, not to request a general tax increase for 1966, and not to publicize the anticipated manpower needs that would be necessary to accomplish U.S. objectives in Vietnam. This guns-and-butter decision, which simultaneously armed soldiers for Vietnam and provided U.S. citizens with the Great Society programs, was tantamount to slow political suicide.

By October 1967, Lyndon Johnson was fighting for his political life: proposing and lobbying for a tax increase to fight a war in Southeast Asia and to send children to school in America. On November 18, 1967, the president privately warned congressional leaders, "If we don't act soon, we will wreck the Republic." This bankruptcy in political credibility was evident in Johnson's personal anguish during the riots that ravaged American cities in the summer of 1967. When he learned that federal troops were to be issued live ammunition in an effort to restore order in Detroit, the president lamented, "I am concerned about the charge that we cannot kill enough people in Vietnam, so we go out and shoot civilians in Detroit."[2]

This book reveals how the president and his principal advisors faced the failure of their military policy in Vietnam. The promised "light at the end of the tunnel" in Vietnam—the point at which North Vietnam would seek peace negotiations—was to be achieved primarily by winning a war of attrition by inflicting losses on the enemy forces at a rate that exceeded their ability to recruit additional forces. Johnson and his advisors expected the enemy to seek negotiations when this crossover point was reached. The Johnson administration became fixated on statistically demonstrating to the press and public progress in a war with an uncertain finish line. Kill-ratios, body counts, defectors, order of battle, weapons-loss ratios, bombing, pacification, died-of-wounds, and population-control data were measured, averaged, and manipulated, allowing the United States government to maintain publicly that the war was being won.

Attrition is often referred to as "the American way of war" because it relies on our superior technology. But it did not account for the extraordinary price North Vietnam was willing to pay. No one in

Johnson's administration really knew when the breaking point in the enemy's will to fight would be reached or how much punishment the Communists would accept before they sought negotiations. By mid-1967 Lyndon Johnson's worst fears were realized when the press raised for public debate the possibility that the war had become a stalemate. If *progress* in Vietnam had meant winning, *stalemate* was the equivalent of losing. The fragile political consensus for building a Great Society at home and defending freedom in Vietnam collapsed under the strains of Lyndon Johnson's credibility gap. As the war became stalemated, the president lost support from both hawks and doves who saw no benefit in the president's policy. A majority of Americans no longer trusted their president.

An important caveat on the nature of primary source materials from the presidential archives. The historical record on Vietnam can seem as bewildering and contradictory as the war itself had been. The documents often contradict the recollections of principal foreign policy advisors who have become quite adept at inventing a history that never was or giving interviews that are of considerably less value than the recollections of amnesia victims.

Nine years after his oral-history interview for the Johnson Library, former presidential assistant William Blackburn attached the following postscript to his original interview: "I unfortunately display a rather cavalier attitude toward our involvement, and while I think that that is more superficial than my views at the time, I must admit to having formed that attitude while working in the highly, and obviously biased, atmosphere of the White House. During the following decade, I have been influenced by discussions, pro and con, over our involvement in Viet Nam, and by the revelation of facts unknown to me, and to most of my associates at the White House, during the period of 1967 and 1968. . . . Unquestionably, one of the aspects of this 'Greek tragedy' was the assumption that our people, our political climate, and our economy could sustain both a full commitment in Viet Nam and the unparalleled commitment to social problems proposed by the Johnson Administration. These difficulties, combined with the moral questions raised by the many citizens who were concerned over the war, especially by a new breed of young people with whom we in the Administration had no dialogue, inevitably led to dis-illusionment and discord."

The recently declassified primary-source materials researched in *Lyndon Johnson's War* include presidential staff assistant and deputy press secretary Tom Johnson's notes from the regular Tuesday luncheons of the principal advisors, as well as other foreign-policy meetings; the weekly cables of Ambassador Ellsworth Bunker to the president; General William Westmoreland's private command history notes; intelligence data declassified in conjunction with the CBS-Westmoreland libel trial; and materials from the Lyndon Baines Johnson Library, which include National Security Council histories, the Vietnam country file, meeting notes, and memos to the president. As a consequence of this rich reservoir of material, I have reprinted, whenever possible, *the world as seen by those who shaped policy between 1967 and 1968.* Readers will find exact quotes (grammatical and spelling errors included) from recently declassified files because I believe that the contradictions in logical thinking made by those in leadership positions ought to be digested without an intermediary. I give you their ink from this watershed period and leave the gift of revisionism to those who shape history.

Acknowledgements

In the span of five years I have incurred many debts which I now acknowledge with gratitude.

At the University of California–Davis I benefitted from the work of several undergraduate research assistants—Dana Callihan, Arthur Combs, Susan Fanelli, Paul Fife, Scott Hill, William Lewis, Liang Tan, Laura Weir, and Diane Yapundich. During the final weeks of the project Stephen McHugh energetically tracked down missing footnotes as well as missing pieces of history. Two graduate-student research assistants provided indispensable service. Paul Hahn organized my CBS-Westmoreland archive and Linda Norman distilled over one hundred oral-history interviews.

Two colleagues at Davis, John Freeman and Bruce Jentleson, endured my queries for clarifying the historical record. Alan Olmstead, director of the Institute of Governmental Affairs, committed his resources and friendship to the project. M. A. Farber, who covered the

CBS-Westmoreland trial for the *New York Times,* helped clarify the issues relating to order of battle.

At the Lyndon Baines Johnson Library I was assisted by archivist David Humphrey who helped navigate me through the documents. I also want to thank Claudia Anderson, Mike Gillette, Ted Gittinger, Linda Hanson, Tina Lawson, Director Harry Middleton, E. Philip Scott, Nancy Smith, Bob Tissing, and Frank Wolfe of the Lyndon Baines Johnson Library. I received generous support from the Guggenheim Foundation, the American Council of Learned Societies, and a travel grant from the Lyndon Baines Johnson Foundation.

My publisher, Donald Lamm, president of W. W. Norton has been a model for what any author might need of a publisher. His reading and detailed comments of the draft provided a cogent perspective. Questions of style and clarification of substance were resolved by Margie Brassil's skillful copyediting.

In preparation of the manuscript I was assisted by a staff at Davis that included Micki Eagle, Pat Johnson, Kathi Miller, and Brenda Peterson. I especially want to thank Eunice Carlson for typing several iterations of the manuscript. Linda Potoski and Pat Richell then completed the task.

Several friends who served in Vietnam, Donald Beeler, Michael Handley, Gary Loveridge, Pete Klemik, and Phil Carmona took time to remind me that Vietnam had been more than the decisions made in Washington. I also want to thank the many Vietnamese students at Davis who have spoken with me about my work and their lives. Most of these young people were forced to flee Saigon in 1975, and they have asked me the hardest questions about the war and our country's commitment. Most were born after the Tet offensive of 1968, after Lyndon Johnson's war.

Thanks also to the Schilling family for making Osprey Cove, their Pacific Coast home, available to me. The extraordinary view and environs rejuvenated, indeed inspired, this weary author.

My family, Janet, Scott, and Lindsay were of great help in providing the proper perspective and diversions. As always I drew strength from their support and encouragement.

This book is dedicated to the generation of young people whose lives were touched by Vietnam.

Abbreviations and Acronyms

ARVN	Army of the Republic of Vietnam
CIA	Central Intelligence Agency
CINCPAC	Commander-in-Chief, Pacific Command
COMUSMACV	Commander, U.S. Military Assistance Command, Vietnam
CORDS	Civil Operations and Revolutionary Development Support
CTZ	Corps Tactical Zone
DOD	Department of Defense
DMZ	Demilitarized Zone
DRV	Democratic Republic of Vietnam
FWMAF	Free World Military Assistance Forces
GVN	Government of Vietnam
HES	Hamlet Evaluation System
ISA	International Security Affairs (DOD)

JCS	Joint Chiefs of Staff
JCSM	Joint Chiefs of Staff Memorandum
MAAG	Military Assistance Advisory Group
MACV	Military Assistance Command, Vietnam
NSAM	National Security Action Memorandum
NSC	National Security Council
NVA	North Vietnamese Army
OB	Order of Battle
OSA	Office of Systems Analysis
PAVN	Peoples Army of Vietnam
PF	Popular Forces
PROVN	Program for the Pacification and Long-term Development of South Vietnam
ROK	Republic of Korea
RVN	Republic of Vietnam
RVNAF	Republic of Vietnam Armed Forces
SEATO	Southeast Asia Treaty Organization
USIA	United States Information Agency
VC	Viet Cong
VCI	Viet Cong Infrastructure

Lyndon Johnson's War

I

Introduction: Vietnam Vogue vs. Vietnam as History

In early February 1966, the U.S. ambassador to Vietnam, Henry Cabot Lodge, cabled President Johnson with an historical analogy that could be used for justifying American involvement in Vietnam. When asked in the House of Commons in 1805 what had been gained in the war against France, the British statesman William Pitt answered, "We have gained everything that we would have lost if we had not fought this war." Ambassador Lodge believed that this analogy "is even truer in our war in Vietnam than it was of the British war against France."[1]

President Johnson and his inner circle of foreign-policy advisors believed that the central achievement of U.S. policy between 1965 and 1967 had been the defeat that had been prevented by Americanizing the war in July 1965. "The fact that South Vietnam has not been lost and is not going to be lost is a fact of truly massive importance in the history of Asia, the Pacific, and the US," wrote the former special assistant for national security and then-president of the Ford

3

Foundation, McGeorge Bundy, to the nation's Commander in Chief in May 1967.[2]

But in 1975 South Vietnam was lost and the bitter aftermath of the war left Americans searching for the whys of initial involvement and ultimate defeat. The first books on the subject were written by participants and were personal accounts of the effects of war. The principals in the decision process often sought penance by rationalizing their roles for future history, while others refused to talk at all about their participation in the war councils. Answers to most important questions bearing on the war remained sealed in the vaults of archival repositories.

Today, a new Vietnam scholarship has emerged alongside a national willingness to understand the war as history. This willingness is symbolized by the over 143 privately financed memorials that have been built or are under construction in 45 states and by the thousands of people who daily visit the Vietnam War Memorial in Washington, D.C. Once referred to as "Jane Fonda's ditch" or "a one-ton condolence card," the Vietnam War Memorial is now the second-most popular tourist attraction in the capital after the Smithsonian Air and Space Museum. Many visit for personal reasons—to touch one of the over 58,000 names or to leave a memento—but no visitor can escape the sense of despair, contradiction, and senselessness of the Vietnam conflict that is captured by the black granite wall built below ground level.

The public's interest in "Vietnam Vogue" is evidenced by the popularity of the films *Platoon, Full Metal Jacket, Hamburger Hill,* and *Hanoi Hilton.* CBS television's "Tour of Duty" brought the war back into prime time as did HBO's 90-minute trilogy "Vietnam War Story." CBS Video Library marketed *The Vietnam War* with Walter Cronkite, with the slogan, "Vietnam. You Have to See it to Understand it." Subscribers were offered *The Tet Offensive* at the introductory price of $4.95. Time-Life Books's multi-volume series *The Vietnam Experience* was marketed for the general public in 1986 with the sales pitch, "Only now can we begin to understand the historical perspective and answers to the questions America has been asking for years."

Yet, ironies from the real war remain unresolved. Those who had served their country did not return to parades or national acclaim. Their reception reflected America's attempt to cast aside, to separate itself from the ugly war. Vietnam veterans were initially stereotyped as societal outcasts. Suicide statistics later confirmed the effects of such unsupportive, even hostile treatment: Suicide rates for army combat veterans of the Vietnam conflict were 72 percent higher within five years of returning to civilian life than of those who served elsewhere during the same period.[3]

The stigma of Vietnam was later passed from one generation to the next in the cruelest irony of Vietnam service. Agent Orange, the herbicide containing dioxin and sprayed in Vietnam to defoliate the jungles, poisoned not only veterans, but their innocent and unborn children, many of whom were born with birth defects attributed to dioxin. "We will always live with what we killed in Vietnam," as one veteran lamented. In September 1987, Federal scientists would not proceed with a congressionally mandated study on the effects of Agent Orange because not enough contaminated soldiers could be identified. When Veterans Administration scientists later released a study of 50,000 Vietnam-era veterans showing excessive rates of death due to lung cancer and non-Hodgkins lymphoma, the senior analyst in the Office of Science and Technology called it "a statistical fluke."[4]

The war as today's history offers other paradoxes. Eleven years following the fall of Saigon, Vietnam initiated an aggressive campaign to attract American tourists. For $2,000 a tourist received a twelve-day package tour that used Ho Chi Minh City, once known as Saigon, as its gateway. Excursions included a tour of the American War Crimes Museum in Ho Chi Minh City. Cam Ranh Bay, once the U.S. naval and air base serving as the logistical hub on Vietnam's coast, is today the largest Soviet naval base for deployment of warships outside the Soviet Union.

For the families of individuals still classified as "missing in action," the war might never be over. In August 1987 General John Vessey, Jr., U.S. special envoy on Americans missing in action in Vietnam, traveled to Hanoi in an effort to gain an accounting for more than 1750 Americans still missing since the war. In April 1988, Republican Senator John McCain, who had spent 5½ years as a prisoner of war in Vietnam, introduced congressional legislation calling upon Vietnam and the United States to establish diplomatic "interest sections" in each other's capitals to help resolve outstanding issues between the once warring nations. "Thirteen years after the fall of Saigon, the time has come for increased efforts to resolve the legacies of the Vietnam war," wrote Senator McCain when introducing his legislation.

With respect to the geo-political justifications for U.S. military involvement, few in 1965 could have envisioned that China and Vietnam would later be at war against one another; Pol Pot's Cambodia at war with Vietnam; and China and the United States engaged in cordial relations. The dominoes in Laos and Cambodia fell, but LBJ's prediction that all Southeast Asia—to Singapore and Djkarta—was wrong. Thailand, Burma, Malaysia, Indonesia, India, and Australia did not fall when America pulled out of South Vietnam.

Was the war a noble or an ignoble cause? Did the United States lack only the will to win? Advocates in the verdict of history compare the consequences of the failed military intervention with the human tragedy exemplified by the boat people of Vietnam and the killing fields of Cambodia. In the war as military history, not one of President Johnson's principal advisors now supports the war as it was fought. In retrospect, everyone who participated now knows better.[5] A Vietnam "could-have" school of thought begins with "ifs": If only LBJ had overruled his civilian advisors and acted on the Joint Chiefs' recommendations for unrestricted bombing; if only he had authorized an invasion of North Vietnam; if only he had sanctioned drives into Laos and Cambodia to clean out enemy sanctuaries; if only he had sealed the border between North and South Vietnam; if only he had bombed the dikes and mined the harbors—then the United States could have forced Ho to accept a negotiated settlement. In the words of Air Force General ("Old Ironpants") Curtis LeMay, who in 1968 joined George Wallace's third-party ticket in quest of the presidency, "We are swatting flies when we ought to go after the dunghill."

The failed intervention in Vietnam has created two types of "never-again" schools of thought with respect to interventionism today. A new generation of 18-year-olds (not born when Lyndon Johnson Americanized the war in Vietnam) have been politicized by the psychic humiliation of losing Vietnam into confirmed hawks with respect to foreign policy forays into Grenada or Libya. Conversely, a majority of Americans have consistently opposed U.S. intervention in Central America because they fear another Vietnam-like quagmire. Yet, the bumper-sticker "No Vietnam war in Central America" trivializes the complex issue of hemispheric security. What percentage of Americans could today locate Nicaragua and Vietnam on a blank map of the world?

Vietnam revisionism has frequently sought to shift responsibility for losing the war from those who made policy to those who pointed out the contradictions in policy. Once a favorite ploy of Lyndon Johnson, this tactic of blaming the messenger has proven useful to Johnson's successors as well. On Memorial Day, 1986, President Reagan referred to the brave "boys of Vietnam . . . who fought a terrible and vicious war without enough support from home." This "pass-the-guilt" school of thought is premised on the supposition that while the United States won the military battles, it lost the larger political confrontation in the corridors on Capitol Hill and in the antiwar protests across America. Accuracy in Media (AIM) has produced two shows narrated by Charlton Heston that maintain that television, not inconsistencies or contradictions in policy, turned Americans against the war: "Who betrayed those who died in Vietnam? Was it our media?" For $32.95 a purchaser could get the answer in two videotapes, "Television's Vietnam: The Real Story and the Impact of Media." President Reagan said that "all Americans should see" both films.

Indeed, the 1984 libel trial involving CBS and General William Westmoreland revealed just how unsettled Vietnam, as history, remained. The CBS broadcast "The Uncounted Enemy: A Vietnam Deception" opened with Mike Wallace's statement that "what went wrong in Vietnam is still one of the great questions of our recent American experience. We still don't know all the answers." The CBS broadcast then charged that General Westmoreland, as Commander, U.S. Military Assistance Command, Vietnam (MACV), actually conspired to deceive President Johnson and the public on enemy troop strength. Had the war been rotten enough that intelligence estimates and analyses had been compromised? Had MACV intelligence officers, because of political pressure from Washington, fudged their estimates in order to show progress? And, had they succeeded in shielding data from their Commander in Chief that might have offset the shock of the massive Tet offensive in January 1968? Had General Westmoreland "cooked the books" and engaged in treasonable offenses? If so, responsibility for the failure of Vietnam policy belonged not with Lyndon Johnson but with General Westmoreland.

When CBS failed to issue a retraction of its conspiracy charge, General Westmoreland brought legal action against CBS and the documentary's producers. The case brought virtually all of the surviving principals into a court of law and the power of subpoena forced declassifications of hundreds of previously classified documents bearing on the subject of enemy troop strength and the cable/memo traffic that encompassed it. The courtroom proved a poor place for General Westmoreland to fight his battle with history, but the subpoenas created conditions for accelerating research into Vietnam as history. The trial ended without a verdict. Before dismissing the jury, however, Judge Pierre Leval explained that "Judgments of history are too subtle and too complex to be resolved with the simplicity of a jury's verdict. It may be for the best that the verdict will be left to history."

II

===

Setting the Stage

> If you're in one, stop digging.
>
> Denis Healey, *Law of Holes*

In July 1965 Lyndon Johnson chose to Americanize the war in Vietnam. Faced with the prospects of losing South Vietnam to the Communists, the president announced that U.S. combat strength in Vietnam would immediately be increased from 75,000 to 125,000 and that additional U.S. forces would be sent when requested by field commander General William Westmoreland. The level of forces needed would be achieved through substantial increases in monthly draft calls but Reserve units would not be called into service. "Now," Johnson wrote in his memoirs, "we were committed to major combat in Vietnam. We had determined not to let that country fall under Communist rule as long as we could prevent it."[1]

Just seven months following the July 1965 decision, President Johnson travelled to Honolulu in February 1966 for a first-hand assessment on the war's progress from General William Westmoreland and to secure commitments for political reform from South Vietnam's prime minister Nguyen Cao Ky. Johnson was accompanied by Secretary of State Dean Rusk, Secretary of Defense Robert McNamara, Chairman of the Joint Chiefs of Staff General Earle Wheeler, Special

9

Assistant for National Security McGeorge Bundy, Secretary of Health, Education and Welfare John Gardner, and Secretary of Agriculture Orville Freeman. In Honolulu they were met by a 28-member South Vietnamese delegation headed by Ky and Chief of State Nguyen Van Thieu. Also waiting in Honolulu were General Westmoreland and Pacific Commander Admiral Ullysses S. Grant Sharp, Jr.

The visit to Honolulu was Johnson's first trip outside the North American continent since becoming president. The decision was made hastily and for political reasons—Senator J. William Fulbright, Democratic senator from Arkansas and chairman of the Senate Foreign Relations Committee, had scheduled televised committee hearings on the war. Johnson outfoxed his political adversary by putting the principal witnesses on *Air Force I* and flying to Honolulu. The president's trip galvanized public attention and South Vietnam's premier Ky was featured on the cover of *Time* magazine. Fulbright was left to question retired General James Gavin and diplomat George Kennan—critics of the war but neither holding an official position in government.

At Honolulu, Johnson learned from General Westmoreland that the July deployments had staved off defeat in the South, but additional troops would now be needed to take the military initiative. President Johnson reluctantly agreed to a dramatic increase in U.S. troop strength from the 184,000 currently deployed to 429,000 by the end of the year. In exchange for the increase LBJ, utilizing his favorite exhortation, told Westmoreland to "nail the coonskin to the wall" by reaching the crossover point by December 1966.

LBJ also told Ky he expected results, especially a plan for a new constitution and free elections. To underscore these expectations, the president related a story for South Vietnam's premier. "There was once two poker players and the first player asked 'What do you have?' 'Aces,' said the second. 'How many aces?' asked the first. 'One aces,' answered the second." Looking directly at Ky the president said, "I hope we don't find out we only had one aces."[2]

Nailing the coonskin proved to be elusive, however, and doubts within the administration on the feasibility of achieving U.S. objectives in Vietnam had begun to surface as early as November 1965. Among the doubters was Secretary of Defense Robert McNamara—the godfather of the Pentagon's computerized methodology and systems analysis that had originally forecast an end to the war within a reasonable period of time.

It was Robert Strange McNamara's exuberance for statistical analysis as a method for finding the code to break Ho's will that was discredited during the war. McNamara had utilized statistics and management/systems analysis to solve tough problems throughout his distinguished public career. A graduate of Harvard Business School, he was best known for almost single-handedly reviving Ford Motor Company and for his meteoric rise at Ford from manager to vice-president and, in 1960, to president—the first person outside the Ford family to hold that title. At Ford, as he would later do at the Pentagon, McNamara surrounded himself with a remarkably talented group of young, energetic, and similarly committed individuals who at various times were referred to as the "quiz kids," "whiz kids," "computer jockeys," "technipols," or "McNamara's band."

McNamara's entire public career had been a success story. After serving only one month as president of Ford, McNamara had accepted John Kennedy's offer to run the Pentagon. Following Kennedy's assassination, and during the period in which President Johnson became preoccupied with the legitimacy of transition and then the 1964 election, responsibility for running the war (which was still a relatively small commitment) had fallen to the civilian secretary of defense. Vietnam was then referred to in laudatory terms as "McNamara's war." President Johnson trusted McNamara and respected him for his ability to get things done. General Westmoreland later recalled that "Mr. McNamara came from American business and he was very statistically oriented. He was very anxious to fight this war as efficiently as possible. I have heard him say that he wanted to end the war without having great stockpiles of material as we had in World War II."[3]

McNamara became an open target for southern conservatives on the Armed Services Committee and military hawks who blamed the military stalemate on the secretary of defense. In part this reaction reflected the belief that more bombing would accomplish what a great amount of bombing and a great number of troops had failed to do—bring security and stability to South Vietnam and convince Hanoi to seek negotiations. The attacks on McNamara also manifested the desire by his political opponents to take that smart son-of-a-gun down a peg or two.

McNamara's initial doubts had surfaced following the battle at Ia Drang Valley in November 1965. The battle had pitted the Army's First Cavalry Division against regimental-size formations of North Vietnamese. In direct confrontation with the enemy, premium firepower had smashed large enemy formations. The battle had left 1200 Communists killed-in-action compared with approximately 200 for the United States. Westmoreland believed that the size of enemy casualties validated the concept of attrition as a military strategy.[4]

McNamara, however, doubted that the enemy would stand toe-to-toe very frequently, and a war of attriting the enemy's manpower base would take time, possibly too long for the American public. The secretary subsequently pressed his case for what became a 37-day Christmas bombing pause and at one point told Johnson that the United States could not win the war in Vietnam. During a December 18, 1965, White House meeting, President Johnson asked McNamara, "Then, no matter what we do in the military field there is no sure victory?" McNamara responded, "That's right. We have been too optimistic." When the bombing pause failed to produce fruitful negotiations, the bombing program was accelerated.

By 1967–68 the Joint Chiefs were in open revolt against the civilians in the Pentagon, and President Johnson, who had always been suspicious of the military, now lost faith in his dovish defense secretary. Vitriolic perceptions of "McNamara's band" permeated the inner war councils. Admiral Sharp later wrote, "We could have flattened every war-making facility in North Vietnam. But the handwringers had center stage. . . . The most powerful country in the world did not have the willpower needed to meet the situation."[5] General John Paul McConnel charged that "I didn't think Mr. McNamara understood air power nor its application very well. . . . In fact, I don't think there was at that time anybody in the Office of the Secretary of Defense who understood the application of tactical and strategic powers. At least, not the way I understood it."[6] Admiral Thomas Moorer added, "I thought that McNamara didn't know what the hell he was talking about because they were claiming that the bombing wasn't effective, see."[7]

The Prognosis is Bad—October 1966

By the final quarter of 1966 the crossover point was nowhere in sight. At President Johnson's behest Secretary McNamara visited Vietnam in October 1966. It had been twelve months since McNamara's last visit—a period during which U.S. troop deployments had more than doubled. The secretary spent his first two days in formal briefings with military commanders and then visited military posts in the field.

Signs of an inconclusive military stalemate were already evident. Military defeat had been prevented, but little progress had been made in rooting out Communist forces and destroying their infrastructure in South Vietnam. Moreover, while unremitting but selective application of air and naval power had inflicted serious damage to war-supporting targets in North Vietnam, it had not reduced Hanoi's capacity to support or direct military operations in the South.

On October 14, 1966 Secretary McNamara wrote LBJ that despite significant increases in U.S. troop deployments and in the intensity of the bombing campaign, Hanoi "knows we can't achieve our goals. The prognosis is bad in that the war can be brought to a satisfactory conclusion within the next two years." The U.S. military escalation had blunted Communist military initiatives, but had not diminished the enemy's will to continue. "Any military victory in South Vietnam the Viet Cong may have had in mind 18 months ago has been thwarted by our emergency deployments and actions. And our program of bombing the North has exacted a price. My concern continues, however, in other respects. This is because I see no reasonable way to bring the war to an end soon." McNamara apparently recognized the limits of U.S. military force in a war with political ends. According to McNamara, Hanoi had adopted a strategy of "attriting our national will."

McNamara identified shortcomings in a military strategy that was seemingly detached from its original political goals. "In essence, we find ourselves—from the point of view of the important war (for the complicity of the people)—no better, and if anything worse off. This important war must be fought and won by the Vietnamese themselves. We have known this from the beginning. But the discouraging truth is that, as was the case in 1961 and 1963 and 1965, we have not found the formula, the catalyst, for training and inspiring them into effective action." The Pacification and Revolutionary Development program—aimed at gaining the hearts and minds of the population—was "thoroughly stalled." Pacification had been a central objective of U.S. policy in Vietnam. It had involved the military, political, economic, and social establishment of local government with the participation of the Vietnamese people. For pacification to succeed, it was necessary to achieve sustained periods of territorial security, economic activity, and political control, yet the Viet Cong political infrastructure still thrived in the South's countryside and provided an enormous intelligence advantage for the enemy. In McNamara's words, "full security exists nowhere (not even behind the US Marines' lines and in Saigon); in the countryside, the enemy almost completely controls the night." The people in rural areas believed that the government of South Vietnam "when it comes will not stay but that the VC will." Moreover, people believed that those who cooperated with the Government of Vietnam (GVN) would be punished by the Viet Cong (VC) and that the GVN was indifferent to the people's welfare. The United States could not do the job of pacification and security for the Vietnamese. "All we can do is massage the heart," warned McNamara.

October 1966 was not, however, the time to pull back or even out. Instead, faced with this unpromising state of affairs, McNamara endorsed a policy of redefining U.S. strategy. "We must continue to press the enemy militarily; we must make demonstrable progress in pacification; at the same time, we must add a new ingredient forced on us by the facts. Specifically, we must improve our position by getting ourselves into a military posture that we credibly would maintain indefinitely—a posture that makes trying to 'wait us out' less attractive." In order to achieve the political objectives of changing Hanoi's long-term strategy, McNamara recommended stabilizing U.S. forces at 470,000. "It is my view that this is enough to punish the enemy at the large-unit operations level and to keep the enemy's main forces from interrupting pacification. I believe also that even many more than 470,000 would not kill the enemy off in such numbers as to break their morale so long as they think they can wait us out." A stabilized U.S. force level would put the United States in a position where negotiations would more likely be productive.

Secretary McNamara also recommended in his report that a portion of the 470,000 troops—perhaps 10,000 to 20,000—should be devoted to the construction and maintenance of an infiltration barrier.
This interdiction system would cost $1 billion dollars and be con-
structed with fences, wires, acoustic sensors, and mines. McNamara
also recommended that Rolling Thunder* attack sorties on the North
be stabilized. Approximately 12,000 sorties a month were currently
directed against the North—double the amount of the previous
year—yet, in Secretary McNamara's opinion, the JCS could not show
what effect the sorties had had on Viet Cong infiltration into the
South. "Furthermore, it is clear that, to bomb the North sufficiently
to make a radical impact upon Hanoi's political, economic and social
structure, would require an effort which we could make but which
would not be stomached either by our own people or by world
opinion; and it would involve a serious risk of drawing us into open
war with China."[8]

The Joint Chiefs of Staff quickly responded to McNamara's recommendations. Chairman Earle Wheeler, the country's highest ranking
uniformed soldier, wrote directly to the secretary that the chiefs
agreed with McNamara that "we cannot predict with confidence
that the war can be brought to an end in two years." Accordingly,
for political, military, and psychological reasons, it would be necessary to prepare openly for a long-term, sustained military effort.
Wheeler warned McNamara that the enemy strategy "appears to be
to wait it out; in other words, communist leaders in both North and
South Vietnam expect to win this war in Washington, just as they
won the war with France in Paris."

But, while the JCS agreed with McNamara's diagnosis, they vehemently rejected the secretary's proposed treatment. A stable and

*Rolling Thunder was the code name for U.S. air operations over North Vietnam.
The program was closely monitored from the White House by President Johnson and
his civilian advisors. This interdiction program started in March 1965 as an attempt to
destroy North Vietnamese transportation routes and thereby slow infiltration of personnel and supplies from North to South Vietnam. Rolling Thunder was expanded in
July 1966 to include ammunition dumps and oil storages, and in the spring of 1967 it
was further expanded to include power plants, factories, and airfields in the Hanoi-
Haiphong area. The Rolling Thunder program was substantially reduced in April 1968
and terminated on November 1, 1968. In the three years of Rolling Thunder, 643,000
tons of bombs were dropped on North Vietnam.

sustainable force level of 470,000 was substantially less than the military envisioned. The JCS were even less enamored with McNamara's plans for an infiltration barrier which was privately derided as an "Alice-in-Wonderland solution to insurgency." Barriers properly installed and defended by ground and air effort could indeed impede infiltration into South Vietnam, but McNamara's air-raid munitions barrier could not accomplish this goal and the diversion of funds would impair ongoing military programs throughout the world.

The very premise for stabilizing Rolling Thunder as a carrot to induce negotiations was rejected by the chiefs. Instead, they claimed that the air campaign needed to be accelerated. "Our experiences with pauses in bombing and resumption have not been happy ones," Wheeler wrote. "Additionally, the Joint Chiefs of Staff believe that the likelihood of the war being settled by negotiation is small; and that, far from inducing negotiations, another bombing pause will be regarded by North Vietnamese leaders, and our Allies, as renewed evidence of lack of US determination to press the war to a successful conclusion. The bombing campaign is one of the two trump cards in the hands of the President (the other being the presence of US troops in SVN). It should not be given up without an end to the NVN aggression in SVN."

General Wheeler concluded with a clear statement that the chiefs believed the war had reached a critical stage in which "decisions taken over the next sixty days can determine the outcome of the war and, consequently, can affect the over-all security interests of the United States for years to come." Wheeler acknowledged the admirable goals of trying to settle the war by peaceful means. "Certainly, no one—American or foreigner—except those who are determined not to be convinced, can doubt the sincerity, the generosity, the altruism of US actions and objectives. In the opinion of the Joint Chiefs of Staff the time has come when further overt actions and offers on our part are not only nonproductive, they are counterproductive. A logical case can be made that the American people, our Allies, and our enemies alike are increasingly uncertain as to our resolution to pursue the war to a successful conclusion."[9]

Meeting in Manila

Would the next sixty days really be as decisive as Wheeler predicted? What did the chiefs mean by "a successful conclusion"? Were the American people really questioning U.S. resolve to succeed in Vietnam? What yardstick could be used to measure success? With an eye towards finding answers, and with the McNamara and Wheeler reports in his hand, the president convened a seven-nation meeting of Asian allies in Manila.

Accompanied by Mrs. Johnson and his official team of advisors, which included Secretary of State Dean Rusk, the president arrived in Manila on October 23, 1966, occupying the same hotel suite used by the Beatles during their historic tour the previous summer. The president's arrival in Manila was preceded by a visit to Australia where hostile demonstrations in Melbourne and Sydney against U.S. foreign policy overshadowed festivities planned by Australian leaders waiting to greet the president.

Upon his arrival in Manila, Johnson declared, "Asia and Asians must lead, but we are prepared to help." The seven-nation conference brought together President Chung Hee Park of South Korea, Prime Ministers Harold Holt of Australia and Keith Holyoake of New Zealand, Premier Thanom Kittikachorn of Thailand, President Ferdinand Marcos of the Philippines, and Premier Nguyen Cao Ky and Chief of State Nguyen Van Thieu, of South Vietnam.[10]

Of particular interest at Manila were the military assessments provided by General Westmoreland and Premier Ky. The two men presented quite disparate personalities. General William Childs Westmoreland was the soldier's soldier. Frequently depicted as a grown-up eagle scout, Westmoreland had been first captain of cadets at West Point. In World War II, he had fought in North Africa and Sicily and led troops in the Normandy landing. Following the war he took paratroop training and commanded a combat regiment in Korea. In June 1964 Westmoreland replaced General Paul Harkins as head of the U.S. Military Assistance Command in Vietnam (MACV).

In contrast, the gaudy and flamboyant Ky was habitually attired in a black flying suit with a purple scarf around his neck and ivory-handled pistols jutting from his pockets. Many Americans had a hard time taking him seriously, but Ky took himself quite seriously. Trained as a pilot by the French, Ky later operated under CIA cover while flying secret agents into North Vietnam. Indeed, his black flying suit was designed by Ky so that he would be less visible if ever forced to parachute against the night sky. Following the June 12, 1965, coup, Ky had been installed as premier by the nineteen-member national leadership council until a constitution could be written and elections held, both of which were yet to be done at the time of the Manila conference.

President Johnson now asked Ky, "What is in the mind of the Viet Cong—do they expect to win?" Ky replied: "No. I don't think so. I believe they will very soon collapse—if we can get to them the facts." He said that General Westmoreland had reported to him the other day that half the prisoners captured in recent military operations still thought Diem (who had been assassinated in November 1963) was running the government in Saigon. "We must improve our information, get to the people, give them the facts, enlarge the open arms program. Then they will come back to us."

The president then asked General Westmoreland for his assessment of the military situation. As recorded in the meeting notes, Westmoreland assured Johnson, "By every index, things were improving." General Westmoreland cited the favorable trend of relative casualty figures, defections, and weapons losses. "Above all, an optimistic spirit was now unmistakable in Vietnam. The ARVN [Army of the Republic of Vietnam] are fighting better and are more aggressive. There was improved outlook for pacification which would become the first task of the ARVN as they were retrained. Improved intelligence from the villages permitted more effective police measures." The president asked if the VC would still seek a major victory in October. Westmoreland thought they would try, but they would not succeed.

The president asked General Westmoreland whether he had enough troops. The meeting notes record that "[Westmoreland] could certainly need more forces. He would like all the allies fighting in Vietnam to increase their forces at least by 35%." The president turned to Secretary of State Rusk and remarked "that [Rusk] had his work cut out for him." The president asked if there were any more troops to be generated from South Vietnam. General Westmoreland replied that he envisaged an increase of about 22,000 by the end of 1967, but basically South Vietnam was a country whose manpower for military purposes was being stretched to the maximum.

General Westmoreland concluded his military assessment by stating "that while there was light at the end of the tunnel, we had to be geared for the long pull. The enemy is relying on his greater staying power. It is only his will and resolve that are sustaining him now, and his faith that his will is stronger than ours."

With respect to bombing, General Westmoreland warned LBJ against taking any actions to stabilize Rolling Thunder. "We should in no case unilaterally quit bombing. Infiltration continues. The price of infiltration has definitely been raised." The president suggested that "General Westmoreland talk with Secretary Rusk, and instructed Rostow to get a fuller version of General Westmoreland's suggestions about the future of the bombing program." The meeting transcripts depict LBJ's suspicion of the press that would later destroy the administration. "Both of us," the president said to Ky, "must be careful not to let the press bait us." The president's last words at the meeting were, "Don't let the newspapermen divide us."

The Manila conference provided President Johnson with the opportunity to send several messages to different audiences. For the Asian nations represented at the conference there was the pledge of support. For Hanoi, there was a signal of determination in U.S. resolve. For the South Vietnamese, there was a signal that the credibility of the U.S. commitment was genuine. Aggression would be repelled; the fledgling government of South Vietnam deserved the loyalty of the Vietnamese people. For the American public there was the signal that these signals had been sent. The United States would continue its support for the objective of a free South Vietnam.

But Johnson then went one step further. Inspired by an October 10 conversation in the White House in which Soviet Foreign Minister Andrei Gromyko had urged President Johnson to be more specific with respect to conditions for a U.S. withdrawal from Vietnam, LBJ pressed his Asian allies to join him in signing the Manila Communiqué. The United States pledged to withdraw all forces from South Vietnam within six months of North Vietnam's ceasing its aggression against the South.

Following the Manila conference LBJ travelled to the U.S. installation at Cam Ranh Bay in South Vietnam. "I wanted to visit our fighting men," Johnson later wrote. "I wanted to tell them how their President and most of their countrymen felt about what they were doing. I have never been more moved by any group I have talked to, never in my life."[11]

Attrition as Strategy

By November 1966 the viability of General Westmoreland's attrition strategy was being questioned. As a military strategy, attrition meant wearing down or grinding down the enemy until the enemy lost its will to fight or the capacity to sustain its military effort. Despite recent deployments, the United States had not been able to attrite the enemy forces fast enough to break their morale and more U.S. forces were unlikely to accomplish that objective. A young CIA analyst, Samuel Adams, believed he had discovered, from captured enemy documents, that possibly twice as many enemy soldiers were in South Vietnam as MACV's current intelligence reported. (Twenty years later Adams's story would be aired in the CBS documentary "The Uncounted Enemy" which resulted in the lawsuit brought by General Westmoreland.) In a guerilla war it was generally agreed that three conventional soldiers were the equivalent of one guerilla. If the United States was fighting an enemy force of half a million, U.S. deployments were woefully insufficient.

Adams communicated his data to George Carver, special assistant to the CIA director for Vietnam affairs. On November 22, 1966, Carver wrote to presidential assistant Robert Komer that "a reappraisal of the strength of communist regular forces which is currently underway indicates that accepted (i.e., MACV) estimates of the strength of Viet Cong irregular forces may have drastically underestimated their growth, possibly by as much as 200,000 persons." The memo had little effect on the ebullient Komer who a week later wrote McNamara, "I suspect that we have reached the point where we are killing, defecting, or otherwise attriting more VC/NVA strength than the enemy can build up."[12]

Komer was certainly not alone in painting optimistic scenarios from the perception of declining enemy strength. On November 21, 1966, Colonel Robert Ginsburgh, the National Security Council's liaison with the Joint Chiefs, wrote Special Assistant Walt Rostow, "You will recall that last December our figures indicated the beginning of a gradual erosion in communist strength. These latest figures indicate that the communists by now ought to be in really serious trouble. In September, my analysis showed that the war would most probably be terminated between June 1969 and 1972. At the time, I felt that I was way out on a limb. If the present trends continue, however,—and this is always a big if—I do not see how they can possibly hold out beyond the summer of 1969." (In a February 9, 1967, memo to the president, Rostow described Ginsburgh as "a thoughtful Ph.D. and not a 'hawk' like me.")

This was precisely the type of analysis that Walt Rostow liked to receive. On March 31, 1966, President Johnson, acting on the strong recommendation of his special assistant, Jack Valenti, had passed over Bill Moyers and Robert Komer and selected Walt Whitman Rostow as McGeorge Bundy's replacement at the National Security Council. Where Bundy had held the imposing title special assistant for National Security Affairs, Rostow's title of special assistant to the president was seen by official Washington as LBJ's intent to have a less imposing role for the national security advisor.

That Rostow had assumed the position at all was somewhat of a mystery. An original member of Kennedy's Brain Trust, it was Rostow who had coined the theme of "New Frontier" and the ringing cry, "Let's get the country moving again." Following JFK's election he had hoped to be appointed chair of the State Department Policy Planning Council, but Secretary of State Dean Rusk had chosen someone less closely tied to the new president. Instead, Rostow had become McGeorge Bundy's aid as deputy special assistant for national security affairs. A few months later he was appointed counselor of the Department of State and chairman of the Policy Planning Council.

Rostow's academic credentials were impeccable. Having finished Yale at 19, he went to Oxford as a Rhodes scholar and later returned to Yale for his Ph.D. During World War II he served as a major in the Office of Strategic Services (OSS). After the war he returned to teaching, first at Oxford, then at Cambridge, and from 1950 to 1961 he was Professor of Economic History at MIT. The *New York Times* praised Rostow's appointment as "an assurance both of professional competence and of continuity in one of Washington's most critical posts. Mr. Rostow is a scholar with an original mind, as well as an experienced official and policy planner . . . the appointment places beside the President an independent and cultivated mind that, as in the Bundy era, should assure comprehension both of the intricacies of world problems and of the options among which the White House must choose. No President could ask for more." Over time, Rostow became excessively optimistic for the case of military victory by the strategy of attrition.

Assessing Future Prospects

In his 1966 year-end report to Admiral Sharp and General Wheeler, General Westmoreland listed enemy strength at 300,575 which actually represented a 42,000 increase in 1966. Westmoreland reported enemy infiltration into the South at 8400 a month plus another 3500 gained from recruiting South Vietnamese. "The conclusion to be drawn from the enemy's strength increase of some 42,000 during 1966 is that despite known losses, he has been able to maintain a proportional counter-buildup to the growth of US/FWMA [Free World Military Assistance] forces. Sources of this increase are in-country conscription and foot infiltration down the trails from NVN through the DMZ [demilitarized zone], but principally through Laos and the Cambodian extension."[13]

General Westmoreland's data was viewed with skepticism within the White House. On January 3, 1967, Rostow wrote LBJ, "I do not for one minute believe the infiltration rate is 8400 per month. I believe it is a MACV balancing figure to give them what I strongly suspect is an inflated order of battle. They are being excessively conservative both as an insurance policy and to protect themselves against what they regard as excessive pressure to allocate more forces to pacification." (Ironically, the CIA would later charge Westmoreland with deliberate underestimation of the data.)

Westmoreland's 1966 year-end assessment led Admiral Sharp to cable both Westmoreland and Wheeler regarding MACV's 1967 operational concept for Vietnam. Sharp believed that while MACV's plan for 1967 was adequate to meet the anticipated enemy threat, it would be necessary to "avoid devoting too great a measure of our effort to anti-infiltration at the expense of more important operations. We should continue and, if possible, expand our air and naval interdiction of his infiltration system."

Sharp took direct aim at the infiltration barrier McNamara had proposed in October. "It is virtually impossible," wrote Sharp, "to stop or appreciably impede infiltration into SVN with ground forces now available or programmed for the theater, especially in light of the contiguous sanctuaries the enemy now enjoys. Although it would be desirable to stop or measurably impede infiltration, such action is not imperative to our winning a military victory. . . . Our air and naval interdiction operations must be continued at the present level and, if possible, they must be expanded. Although not in themselves capable of quelling infiltration, their effects against the enemy and his movement of personnel and equipment to the South are appreciable."

The intrinsic value of the air campaign lay in the cost it imposed on North Vietnam and Admiral Sharp argued that it was time to really punish the enemy.

> Our country harbors a natural desire to ease the hardships in the Vietnam conflict. The military, however, must press to go all out at all levels in SVN if we are to win. We are faced with a full blown and difficult war and our government has committed a huge amount of combat power to this conflict, yet we are still a long way from achieving our objectives. If we are to reach an acceptable military decision in Vietnam, we must not permit our operational tactics to reflect the reticence which currently characterizes some bodies of public and official opinion. Our ground forces must take the field on long term, sustained combat operations. We must be prepared to accept heavier casualties in our initial operations and not permit our hesitance to take greater losses to inhibit our tactical aggressiveness. If greater hardships are accepted now we will, in the long run, achieve a military success sooner and at less overall cost in lives and money."[14]

Sharp's candid appraisal of U.S. military prospects reflected his intent to wage war against the enemy, but the U.S. goal in Vietnam was not military victory in the classical sense. If it had been, the war would have been fought on quite different terms. This became the quintessential Catch-22 for those advising the president. Johnson demanded solutions or strategies for winning the war, but the documentation confirms very little agreement on the definition of winning. What did Sharp mean in his statement that the military "must press to go all out at all levels in SVN if we are to win"? Did Secretary McNamara and President Johnson share that same definition of "to win"?

LBJ never intended to accept Sharp's advice for winning the war. The U.S. goal was to build democratic political stability in the South, not destroy the North. Johnson also feared that further punishment of the North would precipitate Chinese intervention and the possibility of world war. Yet, the president could not stop the bombing since it was the only stick he had, however unwieldy, for hoping to force negotiations. The Joint Chiefs would soon attempt to force Johnson's hand by arguing that only by removing the wraps on the bombing of Hanoi and its environs could the enemy be brought to the conference table.

There were three purposes in selective bombing of military targets in North Vietnam: (1) To back U.S. fighting men by denying the enemy a sanctuary; (2) to exact a penalty against North Vietnam; and (3) to limit the flow or to substantially increase the cost of infiltration of men and material from North Vietnam. But while bombing clearly served these purposes it soon became a substitute for an invasion or an occupation of North Vietnam or an introduction of troops into Laos.

In early January 1967 President Johnson instructed his special assistant, Walt Rostow, to organize a secret committee to examine the overall effects of bombing North Vietnam. Rostow immediately spoke with Washington lawyer Clark Clifford, a personal friend, confidant, and member of the inner circle of unofficial presidential advisors. Clifford was regarded as a hawk, primarily because he had vehemently opposed the 1965 Christmas bombing pause. Clifford now warned Rostow that the existence of such a group might threaten administration credibility. Why was the president reexamining his own bombing program? "There is no substitute, in a matter of this kind, for the President's personal, lonely judgment," Clifford wrote to Rostow. "And the very fact that the President was asking for outside advice in this matter would indicate, to the public and the world, that the President was uncertain. Whatever recommendations the report made would complicate the President's problem."[15]

Rostow took Clifford's advice and wrote to the president that such

a group "would be unsettling and possibly explosive, if made public—among other things, because it would appear you were not confident of JCS and Bob McNamara's advice." In truth, the president
was not very confident in the chiefs' bombing program and he was
beginning to worry about his defense secretary. While it was apparent by late 1966 that major troop deployments had staved off the
defeat that might have occurred without American intervention in
July 1965, increases in troop deployments and the intensity of bombing had not brought North Vietnam to the conference table.

The U.S. objective in Vietnam was the independence of South
Vietnam, its freedom from attack, and a stable, democratic government in the South. By denying the Communists a military victory,
the United States believed it could create conditions under which
negotiations would be viable. But Hanoi saw Vietnam as a single
country that had been split artificially by neo-colonialist intervention. The revolutionary Viet Cong (VC) believed it had an obligation
to free South Vietnam from foreign intervention, while the United
States believed that the Vietnam war was a case of one country trying
to conquer another country covered by our treaty guarantee.

LBJ's policy was slowly slipping the war into a stalemate, yet even
as that became evident, he refused to abandon his no-win policy.
President Johnson would soon learn, as Hanoi's leaders well understood, that a stalemate could undermine a democracy faster than a
Communist régime. A free press, the legitimacy of political opposition, and an attentive citizenry forced Johnson to exaggerate rates of
progress and lights at the ends of tunnels in order to keep the war
going. Operating under restraints imposed by the president, the
military commanders recognized that Vietnam would be a long war.
Hanoi could accept the conditions of a stalemate longer than the
United States. Stalemate was tantamount to victory for Hanoi.

III

The Slippery Slope to Stalemate

progress (n. prog′res or, esp. Brit., pro′gres), n. 1. movement toward a specific goal or a further stage. 2. development or cumulative improvement as of an individual or a civilization. 3. forward or onward movement in space or time.

stalemate (stal′mat′), n. v. -mat-ed, -mat-ing. -n. 1. Chess. a position in which a player cannot move any piece except his king and cannot move his king without putting it in check, the result being a draw. 2. any position or situation in which no action can be taken.

The Random House Dictionary of the English Language. The College Edition

In his January 1967 State of the Union address, the president spoke somewhat guardedly but nevertheless optimistically of the war against aggression in Vietnam. President Johnson assured the American public that General Westmoreland believed the enemy could no longer succeed on the battlefield. "I wish I could report to you that the conflict is almost over. This I cannot do. We face more cost, more loss, and more agony. For the end is not yet. I cannot promise you that it will come this year—or come next year. Our adversary still believes, I think, tonight that he can go on fighting longer than we can, and longer than we and our allies will be prepared to stand up and resist."

The 1967 State of the Union message also provided Johnson with a forum to request that Congress pass a 6 percent tax surcharge in an effort to slow inflation without risking a recession. Only now were the twin effects of the 1964 tax cut and growing expenditures associated with the war threatening to undercut a period of sustained growth. Between 1964 and 1967, the GNP had increased by 7 percent per annum, while inflation and unemployment had remained low. But Johnson's economists recognized that the costs of the war, which now totalled over $17 billion annually, would bring back inflationary pressure—unless a tax was implemented.

The president harbored grave private doubts concerning the politics of war and taxation. In his memoirs, *The Vantage Point,* Johnson explained, "I stuck to the middle ground, for I realized that my Presidency would require dealing simultaneously with major military crises abroad and urgently needed reforms at home. That course was not comfortable. It would have been easier in the short run to break out the flag for an all-out military effort, and perhaps easier still to abandon our commitment in Asia and concentrate on domestic tasks. But I was convinced that the middle ground was the right course for the United States. That was the fundamental approach of my administration, and I was not going to abandon it. Holding to it, however, eroded my popularity from two directions—with those who wanted to do more in the war and with those who wished to do more at home. And Presidential popularity is a major source of strength in gaining cooperation from Congress."[1]

Questions on Enemy Strength

Within the CIA a cloudy picture of military progress was emerging from studies of enemy strength. A January 9 report from the CIA Office of National Estimates described the political health of South Vietnam as "precarious," pacification of the countryside "spotty," the fighting capabilities of the South Vietnamese "generally poor." If this war was to be won with political reform and stability in the South, it would be a long road ahead. Moreover, Hanoi, not U.S. troop increments, controlled the rate of attrition in the South. "There is no evidence of a diminution of Communist will to continue the war." Hanoi expected U.S. resolve to crumble once it became apparent that a viable political structure could not be created for winning mass support in South Vietnam. "We do not know how long the Communists will remain determined to persist," noted the CIA report.

The CIA analysis documented the failure of Westmoreland's strategy of attrition—there would be no imminent crossover point. Not only were the Communists still capable of fighting for at least another year, "they are probably determined to do so." None of the Communist's problems appeared to be critical. The report concluded, "Thus, from the purely military standpoint there are good reasons to believe that the Communists will persevere."

The size of enemy forces was well on its way to becoming an official bureaucratic debate and source of controversy, not a conspiracy by MACV intelligence officers. On January 11, 1967, George Carver, special assistant for Vietnamese affairs, wrote to CIA Director Richard Helms that the MACV Order of Battle (OB) for the size of enemy strength was "far too low and should be raised, perhaps doubled." Raising the OB figure to "a more realistic level would allow the intelligence community to make a better-informed appraisal of what we are up against and would enable it to grapple more effectively with such nuts and bolts problems as communist manpower allocations, desertion rates, casualty estimates, and logistics."

The Order of Battle during the Vietnam war was an estimate of Communist capabilities to conduct military operations. It was an inexact process, arrived at by counting enemy defectors, prisoners, spies, captured documents, reconnaissance photos, etc., and was broken down into the following classifications:

Classification of Forces:

(1) Viet Cong (VC) Main Force (MF): Those military units which were directly subordinate to Central Office for South Vietnam (COSVN), a Viet Cong Military Region, or sub-region.

(2) Viet Cong (VC) Local Force (LF): Those military units which were directly subordinate to a provincial or district party committee and which normally operated only within a specified VC province or district.

(3) North Vietnamese Army (NVA) Units: A unit formed, trained, and designated by North Vietnam as an NVA unit, and composed completely or primarily of North Vietnamese. At times, either VC or NVA units and individual replacements appeared in units that were predominantly NVA or VC at the command level.

(4) Irregulars: These were organized forces composed of guerrilla, self-defense, and secret self-defense elements subordinate to village and hamlet level VC organizations. These forces performed a wide variety of missions in the support of VC activities and, in fact, provided a training and mobilization base for the VC maneuver and combat support forces.

(a) Guerrillas: Guerrillas were full-time forces organized into squads and platoons which did not always stay in their home village or hamlet. Typical missions for guerrillas were collection of taxes, propaganda, protection of village party committees, and terrorist and sabotage activities.

(b) Self-Defense Force: A VC para-military structure responsible for the defense of hamlet and village areas controlled by the VC. These forces did not leave their home area, and they performed their duties on a part-time basis. Duties consisted of conducting propaganda, constructing fortifications, and defending home areas.

(c) Secret Self-Defense Force: A clandestine VC organization which performed the same general function in GVN controlled villages and hamlets as did the self-defense forces in VC controlled areas. Their operations involved intelligence collection as well as sabotage and propaganda activities.

On January 19, General Wheeler instructed members of the intelligence community with responsibility for collecting and analyzing OB figures to meet in Honolulu in order to standardize methods for developing and presenting statistics on the Order of Battle, infiltration trends, and estimates. These concerns certainly reached the president's desk. Rostow wrote to LBJ on January 20, 1967 "as you know, a debate continues on the absolute size of the enemy order of battle in Viet Nam." Rostow reported that "whatever the size, you should know that official statistics now show for the first time a net decline in both VC main force and North Vietnam army units for the fourth quarter of 1966. This is the first reversal of the upward trend since 1960."

At the conference held in February in Honolulu, representatives from MACV, CIA, and other U.S. intelligence agencies agreed that major book increases in the numbers listed for MACV's Order of Battle would be forthcoming. It was generally recognized that enemy strength for personnel in the Irregular and Political categories was much greater than MACV's intelligence estimated showed. High priority was given to updating these new estimates.

General Wheeler soon cabled Admiral Sharp and General Westmoreland that he was becoming "increasingly concerned over the contradictory order of battle (OB) and infiltration statistics which are contained in the numerous documents currently being circulated throughout Washington." Members of Congress, White House officials, and the press were starting to focus on these administrative discrepancies. Part of the problem involved an impression of precision, which did not actually exist in OB and infiltration figures. The fact was, however, that officials in Washington wanted consistent data on the war's progress. "It was a very bad pressure," recalled George Carver. "It came out of the White House."

Relentless pressure continued to build from Washington for demonstrations of further progress in the field. But the data frequently undermined the assumption that the United States held the military initiative in Vietnam. When General Wheeler received General Westmoreland's updated statistics on Battalion and Large-Size Enemy-Initiated Actions he cabled back to Westmoreland on March 11, "I have just been made aware of the figures you now report. If these figures should reach the public domain, they would, literally, blow the lid off of Washington. Please do whatever is necessary to insure these figures are not repeat not released to News Media or otherwise exposed to public knowledge. . . ."

The new figures showed dramatic increases in the number of enemy-initiated attacks. In another cable to Sharp and Westmoreland, General Wheeler wrote:

> I must say I find this difficult to believe and certainly contrary to my own impression of how the war has been going during the past six to eight months. The implications are major and serious. Large-scale enemy initiatives have been used as a major element in assessing the status of

THE SLIPPERY SLOPE TO STALEMATE 31

the war for the President, Secretary of Defense, Secretary of State, Congress, and as well in Washington. These figures have been used to illustrate the success of our current strategy as well as over-all progress in Vietnam. Considerable emphasis has been placed on these particular statistics, since they provide a relatively straight-forward means of measuring the tempo of organized enemy combat initiative. (In cold fact, we have no other persuasive yardstick.) Your new figures change the picture drastically. . . . I can only interpret the new figures to mean that, despite the force buildup, despite our many successful spoiling attacks and base area searches, and despite the heavy interdiction campaign in North Vietnam and Laos, VC/NVA combat capability and offensive activity throughout 1966 and now in 1967 has been increasing steadily, with the January 1967 level some two and one-half times above the average of the first three months in 1966.

Wheeler recognized the political implications of a military stalemate in Vietnam: "I cannot go to the President and tell him that, contrary to my reports and those of the other chiefs as to the progress of the war in which we have laid great stress upon the thesis you have seized the initiative from the enemy, the situation is such that we are not sure who has the initiative in South Vietnam. Moreover, the effect of surfacing this major and significant discrepancy would be dynamite, particularly coming on the heels of other recent statistical problems. I have discussed the whole problem with Secretary McNamara and we agree that urgent action is required." This action involved trying to find new procedures for reporting progress in the war. "I believe we should do this promptly in view of the President's intention to meet with Ambassador Lodge and you in the near future," Wheeler concluded.[2]

Guam: Dramatizing Progress in March 1967

In preparation for the Guam conference on March 20 Lodge cabled Rusk, "I fully concur in the need to accelerate our present rate of progress and to dramatize what has been and should be achieved to meet the heavy pressures I know the president and you are under at home."[3] Two days before the conference an optimistic Rostow wrote to LBJ, "If victory is not in sight, it is on the way."

The Guam meeting was intended to provide a dramatization of unity and support for the U.S. commitment in Vietnam. Joining the president at Guam were Generals Westmoreland and Wheeler, and Admiral Sharp, as well as Chief of State Thieu and Premier Ky, who presented LBJ with a draft copy of the new Vietnamese constitution fulfilling the pledge made at Honolulu. "Their proud looks at Guam said: We have done what we said we would, even though many people thought it was impossible," Johnson later recalled.[4] Ky now promised Johnson that the constitution would be promulgated and that Vietnam would soon hold free elections. President Johnson must have thought that Ky was a man with two, not one, aces.

Changes in the civilian guard in Saigon were announced prior to the Guam meetings. Ellsworth Bunker was appointed to succeed Henry Cabot Lodge as United States ambassador, and Robert Komer, who held the title special assistant to the president, was named deputy to the commander of MACV with the rank of ambassador and was assigned responsibility for the pacification program. Bunker brought a distinguished public service record as ambassador to Argentina, Italy, and India, as well as the Organization of American States (OAS). He had been instrumental in forging a coalition government in Santo Domingo which eventually allowed the United States to withdraw its forces. The Komer appointment was met with dismay by officials in Washington if only because he was already known for his "sunny-side-up" views of the war. Saigon observers described Komer as "a Guildenstern at the court of Lyndon I—willing to please his President at all costs." By 1968 even his friends referred to him as "blowtorch."[5]

In preparation for an evening meeting between LBJ and Thieu and Ky, Walt Rostow suggested that the president emphasize the following points:

> You are counting on these two great patriots to do the job. The war itself; the transition to constitutional government; the future of South View Nam as a nation; the capacity of the US to sustain the war—all these depend on unity among the Vietnamese military. . . . You have put a half million men in Southeast Asia. You intend to see this through. You are not going to sell out the people of South Viet Nam. And remember this: the US has been through many crises; our friends have emerged well—from Greece and Berlin to South Korea. We are shed-

ding blood with them on their soil. We do not intend to give away the fruits of our effort at the conference table. They should do their job with confidence.[6]

The working notes and tape transcripts from the March 20–21, 1967, Guam meetings included a remarkable exchange between President Johnson and General Westmoreland. In February 1966 LBJ had demanded a "coonskin on the wall" by December 1966. Now, three months after the December deadline, the president asked his field commander, "Are they bringing in as many as they're losing?" Westmoreland answered, "Up until now, no, sir. Their gains have exceeded their losses. However, if the present trend continues I think we might arrive at the cross-over point. Perhaps this month, or next month. And by the cross-over point I mean where their losses are greater than their gains." Although the statistics he had sent to Wheeler earlier in the month proved the contrary, Westmoreland now maintained that the enemy's 287,000-man order of battle was leveling off and as of March, had reached the crossover point of attriting more men than Hanoi could recruit or infiltrate each month.

The meeting on March 21 began with General Westmoreland reviewing the enemy order of battle and troop strength. Westmoreland provided a corps by corps review and summarized the overall picture. The general noted progress and achievement but made the point that unless military pressure caused the Viet Cong to crumble and Hanoi to stop its support of southern insurgency, the war in Vietnam could go on indefinitely. Hanoi was still confident of victory and confident that the Communists would wear down the Free World's will to continue the fight. General Westmoreland continued his case against any bombing pause. Also present at the meeting was Admiral Sharp, who argued that bombing had been successful in light of its limited objectives. "It had not stopped infiltration, but no one had ever thought it would. It had made Communist infiltration immensely more difficult and costly for the Communists and also exerted a constant pressure on the North Vietnamese regime."[7]

The Guam conference illustrated the private doubts and disagreements amongst the president's principal advisors. Writing to the president on March 22 Rostow warned "As you are undoubtedly aware, Gen. Westmoreland's presentation at Guam was, evidently, designed to be conservative and non-promissory—which, given his responsibilities, is understandable. He repeated the infiltration estimate of 7,000 per month." Rostow considered 7000 as an upper-end calculation, arrived at by "averaging over the twelve months of 1966 the maximum total of confirmed, probable, and possible; projecting forward at a rate which ignores the downward trend in quarterly totals since the first quarter of 1966." Rostow anticipated a much more optimistic scenario and explained to the president that "I must confess that I am greatly impressed by the fact that the Chieu Hoi [desertion] figures have remained over 1,000 per week for 5 weeks. If that can be sustained for, say, 6 months, I find it hard to believe that the VC infrastructure can hold up."[8]

Following the meeting in Guam, General Westmoreland forwarded to President Johnson a "minimum essential" and "optimum" force plan for American troop strength beyond the 470,000 already approved for 1967. The minimum plan would bring U.S. forces to a total of 550,500; the optimum force to 670,000. The troop request reflected both the debasement of McNamara's call for the stabilization of U.S. forces in Vietnam, as well as a road map to endless escalation. Johnson ordered Wheeler and Westmoreland back to Washington for consultation.

April Consultations at Home

The April 1967 meeting of the principals revealed the slippery slope on which the credibility of the administration's Vietnam policy rested, as well as the serious intramural divisions between the secretary of defense and the Joint Chiefs over the bombing program. The declassified transcripts also document a remarkably barren political base for the president. During their private White House meetings, General Westmoreland painted a much grimmer picture than he had the previous month for President Johnson. Without the additional forces, "we will not be in danger of being defeated, but it will be nip and tuck to oppose the reinforcements the enemy is capable of providing. In the final analysis, we are fighting a war of attrition in Southeast Asia. What is the next step? A second addition of $2\frac{1}{3}$ divisions, another 100,000 men, probably in FY 1969." How much would be enough? "With the troops now in country, we are not going to lose, but progress will be slowed down. This is not an encouraging outlook, but it is a realistic one," Westmoreland explained to his Commander in Chief.[9]

Westmoreland also told Johnson that enemy strength in South Vietnam totaled 285,000 men which was 2000 less than the number he reported in March. "It appears that last month we reached the crossover point. In areas excluding the two northern provinces, attrition will be greater than additions to the force." The president then asked, "Where does it all end? When we add divisions, can't the enemy add divisions? If so, where does it all end?" General Westmoreland answered:

> The enemy has 8 divisions in South Vietnam. He has the capability of deploying 12 divisions, although he would have difficulty supporting all of these. He would be hard pressed to support more than 12 divisions. If we add 2⅓ divisions, it is likely the enemy will react by adding troops. . . . With the present program of 470,000 men, we would be setting up a meat grinder. We would do a little better than hold our own. We would make progress, but we would have to use a fire brigade technique. Unless the will of the enemy was broken or unless there was unraveling of the VC structure, the war could go on for five years. If our forces were increased, that period could be reduced, although not necessarily in proportion to increases in strength. Other factors than increase in strength must, of course, be considered. We now have a professional US force. A non-professional force such as that which would result from fulfilling the requirement for 100,000 additional men by calling Reserves, will cause some degradation of morale, leadership and effectiveness. With a force level of 565,000 men, the war could well go on for three years. With the second increment of 2⅓ divisions, leading to a total of 665,000 men, it could go on for two years.

General Wheeler then informed the president that the chiefs had considered a "possible invasion of North Vietnam." The bombing campaign had reached the point where all worthwhile fixed targets except the ports had been struck. According to Wheeler additional punitive action against the Democratic Republic of Vietnam (DRV) by denying them access to the ports was necessary. When LBJ asked Wheeler, "What if we do not add the 2⅓ divisions?" Wheeler provided an answer the president could not accept: "The momentum will die; in some areas the enemy will recapture the initiative. We won't lose the war, but it will be a longer one."

The next day, in the first address to a joint session of Congress by a battlefield commander, General Westmoreland chose his words carefully. Later he recalled in his book, *A Soldier Reports,* "I consciously avoided using the word 'victory,' for the national goal was not to win a military victory over North Vietnam." The general emphasized in his speech that progress had been made in providing "the shield of security" for the development of a free and independent South Vietnam. Nevertheless, the lack of American resolve and patience could possibly undermine U.S. objectives: "In evaluating the enemy strategy it is evident to me that he believes our Achilles' heel is our resolve. Your continued strong support is vital to the success of our mission. . . . Backed at home by resolve, confidence, patience, determination, and continued support, we will prevail in Vietnam over the Communist aggressor."[10]

MACV's request for additional forces met with skepticism within the Defense Department. Towards what specific goal were these extra forces needed? Was the United States merely trying to again avoid defeat or postpone an inevitable withdrawal? What analysis was available to assess the impact of 470,000 troops compared with 570,000 or 670,000? What forces or factors explained the staying power of the North Vietnamese? McNamara's assistant Alain Enthoven warned the secretary that "we have hurt them with our bombing, and we can hurt them more. But we can't hurt them so badly as to destroy their society or, more to the point, their hope, not only for regaining the material things they sacrifice today, but the whole of South Vietnam."

North Vietnam was willing to endure all sacrifices in order to vindicate nationalism as a policy, noted Enthoven. Governmental stability in the South was woefully inept and Hanoi understood that the punishment it took would ultimately result in triumph against its aggressor. "Hanoi is betting that we'll lose public support in the United States before we can build a nation in South Vietnam," he continued. "We must do what we can to make sure that doesn't happen. We must work on both problems together: slow the loss in public support; and speed the development of South Vietnam. Our horse must cross the finish first."[11]

Crossing the finish line first posed serious problems. The July 1965 decision to Americanize the war had apparently eroded whatever incentives the South Vietnamese people may have held to help themselves. Opponents of escalation believed that the additional forces being requested by Westmoreland would not solve pacification problems; nor would they slow the horse carrying U.S. public opinion towards rejecting the war. Additional forces were not needed for military security and could not control the rate of attrition. No one could show what 200,000 more American troops would accomplish beyond increasing the enemy's weekly losses by 400 a week. "In theory, we'd then wipe them out in 10 years," Enthoven wrote McNamara.

It was now evident to Secretary McNamara that attriting the enemy's manpower strength would ultimately fail as a military strategy as well as a presidential policy for political survival. "The point is that it didn't add up," recalled McNamara. "If you took the strength figures and the body count, the defections, the infiltration and what was happening to us, the whole thing didn't make, didn't add up. I tried to make it add up in, in a judgmental way rather than an arithmetic way. . . . What I was trying to find out was how the hell the war went on year after year after year when we stopped the infiltration or shrunk it and when we had a very high body count and so on. It just didn't make sense. And the fact is that it didn't add up."[12]

It didn't add up because the enemy, and not the U.S. deployments, controlled the size of their losses. Enemy forces initiated over 90 percent of the company-sized fire fights; over 80 percent began with a well-organized enemy attack. The enemy's losses rose and fell with their choice of whether or not to fight; they could hold their losses to about 2,000 a week regardless of U.S. force levels. Hanoi could prolong the war indefinitely by strategically controlling the rate of their losses.

President Johnson said no to Westmoreland's 200,000 upper-limit request of April 1967. Yet the president's reasoning bordered on the outer limits of logic. This remarkably experienced political man chose a slow and steady course that was lined with domestic political uncertainties. How long did President Johnson believe he could get away with building a Great Society at home and waging a war in Vietnam? Rostow later recalled, "The critical decision, for example, in April of '67 when he turned down the request for 200 thousand, was not made by any such arithmetic counting of the orders of battle. It was made on the basis . . . about as follows: We're now making slow, steady, attritional progress as of early '67 that was very clear. . . . The judgment that was made there was, well, we're making slow progress now . . . with the forces that we now plan and the extra forces are not needed."[13]

The Question of Conspiracy?

Returning from Washington to Saigon, General Westmoreland was briefed by MACV intelligence officer Kelly Robinson. The briefing officer reported that some MACV analysts also believed that enemy strength for the political cadres (quasi-military and self-defense militia) category in the Order of Battle was higher than the official estimates Westmoreland had just used to brief the president. According to Robinson, Westmoreland expressed "shock" and "concern" and repeatedly said "what am I going to tell the press?" When Westmoreland had the estimate confirmed he bemoaned, "What am I going to tell Congress? What is the press going to do with this? What am I going to tell the President?"

At the center of Sam Adams's charge, made in the CBS documentary, that General Westmoreland conspired against President Johnson by withholding the actual size of the enemy's order of battle was the subsequent decision by General Westmoreland to remove self-defense and secret self-defense forces as well as political cadre from the official North Vietnamese Order of Battle on the grounds they constituted no military threat. While CIA analysts believed that these groups constituted important components of the enemy's overall military strength and served as a source of manpower for main-force units, General Westmoreland believed these groups did not belong in an estimate of armed strength, and he chose not to forward his reasoning to Washington because, "the people in Washington were not sophisticated enough to understand and evaluate this thing and neither was the media."

The official MACV Order of Battle for May 15, 1967, listed enemy strength at 292,000, but many CIA analysts believed that the figure was in the half-million range. If the CIA was correct, how could

MACV and the president claim progress in the war of attrition? How could the crossover point have been reached if the size of the enemy was really 500,000, not 285,000? On May 23, 1967, the CIA prepared and distributed on a classified basis an official memorandum entitled "The Vietnam Situation: An Analysis and Estimate," which stated in part that the Viet Cong paramilitary and political structure was considerably larger than carried in the official U.S. Order of Battle. Rostow, McNamara, and Rusk knew about this memo, LBJ did not.

Expanding the Bombing?

On May 4, 1967, McGeorge Bundy, who since leaving government to direct the Ford Foundation had offered regular counsel to LBJ, wrote in favor of limiting the bombing of North Vietnam (adding the personal disclaimer, "but you know me too well to mistake this for a sudden switch to appeasement").

Bundy now maintained that bombing would not bring the United States any closer to a political solution and, of more concern, American public opinion had become "increasingly uneasy about Vietnam because there appear to be no defined limits to the levels of force and danger that may lie ahead." The irony of U.S. policy vis-à-vis the political debate in the United States was that Johnson's decisions constituted restraint, not mindless escalation. Nevertheless, fear of what the next move would be worried people. "But the caution and restraint of the top men are better known to the few than to the many. There is also obvious pressure from the military for further reinforcements in the South, although General Westmoreland has been a model of discipline in his public pronouncements. One may guess, therefore, that the President will soon be confronted with requests for 100,000–200,000 more troops and for authority to close the harbor in Haiphong. Such recommendations are inevitable, in the framework of strictly military analysis."

Bundy urged LBJ to reject such recommendations and to place a publicly stated ceiling on the level of American participation in Vietnam, so long as there was no further escalation on the enemy side. Bundy echoed arguments being marshalled in the chambers of the Defense Department: Further intensifications of bombing in the

North or major increases in U.S. troops in the South were not good ways for bringing the war to a satisfactory conclusion. Uncertainty about the future size of the war was having destructive effects on the national will.

Bundy maintained that major troop reinforcements offered diminishing political and military returns. "I think there is no one on earth who could win an argument that an active deployment of some 500,000 men, firmly supported by tactical bombing in both South and North Vietnam, represented an undercommitment at this time," he argued. "I would not want to be the politician, or, the general, who whined about such a limitation."

Bundy focused on the need to improve pacification programs and the overall effort in the South. "This war will have no end as long as it merely pits foreign troops against Communists. In the end, it is safety in the villages that is the object of the war." The forces currently deployed were sufficient to punish Communist aggression. "But where the requirement of 1965 was for proof of the American effort, the requirement of 1967 is for re-emphasis upon the role of the Vietnamese themselves, always with our advice and support."

Bundy then raised the political context that constrained LBJ's choices. Hanoi was going to do everything possible to keep its position intact until after the 1968 elections. Having held on for so long they were bound to keep on fighting. "Since only atomic bombs could really knock them out (an invasion of North Vietnam would not do it in two years, and is of course ruled out on other grounds), they have it in their power to 'prove' that military escalation does not bring peace—at least over the next two years. They will surely do just that. However much they may be hurting, they are not going to do us any favors before November 1968."[14]

President Johnson was already boxed in, and the bombing program became the focus of intense public and congressional scrutiny. Uncertainty about what to do next in Vietnam threatened to derail administration policy. It was unlikely that a dramatic escalation in the intensity of bombing would bring the enemy to the conference table. Any evaluation of the bombing campaign needed to be understood within the context of the limited U.S. goals. Bombing electrical power plants in the North was not going to affect Ho's strategy in the South; Ho was not going to change his long-term policy on the basis of losses from the air in North Vietnam. The original rationale for the bombing had been its value for southern morale and its relation to infiltration from the North. The United States bombers had started to hit power plants because, in Bundy's opinion "we have 'run out' of other targets."

The president was torn with respect to his military commanders. The president often repeated his mentor Sam Rayburn's observation that political leaders ought to accept military advice otherwise a lot of money had been wasted training commanders at West Point. On the other hand, he held a deeply rooted suspicion that the military mind knew only how to bomb and escalate. The president needed to take control of the key discussions involving policy in Vietnam. Johnson instructed Secretary McNamara to get General Wheeler's response to Bundy's May 4 memorandum. In a memo directly to LBJ, Wheeler took issue with Bundy's narrow justification for the bombing. Not only was bombing important for its value to southern morale and its relation to northern infiltration, but bombing caused North Vietnam to "pay a price for its continued aggression against South Vietnam."

Wheeler took the initiative in recommending a series of actions against Haiphong harbor, which were opposed by Bundy and McNamara. "As a matter of cold fact," Wheeler wrote to LBJ, "the Haiphong port is the single most vulnerable and important point in the lines of communications system of North Vietnam." During the first quarter of 1967 general cargo deliveries through Haiphong had set new records. "Unless and until we find some means of constructing and reducing the flow of war-supporting material through Haiphong, the North Vietnamese will continue to be able to support their war effort both in North Vietnam and in South Vietnam."

The recommendation to strike Haiphong Harbor was a major change in the chiefs' military action program. They had previously rejected mining the ports and coastal waters on grounds that North Vietnam might in turn mine Tonkin Gulf or close the channel to Saigon. Moreover, China might use mining the ports as justification for taking military action in South China or along the Taiwan Strait. In addition, the USSR had moved 535,000 tons of goods into North Vietnam by sea. Would the Soviets move militarily to open the ports? Would they provide China with floating mines and Cruise missiles?

Wasn't the primary purpose of the bombing to stop infiltration into South Vietnam and to punish the enemy with strategic attacks on military targets in their heartland?

Moreover, the Joint Chiefs' recommendation for mining the ports was accompanied by two ambitious proposals: the first was to attack enemy infiltration at the source by expanding covert operations into Laos; the second was to seed clouds over Laos in order to induce heavy rains which would disrupt infiltration. But General Wheeler warned President Johnson that, should the plan become operational and news of its existence leak out, "international and domestic reaction, asking whether this is a new form of warfare akin to biological and nuclear warfare, might be great."[15]

The president was facing grim prospects ahead; his choices offered very little opportunity for improving either the military situation in Vietnam or his political base at home. The U.S. military effort had frustrated hopes for a Communist victory, but U.S. objectives in the South were stalemated. The bombing campaign and over 425,000 U.S. troops had not brought the enemy to the conference table. Moreover, the bombing campaign had reached the point where all worthwhile fixed targets except the ports had been struck. Progress had been made, but the war was no closer to an end point. North Vietnamese infiltration into South Vietnam continued at the high rate of approximately 8000 a month. The president was now being asked to authorize the mining of Haiphong Harbor. Had the prophets of gloom been correct? Was escalation merely a replacement for critical analysis that might identify the failure of policy? How could the present active deployment of troops and bombing not be enough to accomplish the limited objectives in Vietnam?

IV

Choosing among Imperfect Alternatives

The war in Vietnam is acquiring a momentum of its own that must be stopped.

Secretary of Defense Robert McNamara to the President, May 19, 1967.

On May 19 General Westmoreland renewed his request for an additional 200,000 troops (100,000 ASAP, the rest by 1968) plus 13 tactical air squadrons. The request ignited another fire of dissent within the Pentagon. John McNaughton, assistant secretary of Defense for International Security Affairs, reflecting the prevailing views within the Defense Department, wrote to Secretary McNamara in opposition to any additional troop deployments "unless the situation changes substantially for the worse." McNaughton's premise was that the United States currently had "enough troops to do the job we should be doing." Moreover, the enemy could avoid contact when necessary and "his intention is a stalemate; he can get it at whatever level we choose to deploy."[1]

Secretary McNamara then wrote to the president that General Westmoreland's new request proved that "there appears to be no attractive course of action." Hanoi had decided not to negotiate until the American election in November 1968. "Continuation of our present moderate policy, while avoiding a larger war, will not change Hanoi's mind, so it is not enough to satisfy the American people; increased force levels and actions against the North are likewise unlikely to change Hanoi's mind, and are likely to get us in even deeper in Southeast Asia and into a serious confrontation, if not war, with China and Russia; and we are not willing to yield. So we must choose among imperfect alternatives."

McNamara voiced serious reservations on Westmoreland's request. How could LBJ possibly justify a program which required congressional action authorizing a call-up of the Reserves, the addition of approximately 500,000 men to the military force, and an increase of approximately $10 billion for the 1968 Defense budget? Moreover, once this threshold was crossed, there would be irresistible pressures for ground actions against sanctuaries in Cambodia and Laos; for intensification of the air campaign against North Vietnam; for the blockage of rail, road, and sea imports into North Vietnam; and ultimately for the invasion of North Vietnam. These actions might then cause the Soviet Union and Red China to apply military pressure against the United States in other parts of the world, such as in Korea or Western Europe. McNamara explained to the president that "the new request would increase the total of US forces in Vietnam to 670,000 and the total in the area to 770,000."

Someone had to plug the faucet. "The Vietnam war is unpopular in this country. It is becoming increasingly unpopular as it escalates—causing more American casualties, more fear of its growing into a wider war, more privation of the domestic sector, and more distress at the amount of suffering being visited on the non-combatants in Vietnam, South and North. Most Americans do not know how we got where we are, and most, without knowing why, but taking advantage of the hindsight, are convinced that somehow we should not have gotten this deeply in. All want the war ended and expect their President to end it. Successfully. Or else."

In his letter McNamara quoted from General Westmoreland's taped remarks at Guam that " 'in the final analysis we are fighting a war of attrition. The VC/NVA 287,000-men order of battle is leveling off,' and General Westmoreland believes that, as of March, we 'reached the cross-over point'—we began attriting more men than Hanoi can recruit or infiltrate each month." So why were more troops being requested? McNamara asked the president. If the enemy was really losing between 1500 and 2000 killed-in-action a week, while U.S. and South Vietnamese losses were 175 and 250, respectively, why weren't we doing any better?

McNamara then focused on "the other war"—pacification in South Vietnam—which had also been a failure; corruption in the South Vietnamese government was widespread and real government control was confined to enclaves. "There is rot in the fabric. Our efforts to enliven the moribund political infrastructure have been matched by VC efforts—more now through coercion than was formerly the case." The enemy believed that the United States could not translate military success in the "big war" into the desired "end products"— namely, broken enemy morale and political achievements by the Republic of Vietnam.

Secretary McNamara's opposition to escalation was yet another warning based on his growing doubts about the war situation. In December 1965, when the United States had 175,000 men in Vietnam, he had reported to LBJ that "the odds are even that, even with the recommended deployments, we will be faced in early 1967 with a military standoff at a much higher level. . . ." Again in October 1966, when U.S. deployments had reached 325,000, McNamara had said, "I see no reasonable way to bring the war to an end soon," and now in May 1967, McNamara believed "that remains true today. . . . This is because the enemy has us 'stalemated' and has the capability to tailor his actions to his supplies and manpower and, by hit-and-run terror, to make government and pacification very difficult in large parts of the country almost without regard to the size of US forces there; and . . . the enemy can and almost certainly will maintain the military 'stalemate' by matching our added deployments as necessary."

McNamara also believed that the addition of the 200,000 men, involving a call-up of Reserves and an addition of 500,000 to the military strength, would almost certainly set off bitter congressional debate and irresistible domestic pressures. "Cries would go up— much louder than they already have—to 'take the wraps off the men in the field.' " President Johnson might find himself forced into accepting around-the-clock bombing of military targets as well as such strategic targets as locks and dikes, and mining of the harbors against Soviet and other ships. Associated actions might involve major ground actions into Laos and Cambodia, and probably into North

Vietnam. Finally, "the use of tactical nuclear and area-denial radio-logical-bacteriological chemical weapons would probably be suggested at some point if the Chinese entered the war in Vietnam or Korea or if US losses were running high while conventional efforts were not producing desired results."[2]

Johnson now confronted two imperfect alternatives. He could grant Westmoreland's request and intensify military actions outside the South, especially against the North. This would involve adding a minimum of 200,000 men in 1968 and another 100,000 in 1969. Or, the president could limit the force increases to no more than 30,000 and stabilize the commitment at 500,000.

McNamara threw his weight behind the latter. The momentum of endless escalation needed to be stopped. Dramatic increases in U.S. troop deployments were not the answer. The enemy could absorb and counter them, "bogging us down further and risking even more serious escalation of the war." To choose the first option would "lead to a major national disaster; it would not win the Vietnam war, but only submerge it into a larger one." The second course "will not win the Vietnam war in a military sense in a short time; it does avoid the larger war . . ."

As if these imperfect alternatives were not enough, the Joint Chiefs used the stalemate argument to press for an immediate expansion of air and sea campaigns against North Vietnam. In a detailed report to the president the chiefs endorsed attacks on all airfields and port complexes, all land and sea lines of communication in the Hanoi-Haiphong area, and mining the coastal harbors and coastal waters. The Chiefs also recommended the immediate selective call-up of Reserves and the extension of tours of service for twelve months. The JCS paper, "Worldwide US Military Posture," focused on measures that would enable the United States "to regain the strategic initiative in Southeast Asia, and to achieve a worldwide military posture." The United States had lost the strategic initiative in Southeast Asia and the chiefs blamed civilian leadership in the Pentagon. "Application of US power in Southeast Asia, incrementally and with restraint, has inhibited the effective exploitation of the superiority of US military forces and allowed the enemy to accommodate to the military measures taken. This has contributed to the extension of the war."

This report shows that the chiefs had spoken up against the president's policy, but they took their protest no further than chronicling their dissatisfaction with target system limitations, rules of engagement, and force curtailments which combined to militate against widening the gap between the total Free-World-force capability and the capability of the enemy to generate, deploy, and sustain his forces. Haiphong and other ports in North Vietnam remained active seaports, and rail lines from Communist China remained open. The North Vietnamese Air Force had become increasingly active and aggressive. Cambodia provided a haven and an avenue of infiltration for North Vietnamese/Viet Cong forces and supplies, and the Laos Panhandle supply routes were effectively controlled by North Vietnam. "The rate at which US power has been applied has permitted North Vietnamese and Viet Cong reinforcements and force posture improvements to keep pace with the graduated increases in US military actions. It is fundamental to the successful conduct of warfare that every reasonable measure be taken to widen the differential between the capabilities of the opposing forces."

The chiefs then raised a chilling spectre of falling dominoes. Mobilization was necessary because during the past several months, there had been a marked increase in deliberately flagrant North Korean activities. "Korea provides an attractive place for the communist Chinese to stage a diversionary effort. In the event of a major CHICOM/North Korean attack on South Korea, the US strategic reserve might not be capable of adequate, timely reinforcement. Under these circumstances, the prompt use of nuclear weapons, coupled with air and naval operations against bases and LOCs [lines of communication] in Manchuria, would probably become necessary to preserve the integrity of South Korea." Moreover, a Chinese attack on Thailand could trigger the use of nuclear weapons against lines of communication and supply bases in southern China. Similarly, should the Chinese intervene overtly with major combat forces in Vietnam, "it might be necessary to establish a strategic defense in South Vietnam and use tactical nuclear weapons against bases and LOCs in South China."[3]

The alternatives as outlined by McNamara's letter and the JCS report, were not pleasant ones. As usual, the president sought Rostow's counsel. Rostow wrote directly to LBJ that McNamara's May 19 memorandum "appears a reaction against the JCS position as he understands it and projects it—a reaction that goes a bit too far." Rostow's intermediate strategy involved mobilizing the Reserves in order to "seriously impress Hanoi that the jig was up." Rostow had long favored "the shallow invasion of North Viet Nam" and again endorsed such an action as necessary and advisable.

Rostow identified fundamental differences between his position and Secretary McNamara's: "Like him, I do not wish to see progressive and mindless escalation of the bombing in the Hanoi-Haiphong area; but I am anxious that we not take the heat off that area without an adequate return and would, therefore, like to see continuance of a selective attack based on an examination of what we have achieved thus far and a reexamination of targets." Rostow also favored deploying more troops in Vietnam to be used in rooting out "the provincial VC battalions, permitting the South Vietnamese to begin to put pressure on and even mop up guerrillas at the local level."

With respect to a Reserve call-up by summer; "I think it would be unwise," wrote Rostow, "for us to go into the 1967–68 shooting season without some forces in reserve." But having effective forces in the field took time and training of the Reserves now. "If you want Reserves in 1968, you must decide soon." Rostow advised Johnson that "those thoroughly professional men in Hanoi would, I believe, be profoundly impressed by a call-up. They would know that even if you did not use much of that call-up immediately, you were in a position to deal with whatever manpower requirements emerged. For all these reasons, then, I have a feeling that it would be wise to have some sort of Reserve call-up this summer if you judge it politically possible."[4]

It was now evident to Johnson that Westmoreland's request for another 200,000 men would not make the difference between victory and defeat, but rather the difference between victory in three, five, or some indefinite number of years. The United States was in this for the long haul.

Bombing had become an emotional as well as a technical issue within the Johnson administration. "There are dangerously strong feelings in your official family which tend to overwhelm the strictly military factors," Rostow wrote to the president. Secretaries Rusk and McNamara felt that the domestic and diplomatic risks of bombing Hanoi-Haiphong were not cost-effective, if its effectiveness was measured against Communist operations in the South. General Wheeler felt "a withdrawal from Hanoi-Haiphong bombing would stir deep resentment at home, among our troops, and be regarded by the Communists as an aerial Dien Bien Phu."*

The issue of internal disagreement threatened to derail the administration. Rostow phrased the issue as finding what "kind of scenario can hold our family together in ways that look after the nation's interests and make military sense?" Rostow recommended one final attack at Hanoi power plants to be followed by a radical cut-back on attacks in the Hanoi-Haiphong area. During that time McNamara and Wheeler would visit Vietnam in order to assess manpower needs for the coming year. "We could then reexamine our future bombing policy in the light of the total policy you then adopt towards the next phase of the war in Viet Nam." This scenario would give Rusk and McNamara "a break in what they feel is a dangerous pattern of progressive bombing escalation; Rusk and the State Department a chance to prove if they can buy anything important to us through diplomacy at this time. General Wheeler would get a temporary rather than a permanent change of bombing pattern, with the opportunity to refine his case and make it to you in, say, a month's time."[5]

Special National Intelligence Estimate 14.3-67

While debate on the bombing program was gaining momentum, the dispute on the size of enemy strength continued to simmer between bureaucratic agencies. By mid-June a draft of a new Special National Intelligence Estimate (SNIE) had been completed by the CIA. This detailed study sought to estimate the capabilities of the Vietnamese Communists for prosecuting the war in South Vietnam over the next two years. (The final SNIE, titled "Capabilities of the Vietnamese Communists for Fighting in South Vietnam," would not be published until November.) This first draft estimated enemy strength at between 460,000 and 570,000, and concluded, "We tend to believe that

*Dien Bien Phu was the site of the last great battle between the French and Ho Chi Minh's Viet Minh forces in 1954. French forces surrendered following the 56-day seige by the Viet Minh, ending French power in Indochina. Dien Bien Phu became analogous to defeat and surrender in the view of U.S. military pursuing the war.

the higher figure is closer to the actual total communist strength in South Vietnam." A comparison of the MACV and CIA figures is presented below:

	CIA Figures	MACV Figures
NVA Troops	53,000	53,000
VC Main and Local Forces	63,000	63,000
Irregulars		100–120,000
Guerrillas	60–120,000	(not broken down)
Militia	125,000	
Admin Services	75–100,000	23,000
Political	80,000 [minimum]	40,000
Totals	456–541,000	279–299,000

The draft SNIE had a disquieting effect on all of the principals. Admiral Sharp cabled General Westmoreland registering concern regarding revised strength estimates of Viet Cong Irregular Forces. "Continued close coordination would be essential in order to avoid public disclosure of this sensitive and potentially explosive subject."[6]

Was MACV keeping their official Order of Battle below 300,000 in order to show progress in the war of attrition? In order to accomplish this arithmetically, it was necessary to drop the self-defense and secret-self-defense categories from the official Order of Battle. General Westmoreland did not believe these categories constituted a military threat. CIA analysts viewed self defense and secret defense militia as important components of the enemy's overall military strength and a source of manpower for main forces. Yet, the CIA was to confront intense opposition. In early June 1967, following a trip to South Vietnam, Robert Komer, wrote to the president that a month in-country had reinforced his view that "we are gaining momentum and that by the end of next winter it will be clear for all to see that we have gained the upper hand. In other words, while the war is not being 'won' we will clearly be winning it. The real question is not whether we need more US troops to 'win' the war in the south, but rather how fast we want to win it." Komer envisioned a 50–50 chance of a "clear upper hand" by mid-1968 without major U.S. add-ons—"if everything else breaks our way. By then the deterioration of the VC should be amply evident."

McNamara Responds to the Chiefs

On June 12, 1967, (5 days before commissioning the "Pentagon Papers") McNamara forwarded a revised draft presidential memorandum, titled "Alternative Military Actions Against North Vietnam," to the president. McNamara continued his battle against the Joint Chiefs' recommendation for intensified attacks on the Hanoi-Haiphong logistical base as well as bombing and mining of the ports close to Hanoi and Haiphong. Such escalatory actions would not substantially reduce the flow of men and supplies to the South nor pressure Hanoi into settlement, McNamara asserted. "The real damage, however, rests in the inexorable pressure towards further escalation and in the serious risk of enlarging the war into one with the Soviet Union and China," argued the secretary of defense.

McNamara's analysis reiterated the questions the Defense Department had raised in May. Combat operations in South Vietnam had reached a high level of intensity with only slow progress by friendly forces, "a situation which it is within the power of the enemy to perpetuate." The pacification program was stalled and the South Vietnamese government "is still largely corrupt, incompetent and unresponsive to the needs and wishes of the people."

Seeing little progress from Vietnam, McNamara asked where would it all stop? "Implicit in the [JCS] recommendation is a conviction that nothing short of toppling the Hanoi regime will pressure North Vietnam to settle so long as they believe they have a chance to win the 'war of attrition' in the south." McNamara argued that major entities of the U.S. government could no longer agree on U.S. goals much less strategy and that American public opinion was moving towards rejecting the war. The rising U.S. casualty rate and the increasing proportion of losses being suffered by U.S. forces, would result in substantial disfavor with the public.

The U.S. objective in Vietnam had always been a limited one, and in McNamara's opinion the policy decisions required narrowing, not broadening, the level of commitment. "The limited over-all US objective, in terms of the narrow US commitment and not of wider US preferences, is to take action (so long as they continue to help themselves) to see that the people of South Vietnam are permitted to determine their own future. Our commitment is to stop (or generously to offset when we cannot stop) North Vietnamese military intervention in the South, so that 'the board will not be tilted' against Saigon in an internal South Vietnamese contest for control."

In other words, the U.S. goal in Vietnam was to build democracy and stability in the South, not pulverize the North. Besides, pulverizing hadn't worked with respect to the limited U.S. objective, McNamara wrote. Hanoi had already decided to hold out so long as a prospect of winning the war of attrition in the South existed. Moreover, nothing "short of destruction of the regime or occupation of North Vietnamese territory, will with high confidence reduce the flow of men and material below the relatively small amount needed by enemy forces to continue the war in the South."

How had the North Vietnamese withstood the psychological, physical, and economic pressures of air attacks? McNamara pointed out that the North Vietnamese economy was essentially agrarian, at a comparatively primitive stage of development; the people had simple needs, most of which were satisfied locally; the economy provided little direct input, other than manpower, for the war in the South. The flow of economic and military aid into North Vietnam from Russia and China far surpassed the total damage resulting from air attacks and provided the overwhelming bulk of materials necessary to continue the war. Finally, the North Vietnamese had devised and implemented an elaborate and highly successful system of counter-measures that negated most of the impact of air attacks on the flow of men and supplies in the South.

Cleverly turning the JCS recommendation around, McNamara asked, "Why not escalate the bombing and mine the harbors and perhaps occupy southern North Vietnam—on the gamble that it would constrict the flow, meaningfully limiting enemy action in the South, and that it would bend Hanoi?" Because American lives would be the ante for such a policy, and public opinion would reject the American actions, he then answered. "There may be a limit beyond which many Americans and much of the world will not permit the United States to go. The picture of the world's greatest super-power killing or injuring more than 2,000 non-combatants a month while trying to pound a tiny backward nation into submission on an issue whose merits are hotly disputed, is not a pretty one. It could conceivably produce a costly distortion in the American national consciousness and in the world image of the United States—especially if we increase the damage to North Vietnam greatly in an effort to achieve their capitulation."

McNamara favored a program that would concentrate bombing on infiltration routes in the southern neck of North Vietnam south of the twentieth parallel. The plan reflected the secretary's belief that the outcome of the war hinged on what happened in the South, and it was necessary to start improving the negotiating environment. The secretary warned President Johnson that in the eyes of the world the bombing was not only unproductive, it was morally repugnant. Mining the ports would be unproductive and costly in domestic and world support, and faced with the frustrations of stalemate, the United States would have no choice but to escalate further.

With Westmoreland's request still pending and doubts beginning to emerge on the viability of the U.S. commitment, Secretary McNamara and General Wheeler now headed to Vietnam for a first-hand appraisal of the military situation. Ambassador Bunker was buoyed by McNamara's impending visit, cabling the president, "It gives all of us here new encouragement and enthusiasm in our determination to bring to a successful conclusion the policies and goals you have set for us. We are making progress. We are deeply conscious of the heavy burdens you bear. Please be assured you can count on us."[7]

V

The Summer of Discontent

We all make mistakes. But, as you know, the buck stops here.

President Johnson's remarks to a delegation of Republican
Congressmen visiting the White House, August 17, 1967.

Accompanied by Undersecretary of State Nicholas Katzenbach and
Chairman of the Joint Chiefs General Earle Wheeler, McNamara
arrived on the morning of July 7, 1967, at Tan Son Nhut Airport, the
major air base and commercial airport in South Vietnam, located on
the outskirts of Saigon. The delegation immediately began ten hours
of meetings in the air base's "High Noon Conference Room."
MACV's headquarter's on the air base was referred to as "Pentagon
East." Two days of intensive briefings were followed by visits to
combat zones, a tour of pacification programs in the Mekong Delta,
and private meetings with Thieu and Ky.

While McNamara was assessing the situation in Vietnam, speculation was rampant back home that Westmoreland would get the
troops he had requested. The front page of the July 8 *New York Times*
reported, "Westmoreland asks M'Namara for more troops. Says US
forces are slowly winning the war but must 'step up the pressure.' "
Indeed, the headline mirrored the private meeting during which

Westmoreland insisted, "The war is not a stalemate. We are winning slowly but steadily. North Vietnam is paying a tremendous price with nothing to show for it in return."[1]

McNamara returned to Washington voicing a new outlook, however temporary. During a July 12 secret meeting of the president's principal foreign policy advisors, McNamara stated, "there is not a military stalemate" in Vietnam. During a July 19 Cabinet meeting McNamara again said, "there is no evidence of a stalemate." President Johnson was clearly buoyed by McNamara's news. During a private White House meeting with journalist Peter Lisagor, Johnson boasted, "We've begun to turn defeat into victory. I'm not distressed. There is no truth in the stalemate theory. The McNamara report this time was the best of his nine."[2]

The president was soon presented with an important opportunity to dispel any claims of disharmony between his principal advisors. McNamara and Wheeler had just returned from Vietnam and presented their report to the president. General Westmoreland had also returned to the states in order to attend his mother's funeral and had then flown to Washington for a meeting with the president. During a hastily called White House news conference from the second-floor private sitting room, the president pointed to General Wheeler, General Westmoreland, and Secretary McNamara, who were all seated on a sofa. "We have reached a meeting of minds," declared President Johnson. Looking directly at his three principal advisors, LBJ asked each rhetorically, "The troops that General Westmoreland needs and requests, as we feel it necessary, will be supplied. Is that not true, General Westmoreland?" "Yes sir." "General Wheeler?" "Yes, sir." "Secretary McNamara?" "Yes, sir."

President Johnson then explained to the assembled reporters that the exact number of troops would not be announced until it was ascertained how much of an additional commitment would be made by U.S. allies. For the moment the Reserves would not be mobilized. General Westmoreland told reporters that all reports of stalemate were "complete fiction" and "completely unrealistic." Moreover, tremendous progress had been made—which had been easily observable to the secretary during his recent visit. Westmoreland likened the perception of the lack of progress in the war to the example of parents who sometimes could not see the growth of a child as much

as visiting grandparents who could detect progress much more readily than those who saw the child every day. McNamara, like a visiting
grandparent, had now seen real progress in Vietnam.

President Johnson also announced that he was sending two personal representatives, Clark Clifford, chairman of the President's
Foreign Intelligence Advisory Board, and presidential consultant
General Maxwell Taylor, on a tour of the allied nations involved in
the war. The goal of the mission was to get commitments for additional support from Thailand, Australia, New Zealand, the Philippines, and South Korea.

Clifford and Taylor returned to Washington on August 6 and reported that the allies strongly supported increasing the pressure on
the enemy. Clifford told reporters that some of the allies believed the
war should be called "the war of Southeast Asia," because that best
approximated the stakes. Political satirist Russell Baker described the
Clifford/Taylor mission as the famous "Jim Dandy report." "The
purpose of their journey," he wrote, "which had been puzzling at
first, emerged only upon their return to Washington with the report
that the Johnson Administration's conduct of the Vietnam war was
just right. Vietnam's neighboring states, they said, agreed that American bombing of North Vietnam was perfectly correct and Asian
statesmen applauded the President's over-all war policy with cries of
'Jim Dandy!' the traditional Oriental phrase for telling Westerners
what they want to hear."[3]

The trip had made a powerful impression on Clifford, and despite
what he had told reporters, Clifford knew the allies were not really
ready or anxious to ante up. Nor did they seem terribly troubled by
the possibility of a Communist victory. "I returned home puzzled,
troubled, concerned," Clifford wrote two years later in "A Viet Nam
Reappraisal." "Was it possible that our assessment of the danger to
the stability of Southeast Asia and the Western Pacific was exaggerated? Was it possible that those nations which were neighbors of
Vietnam had a deeper perception of the tides of world events in 1967
than we?"[4]

There were certainly Jim Dandys within the president's circle of
advisors. Throughout July and August Rostow provided President
Johnson with overwhelming documentation that the Communists
faced serious manpower problems. The most observable trend according to Rostow was the "slow decline of the Viet Cong manpower

pool—which has yielded stagnation or reduction in the size and effective strength of Viet Cong main force units and impairment of the Viet Cong infrastructure . . ." Rostow added that he had spent time "reading literally hundreds of particular intelligence reports on the situation in the various provinces of South Vietnam." These reports showed strain in VC morale and manpower and a weakening in military effectiveness, "but no definitive break in the resilient Viet Cong structure."[5]

On July 26, Bunker's weekly cable, which Rostow described in a covering memorandum to LBJ as "the most solid piece of analysis in a single place of progress in Vietnam," arrived in the White House. "I do not want to appear to be over optimistic . . . ," Bunker wrote. "I do not believe, however that there is any evidence that things are in a 'stalemate' here or that we have lapsed into a static situation. I and my colleagues are all convinced that we are moving steadily ahead and moving in the right direction. I do think we need to do more intensive work in educating the press here and I intend to concentrate on this."[6]

On August 7 Rostow reported to LBJ, "All the evidence we have indicates bombing North Viet Nam (and Laos) helps cut down the level of infiltration below the level it would otherwise attain." There certainly was evidence to suggest otherwise, but Rostow, choosing to give Johnson only optimistic reports, said "all" not "some" of the evidence. Rostow concluded for the president, "The evidence is that the Viet Cong are having severe manpower problems in the south and facing real difficulties in maintaining both their guerrilla and their main-force units. . . . All the evidence we have indicates that Hanoi does not now expect to win the war in the south on the battlefield. They are hanging on hoping that there will be a break in the will of the U.S. to continue the war."

The public's perception of the war, particularly of the lack of military progress, was creating additional burdens for the administration. The summer approval polls all showed a decline in support for the war and for LBJ's handling of it. An August 2, 1967, cable from General Westmoreland to General Wheeler, General Harold K. Johnson, Army Chief of Staff, and Admiral Sharp reflected these concerns. It was necessary to orchestrate a public relations campaign to rally public support for the war, he told them. "Of course we must make haste carefully in order to avoid charges that the military establishment is conducting an organized propaganda campaign, either overt or covert." The nation's highest ranking military advisors believed the United States was winning the war. The public, on the other hand, was growing increasingly uneasy with the growing nature of U.S. commitment. The lack of major combat operations was creating a false impression of stalemate. "Nothing could be farther from the truth, of course. Every indicator belies either stalemate or loss of initiative." Westmoreland explained that he had already taken steps to clarify military progress. "While we work on the nerve ends here we hope that careful attention will be paid to the roots there— the confused or unknowledgable pundits who serve as sources for each other."[7]

In August President Johnson approved an additional 45–50,000 troops for General Westmoreland and imposed a new troop ceiling of 525,000. The evidence shows that LBJ chose reluctantly to push ahead his new threshold, but he breathed a sigh of relief when not forced to mobilize the Reserves. During this same period, General Johnson returned from a trip to Vietnam. Rostow wrote to LBJ, "I am told that he comes back with the most optimistic reports. Recommend that you have him give you his report in person. After meeting with him, you might wish to unleash him on the White House Press Corps." Which was exactly what happened. General Johnson vigorously challenged the stalemate thesis and declared, "We're winning the war." The general told the press corps that "this was the first trip where I could see significant evidence of progress." When asked whether the 45,000 troops recently approved by the president would be the "last increase," the general replied, "This should be, with circumstances substantially as they are now, adequate to provide a degree of momentum that will see us through to a solution in Vietnam."

An August 8 cable from General Wheeler to General Westmoreland illustrated the growing problems confronting the administration. The previous day's *New York Times* had carried an article by correspondent R. W. Apple, "Vietnam, the Signs of Stalemate," which quoted from an unidentified military source, "Every time Westy makes a speech about how good the South Vietnam army is, I want to ask him why he keeps calling for more Americans. His need for reinforcement is a measure of our failure with the Vietnamese." Wheeler was repulsed by the quote: "On the assumption that the above extract is in fact a quote, I must say it is regrettable that a senior officer felt compelled to respond to a press query of this type and tragic that he was disloyal to his commander in the process."

Westmoreland quickly cabled Wheeler and Sharp that it was "inconceivable to me that any general officer in Vietnam would make such a statement. Any general who is serving here or who has made an honest appraisal as a result of a professional visit could not come to the conclusion that a need for reinforcements is a measure of our failure with the Vietnamese. Progress is not a failure and by every measure there is increasing progress, as you know." Westmoreland then attacked the messenger: "He [Apple] is pessimistic and suspicious . . . [He] still is convinced that we are not honest about casualties and are manipulating the figures. I have watched Apple become more critical and more argumentative during recent months. Barring some dramatic and irrefutable turn for the better here we can expect him to continue to play the role of doubter and critic. He is probably bucking for a Pulitzer Prize."[9]

Finding a workable answer to the public debate over the question of a stalemate dominated the agenda. During one White House meeting the president asked his advisors, "What is the answer to the stalemate issue?" Wheeler responded that there was no stalemate, but the president persisted. "That's not a good enough answer. McNamara gets ridiculed when he says it. I answered it today by saying it was pure communist propaganda. We should have some colorful general like MacArthur with his shirt neck open to go in there and say this is pure propaganda . . . we have no songs, no parades, no bond drives and we can't win the war otherwise." President Johnson then instructed Walt Rostow to get "a colorful general to go to Saigon and argue with them [the press]. We've got to do something dramatic."

The president also asked General Wheeler "How many in South Vietnam—12–15 million?" The declassified meeting notes detail the barren terrain of logic: Wheeler answered, "about 15 million and the Vietcong are about 4 million." The president wondered aloud, "It seems like with all of the South Vietnamese and all the American troops, we could whip 'em."[10]

The Sick Society

Nothing symbolized the potential bankruptcy of a guns-and-butter policy more than the outbreak of racial violence in urban cities throughout America during the summer of 1967. Rioting in late July left 26 dead in Newark; 40 killed in Detroit, where for the first time in twenty-four years federal troops were needed to stop the rioters. Federal paratroopers ultimately restored order, arresting over 7000 looters and snipers. In the words of Senator J. William Fulbright, the Great Society had become a "sick society." "Each war feeds on the other, and, although the President assures us that we have the resources to win both wars, in fact we are not winning either of them." Johnson soon learned that the constituency that supported his Great Society did not support him on Vietnam.

That summer the president refused to abandon his guns-and-butter strategy. Instead, he renewed his request that Congress pass an across-the-board surtax, raising the amount to 10 percent, a request that pitted Johnson against House Ways and Means chairman, Wilbur Mills. In a battle between two politicians who had been tutored under the wings of former House Speaker Sam Rayburn, it was the president who came up empty. Mills insisted that any tax be accompanied by domestic program cuts of the same magnitude. Johnson resisted and no tax bill was reported out of committee in 1967.

LBJ's political coalition in Congress and credibility with the general public began unraveling. The president's overall job rating, as reported in the Gallup poll, dropped from 47 percent in mid-July to 39 percent in early August. His job rating on Vietnam showed 54 percent disapproval, an all-time high. In effect, the administration was now caught in a self-made trap.

Lobbying Democratic congressmen on August 8 for their support of the administration's tax bill, the president emphasized that "the military situation and pacification are improving. Intelligence shows that we are moving up and Vietcong and North Vietnamese are moving down. Westmoreland has turned defeat into what we believe will be a victory. It's only a matter now of will. . . . There is no stalemate. We are moving along. The kill ratio is 10 to 1."

President Johnson receiving a briefing on Vietnam from Ambassador Henry Cabot Lodge, Secretary of State Dean Rusk, Secretary of Defense Robert McNamara, and Undersecretary of State George Ball. November 1963.

Military and civilian advisors conferring at the LBJ ranch. December 1964.

Secretary of State Dean Rusk.

Secretary of Defense Robert McNamara conferring with Secretary of State Dean Rusk. July 1965.

The president making a point at the Honolulu Conference. February 1966.

The president meeting with Prime Minister Nguyen Cao Ky and Chief of State Nguyen Van Thieu at the Honolulu Conference. February 1966.

Secretary of State Dean Rusk, National Security Advisor Walt Rostow, and President Johnson in the Oval Office. May 1966.

The president reviewing the troops at Fort Campbell, Kentucky. July 1966.

The president confering with Prime Minister Ky at the Manilla Conference. October 1966.

A cabinet meeting. May 1967.

Generals Earle Wheeler and William Westmoreland and Secretary Robert McNamara in the White House. July 1967.

The president with General William Westmoreland visiting the wounded at Cam Ranh Bay. December 1967.

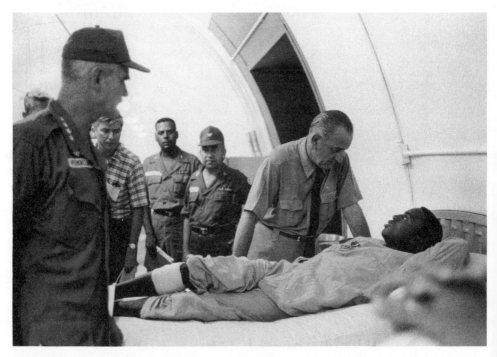

*President Johnson studying a
congressional head count.*

President Johnson and Vice President Hubert Humphrey.

The president with Senator Mike Mansfield.

President Johnson meeting with Senate Minority Leader Everett Dirksen.

House Speaker John McCormick.

House Minority Leader Gerald Ford challenging the president's policy.

The president with Senator J. William Fulbright.

Congressman Wilbur Mills responding to a briefing on the 1968 tax bill.

The meeting quickly turned vitriolic when New York Congress-man Lester Wolff told Johnson, "Nobody sees the light at the end of the tunnel in Vietnam. We are the victims of a poor public relations program." Wolff cited Congressman Gerald Ford's criticisms that the United States was not using its strategic bombing effectively in the North. The president responded, "We are taking out half of the infiltration with our bombing, some reports show. We are reducing infiltration, but we haven't stopped it. I am not going to do what Ford says, because we would be in a war with China tonight if we did. Much as we want it, there is no easy way out."

Johnson reserved his harshest observations for those who wanted the shackles of restraint removed from the military. "Well, I want you to know that I believe in civilian government, and we will have civilian government as long as I am President. Second, what Ford has said is untrue. We don't want to hit targets near China or targets in civilian areas or targets in ports. We get over the China border now even though there is a buffer zone. It doesn't take long when jets fly at 1200 miles per hour. We have hit two ships. You know how emo-tions run in this country when ships are hit. Remember the *Lusi-tania*. We do not want to get the Soviet Union and China into this war."

The Joint Chiefs had recommended 242 targets to be bombed in North Vietnam, and all but 39 that were in the buffer zone along the Chinese border had been authorized. Manifesting his distrust of the military, Johnson told his congressional visitors, "The generals are ready to bomb there but I'm not—there's a difference in judgment." According to Tom Johnson's notes from the meeting, "We'd already hit two Russian ships in the Haiphong harbor, and feared that if we hit more, we'd get more trouble than we got gains. We'd bombed Hanoi within half a mile of Ho Chi Minh's house. (The President pointed toward the Washington monument as he said, 'That's as close as those people down there, and him sitting there on his front porch.') That was too close."

McNamara Testifies on the Bombing Program

In August Secretary McNamara testified before Senator John Stennis's subcommittee of the Senate Armed Services Committee on the subject "Air War Against North Vietnam." The secretary reported that on the operating target list used by the Joint Chiefs for planning attacks on fixed targets, only a handful of targets had been recommended against which strikes had not yet been authorized. The secretary repeated his long-held belief that bombing was never intended as a substitute for success in the South and expanding the target list would not shorten the war. McNamara told the Stennis subcommittee that bombing could not be expected to break the will of North Vietnam nor force Hanoi to the conference table. Instead, bombing had fortified the South in a time of need and increased the cost of the continued infiltration of men and supplies from North to South Vietnam.

Bombing needed to be considered as a supplement to and not as a substitute for counterinsurgency in the South, said McNamara. When evaluated within these limited objectives, the bombing campaign had been successful: Hanoi had paid a price for its aggression, morale in the South had clearly been bolstered, and infiltration hampered. Bombing North Vietnam out of the war would be accomplished only by the systematic annihilation of North Vietnamese population centers, a plan favored by some members of the Joint Chiefs and hawks in Congress but rejected by McNamara and the president. McNamara faced tough grilling by committee members, but he was merely voicing the president's views. (In a revealing letter written in August 1967 to former British Prime Minister Anthony Eden, former Secretary of State Dean Acheson explained McNamara's trauma: "Bob McNamara told me all about the situation a week ago. This report [to Congress] is the truth, but not the whole truth. Rather, a loyal lieutenant putting the best face on a poor situation. The fact is that the bombing of the North started as morale builder for the South when things were very bad there. We have now run out of targets but the Republican hawks keep calling for more which produces useless casualties and encourages some Air Force fire-eaters to urge population bombing. LBJ has not HST's [Harry S. Truman] courage to say no to political pressures. . . .")[11]

The Senate subcommittee included many hawks who felt that the military had been held down by handwringing civilian advisors; Senator Strom Thurmond actually accused McNamara of placating the Communists. This view was reflected in the subcommittee's August report which charged that "diametrically opposed views" of the Joint Chiefs and Secretary McNamara had created the "unsatisfactory progress of the war." The subcommittee faulted civilian control of the war which had rejected "the unanimous weight of professional military judgment." The report criticized the policy of the civilian advisors: "It is not our intention to point a finger or to second guess those who determined this policy. But the cold fact is that this policy has not done the job and it has been contrary to the best military judgment. What is needed now is the hard decision to do whatever is necessary, take the risks that have to be taken, and apply the force that is required to see the job through."

The subcommittee cited civilian control over bombing policy as the reason the air campaign had not achieved its objectives. The imposed doctrine of gradualism prevented U.S. forces from waging the air campaign to best calculate and achieve maximum results. The Senate subcommittee agreed with the JCS that the effects of the air campaign were cumulative; no one could predict which blow would be the crucial one. Every attack stretched enemy resources. No one knew which attack would break the enemy. But the committee had actually misdirected its hostility. McNamara was still the president's agent. Responsibility for the limited bombing policy belonged with President Johnson.

MACV Confronts SNIE 14.3-67

Publication of the new intelligence estimate on enemy strength was scheduled for September 1. The CIA was insisting on the inclusion of 120,000 Self-Defense (SD) and Secret Self-Defense (SSD) forces in the new SNIE, for a total 435,350 Order of Battle. While MACV maintained that the SD and SSD did not belong in the overall total figure, CIA analysts saw the self-defense forces as defenders of their home areas by planting mines, booby traps, and grenades. When SD and SSD strength figures were included in the overall enemy strength, the total contradicted MACV's overall strength figures, which had already been given to the press. The disagreement was politically charged and controversial since MACV could hardly be expected to endorse a new set of figures showing a larger Communist force at a time when Westmoreland was asking for more troops.

Pressure was now brought on the CIA to compromise with MACV. The NSC's Robert Ginsburgh suggested to Rostow that Director Helms be told that it was "time to 'bite the bullet.'" Including SD and SSD figures in an estimate of the enemy's military capabilities made little sense to MACV analysts. These support groups operated in their own hamlets, were rarely armed, had no discipline, and possessed little military capability. An August 19 cable from Komer to Carver sided with MACV's position: "I cannot see case for including vague estimates of low-grade part time hamlet self-defense groups, mostly weaponless, in new O/B."[12]

On August 20, McNamara's deputy, General Creighton Abrams, cabled General Wheeler expressing MACV's opposition to surfacing any estimate that contained SD or SSD strength figures. "The press reaction to these inflated figures is of much greater concern. We have been projecting an image of success over the recent months, and properly so. Now, when we release the figure of 426–531,000, the newsmen will immediately seize on the point that the enemy force has increased about 120–130,000. All available caveats and explanations will not prevent the press from drawing an erroneous and gloomy conclusion as to the meaning of the increase." On the same day, Westmoreland cabled Wheeler with a similar message: "I do not concur in the inclusion of strength figures for the self-defense and secret self-defense. It distorts the situation and makes no sense. No amount of caveats will prevent the erroneous conclusion that will result."[13]

Johnson apparently liked MACV's version of enemy strength. Meeting privately on August 24 with members of the press, the president referred to reports in his possession which showed "that the guerrilla infra-structure is on the verge of collapse. All I can say to that is that if there is a stalemate, as the press reports, then every single one of our men we have out there is wrong. Bunker and Westmoreland do not agree, nor does anybody else who works for us out there—and they have no other purpose than to report the facts. The reporting debate is not one that I can win. Nobody reports we have a stalemate, but this is one where I do not want to win the argument and lose the sale." (Bunker's weekly cable had advised Johnson, "General Westmoreland also reports progress in the very difficult but absolutely essential task of destroying the Viet Cong infrastructure which for many years has been working under deep cover in the villages and hamlets.")[14]

The next day Westmoreland cabled Wheeler and Sharp reiterating his concern that the latest draft of SNIE 14.3–67 contained an enemy strength figure of 461,000 including self-defense, secret self-defense forces, and assault youth. "This command cannot support these latest NIE figures with the intelligence at hand." Westmoreland requested that a team representing all Washington intelligence agencies concerned with the SNIE visit Vietnam "as soon as possible to develop a common and valid set of enemy strength statistics."[15]

In order to resolve these statistical disagreements, George Carver went to Saigon with instructions from CIA Director Helms to reach agreement that would eliminate any appearance of dispute on this politically touchy subject. Records from an August 25 meeting of the Joint Chiefs reveal a similar preoccupation with public relations, and not with the numbers themselves. The chiefs discussed "sending a team to MACV to arrive at acceptable force figures and to coordinate the plan for release of information to the public. . . . The JCS fully appreciate the public release problem and view it as the major problem. While concerned about the figures, they consider them of lesser importance."[16]

Ambassador Bunker also cabled Walt Rostow to voice what he regarded to be a "potentially serious problem created by the new NIE on verge of completion." If the CIA estimate of enemy strength was published with an Order of Battle in the 430–490,000 range, the political implications would be devastating. "Despite all our success in grinding down VC/NVA here, CIA figures are used to show that they are really much stronger than ever. Despite all caveats, this is inevitable conclusion which most press would react," Bunker said. "I intend to mention it to the President in my coming weekly. The credibility gap would be enormous, and is quite inconsistent with all the hard evidence we have about growing enemy losses, declining VC recruitments and the like."[17]

All work on the SNIE was suspended until these disagreements could be worked out. Everyone recognized the need to develop common and valid sets of statistics and to retain credibility in doing so. Yet most of those involved in the process recognized that the numbers were being manipulated for political purposes. Like the proverbial emperor with no clothes, President Johnson was about to be discovered stripped bare of all credibility.

VI

Signs of Optimism

The elections thus constitute the successful end of one process and the beginning of another important one, namely the successful prosecution of the war and the conclusion of an acceptable settlement.

Ambassador Ellsworth Bunker's weekly cable to President Johnson, September 5, 1967.

In the fall of 1967, as progress on the ground churned to a halt, and with no large increments of troops on the way, bombing the North and mining the ports became the war—at least in public debate. It was understandable for the average citizen to expect that removing target restrictions would improve the military stalemate, but President Johnson recognized the tenuousness of that link. Whatever progress was attained from bombing the North needed a correlative in the political and economic aspects of pacification in the South.

The Joint Chiefs believed that bombing would create additional difficulties for North Vietnam and that the additional pain caused by such bombing would be worth the risk of hitting Soviet ships and possibly widening the war, even though this pain would not be decisive for ultimate victory in the South. Secretary McNamara, on the other hand, believed that such bombing could not prevent North Vietnam from carrying on its present level of military operations in

77

the South and would not be worth the risk of widening the war. He also believed that in a country with a coastline 400 miles in length, bombing the port facilities would not eliminate seaborne imports. And even if seaborne imports were totally eliminated, North Vietnam would be able to import over rail, road, and by inland waterway all that it required.

Secretary McNamara continued to argue against hitting the Haiphong and Hanoi ports because foreign vessels frequented them regularly. But LBJ was now ready to expand the bombing program by removing restrictions at Cam Pha and Hong Gai. During a long private meeting of the principal advisors in the White House, LBJ asked McNamara "why he could not give a conditional order that as long as there are no ships left in either of these two harbors—they could get hit." Secretary McNamara said "he did not know if this was feasible." But Johnson rejected McNamara's advice and told General Johnson (who had temporarily replaced Wheeler who was recovering from a heart ailment) to "put our best man in there to see if there are any ships, and if not, hit the ports." General Johnson thanked the president by explaining that "theatre commanders would welcome this kind of latitude."[1]

Secretary McNamara then instructed General Johnson that he needed to make it crystal clear that "if there are no ships in the port then they can be hit" and leave it to the commander to figure out how to be certain that there were no ships. But no authorization was being issued to hit Haiphong harbor because it "always has Russian ships in there." In mid-September, Cam Pha, a target that McNamara had long argued should not be hit, was struck for the first time.

The targets represented a bone to hawks in Congress and to the Joint Chiefs; few in Johnson's private councils really expected the expansion to improve the military situation. Several days later, during the regular Tuesday luncheon of the principals, President Johnson told General Johnson the Joint Chiefs should "search for imaginative ideas to put pressure to bring this war to a conclusion—he did not want them to just recommend more men or that we drop the Atom bomb. He could think of those ideas."[2]

A New Beginning: A First Test of Democracy for South Vietnam

On September 3, 1967, South Vietnam's Chief of State Nguyen Van Thieu was elected president and Prime Minister Nguyen Cao Ky vice-president in South Vietnam's first election under its new constitution. The 44-year-old Thieu was the antithesis of the flamboyant Ky. A graduate of the U.S. Command and General Staff College at Fort Leavenworth, Kansas, in 1957, Thieu, as a colonel and later as Major General, quickly became a respected military leader in Vietnam. Beneath the self-effacing exterior was the personality of a political survivor. Thieu had personally led his Fifth Infantry Division troops in the decisive coup attack against President Diem's bodyguards in November 1963. As chief of state, Thieu had forged a number of political coalitions which had allowed him to emerge with majority support from the military council that had been ruling South Vietnam since 1965.

The Thieu-Ky slate received 35 percent of the total votes cast. The election itself was carried out under restrictive rules that barred any Communist or pro-Communist "neutralist" from appearing on the ballot. The turnout was deceptive since two-thirds of those running had been disqualified from voting as "neutralists" or "Communists." The Armed Forces council had forced Ky to withdraw from the presidential ticket and run with Thieu as vice-president, thus consolidating their strength.

While the Thieu-Ky victory was expected, the margin was generally weaker than anticipated. Moreover, Truong Dinh Dzu, a civilian lawyer, finished second with over 800,000 votes on a platform critical of the government and favoring peace negotiations. Dzu favored ending American bombing of the North, direct negotiations with Hanoi, and private talks with the Vietcong.

In Saigon as in most South Vietnamese cities, the Thieu-Ky ticket ran well behind former premier Tran Van Huong, another civilian candidate. The Thieu-Ky ticket controlled the voting in the outer provinces where military commanders arranged with major ethnic groups to deliver their votes. One official on the scene described it as "Chicago politics, but with circumspection."[3]

President Johnson had sent 22 prominent Americans to observe the Vietnam elections. Finding no ballot boxes with false bottoms, the group issued statements of praise for a fledgling democracy and its honest election. Ambassador Bunker then cabled LBJ, "When we recall that President Diem was officially recorded as having obtained 89.9 percent of the vote in the 1961 presidential election, we can see how far the government of Vietnam has come in conducting a generally fair election and in the compilation of the results." Bunker also warned the president, "All in all, while the elections have taken a considerable step farther down the road, there are still plenty of potholes ahead."[4]

The election in South Vietnam was certainly good news for LBJ, and the president now turned to his own forthcoming electoral chances. During a September 6 Cabinet meeting Johnson spoke optimistically of the political situation: "No matter what the polls show, we are still leading every Republican . . . Romney, with or without Wallace . . . Reagan, Rockefeller, Nixon. . . . Though we're down, we're still 40% ahead of any Republican. . . ." The president told his Cabinet, "We don't take the offensive enough. We have got to speak up and not tuck tail."

On September 8, 1967, General Omar Bradley, who had just returned from Vietnam, provided Walt Rostow with a report that Rostow couldn't wait to send the president: "In general, he emerged with a sense of great optimism. . . . He said, in fact, we must 'fight to keep from expressing over-optimism.' There is not the slightest doubt in his mind that the war is not stalemated. We are moving forward. He found among senior officers—even strong Republicans—a deep appreciation for the support being given to the men in the field by the President. He emerged convinced that we were well on the way to winning the war. The only serious problem was to keep a base of public support in the United States for the effort in Viet Nam."

SNIE 14.3-67, AGAIN

The unrestrained optimism of Rostow and Bradley could not be found at the Order-of-Battle conference, reconvened on September 9 in Saigon. All work had been suspended until the CIA's representative George Carver arrived. After a day of meetings, Carver wrote CIA Director Helms that MACV was "stonewalling," because of "political public relations." MACV was sticking with 119,000 main force, 29,000 administrative services, 65,000 guerrillas, and 85,000 political cadre for a total of 298,000. CIA was insisting on 121,000 main force, 40–60,000 administrative services, 60–100,000 guerrillas, 90,000 political cadre, and 120,000 others for a minimum total of 431,000. "MACV was adamant," wrote Carver, "that no figure or quantified estimate be given for other elements [of] VC organization such as self-defense, secret self-defense, assault youth, etc."

Carver, identifying his frustrations in dealing with MACV, told Helms he had become aware from a "variety of circumstantial indicators" such as "tacit or oblique lunchtime corridor admissions by MACV officers," that "all point to the inescapable conclusion that General Westmoreland (with Robert Komer's encouragement) has given instruction tantamount to direct order that VC strength total will not exceed 300,000 ceiling. Rationale seems to be that any higher figure would not be sufficiently optimistic and would generate unacceptable level of criticism from the press." Carver informed Helms he would see Komer and Westmoreland the next day "and will endeavor to loosen this straightjacket. Unless I can, we are wasting our time. . . . If I can budge Westmoreland, the whole matter can be resolved to everyone's satisfaction in a few hours of serious discussion. If I can not, no agreement is possible."[5]

During the subsequent session, Komer belittled the CIA for having analysts with little experience on the Order of Battle. "The agency's analysis," claimed Komer, "consequently, could not expect to compare in depth and quality to that of MACV." Carver listened to Komer's hour-plus monologue, which focused on "Westmoreland's problems with the press, their frustrating inability to convince the press (hence the public) of the great progress being made, and the paramount importance of saying nothing that would detract from the image of progress or support of the thesis of stalemate."[6]

MACV would never accept an OB of over 400,000 so CIA Director Richard Helms decided to accept General Westmoreland's position on enemy strength. Helms instructed Carver to reach accommodation on MACV's terms. Self-defense and secret self-defense forces were to be removed from the OB and the remaining categories kept in the 300,000 range.

Carver wrote Helms: "Circle now squared"; MACV had accepted the CIA's compromise. Nevertheless in his affidavit in the CBS-Westmoreland trial, CIA Director Helms swore under oath, "I never received any instruction or pressure, either overt or covert, from President Johnson, from members of his staff, or from anyone else to present optimistic reports on the conflict in Vietnam or to present reports which were in any way inconsistent with my evaluation of the intelligence information available to me. I never was given any instructions from President Johnson or from anyone else in his Administration to 'cave in' or capitulate to any estimate by military intelligence analysts or to use the military's estimates of the strength of the South Vietnamese Communists in South Vietnam in Special National Intelligence Estimate (S.N.I.E.) 14.3–67."[7]

General Westmoreland was clearly elated with the compromise, and he cabled to Sharp, "The Washington representatives agree with MACV that the NIE should not quantify the categories of self defense, secret self defense and other similar VC organizations. . . . I am satisfied that this is a good estimate and the best that can be derived from available intelligence."[8]

The "irregulars" (self-defense, secret self-defense, assault youth) would not be quantified; instead, the issue would be treated in narrative form in both the SNIE and in MACV's Order of Battle. From Carver's perspective, the atmosphere had been cleared; Washington and Saigon would now be on the same wavelength, "something that will greatly benefit all aspects of our common endeavor," Carver wrote Helms.[9] A month later Ambassador Bunker, worried about questions that the press might raise, cabled Rostow, "Given the overriding need to demonstrate our progress in grinding down the enemy, it is essential that we do not drag too many red herrings across the trail." By red herrings Bunker meant that it would be a mistake to refer to old estimates of shadowy self-defense and secret self-defense forces and to then say they were dropped from the Order of Battle.

In mid-September 1967 events seemed to be going well for the administration. The bureaucratic dispute over enemy strength had seemingly been resolved, the Joint Chiefs had received authorization to hit previously restricted ports, and the Vietnam elections were over. Rostow now provided LBJ with one of his most optimistic reports on the war. With respect to battlefield and terrorist initiatives, "their curve went to a peak in 1966, now there is sliding even on the battalion levels. . . . They are down-slope now. . . . Hanoi's leaders are elderly men. They are living on their French Indo-Chinese memories. They're hanging on. They lost their winning strategy between the 1964 buildup and now—now they are just hoping we cave in. Hanoi is suffering a growing manpower shortage."[10]

The San Antonio Formula

During a September 29, 1967, address to the National Legislative Conference in San Antonio, Texas, President Johnson restated his administration's position on negotiations and the conditions under which he would agree to halt bombing North Vietnam. The president certainly hoped to find the right lever which might bring both sides to the conference table before the 1968 election. LBJ now made public his proposal to North Vietnam for peace: "The United States is willing to stop all aerial and naval bombardment of North Vietnam when this will lead promptly to productive discussion. We, of course, assume that while discussions proceed, North Vietnam would not take advantage of the bombing cessation or limitation."

The San Antonio formula had been authored by Secretary of Defense McNamara, Assistant Secretary of Defense for International Affairs Paul Warnke, and Deputy Secretary of Defense Paul Nitze. The proposal represented a modification in the Johnson administration's demand that Hanoi halt infiltration into the South as a precondition for a bombing halt. Now, all Hanoi had to do was show an interest in productive discussions and the bombing would be halted. Johnson later wrote in *The Vantage Point*, "We were not asking him [Ho Chi Minh] to restrict his military actions before a bombing halt, and once the bombing ended we were not insisting that he immediately end his military effort, only that he not increase it."[11]

The Vietnamese elections had allowed LBJ to make the overture at San Antonio. The president was almost desperately looking for a way out that would not involve humiliation for the allies and his administration. But Ho Chi Minh had nothing to gain by negotiating with an American president facing re-election, and knowing LBJ had more to lose, Ho rejected the San Antonio proposal. During a mid-September meeting with members of an Australian Broadcasting Group visiting the White House the president had openly expressed his private misgivings about how he had conducted the war:

> I don't want to be misunderstood, so I'll measure my words. I think we may have made two mistakes in Vietnam. . . . First, our posture at home and abroad may have been too moderate, too balanced, not strong or assertive enough from the first. It is possible that we may have moved into Vietnam too slowly—that we have been too restrained in our bombing policy—too gradual across the board. In retrospect, we may have been too cautious for too long. Second, we may have helped to create mistrust or misinterpretation of our peace proposals. If the sincerity of our overtures are questioned, it could be that we have crawled too often. History will record the lengthy and imaginative list of U.S. peace initiatives. It will record how they met nothing but arrogant rebukes by Hanoi . . . Eisenhower may be right. If gradualism does not pay off early, then the enemy must be regarded as the enemy and fought with all resources, with no sanctuary or quarter given."[12]

Selling Progress

On September 27, 1967, Rostow cabled Westmoreland, Bunker, and Komer that they now needed to "search urgently for occasions to present sound evidence of progress in Vietnam." Press and TV reports were dominated not by the optimism that was seen by the White House, but by bad news from Vietnam. "We must somehow get hard evidence out of Saigon on steady if slow progress in population control, pacification, VC manpower problems, economic progress in the countryside, ARVN improvement, etc. All are happening. Little comes through despite what we know to be most serious efforts out our way. President's judgment is that this is at present stage a critically important dimension of fighting the war." Rostow created an interagency task force "to develop new ways of measuring the progress of the war in all its facets." In the interim, however, he wrote, "We must proceed as rapidly as possible to purify existing data so that our present displays can be refined and new, more valid statistical displays can be developed. Individual new statistical series should be added to those currently in use as they become ready."

Some advisors counseled restraint in the administration's search for statistical evidence that would dramatize progress. Philip Habib, deputy assistant secretary of state, warned that, "Our problem is not that the public has not been exposed to this kind of material before. The problem is that they do not accept this evidence as sufficient. Better statistics will help, but not enough to meet the basic problem. The data do not explain away dismay at our own casualty figures (the level and the cumulative total). They do not answer charges of Vietnamese corruption, inefficiency, and inadequate performance. They do not answer the question of how much longer we will be required to maintain our effort. They do not answer those who doubt that it is in our national interest to do what we are doing at the price we are paying. They do not satisfy those who are not looking for military success but who are hoping for a short-run political solution."[13]

In early October, the president received Saigon Report #7867, "Measurements of Progress in South Vietnam." This massive report from the United States Embassy in Saigon sought "to demonstrate to the press and the public that we are making solid progress and are not in a stalemate." Secretary Rusk believed that "Saigon 7867 presents powerful evidence of solid progress." In a letter to Bunker the secretary wrote:

> Precisely because it presents such powerful evidence, we anticipate that critics will seize any possible opportunity to attack its credibility. Therefore, we must be doubly sure that we are fully prepared in Washington and Saigon to back up every statement. . . . The whole question of enemy strength, recruitment and infiltration will certainly be controversial on the basis of past experience. Before these figures are used any more widely, we feel that it is absolutely essential that Washington and Saigon are in agreement on Order of Battle figures and recruitment. As you know the Order of Battle statistics are in the process of coordina-

tion. . . . Given the present exercise re Order of Battle statistics and past and present problems with infiltration and recruitment estimates plus difficulties cited above, we feel that surfacing "balance sheets" and "crossover-points" at this time would not be useful.[14]

But before the Saigon Report could be published the Harris opinion survey for October appeared showing that support for the Vietnam war had dropped to another all-time low of 58 percent—down from 72 percent in July and 61 percent in late August. Modest but steady military progress was no longer politically acceptable. On October 10, presidential special assistant and speech writer Harry McPherson warned LBJ that the administration had to present its case more convincingly to the public, but that "Bob McNamara thinks he and Secretary Rusk have pretty much lost their credibility on the subject and I'm afraid I agree."

Adding to the precarious balance of the administration's credibility, the Order of Battle debate again threatened to derail the public relations purification program. Just when it appeared that a resolution on SNIE 14.3-67 had been achieved, MACV circulated its proposed press briefing explaining the new Order-of-Battle figures. The circulation of the proposed briefing was standard operating procedure within bureaucratic channels. But when it was read by Paul Walsh, acting deputy director for economic research in the CIA, he cabled George Carver that the briefing was "one of the greatest snow jobs since Potemkin constructed his village." Walsh believed that "this briefing and similar fictions that MACV proposes to present in the near future, present a series of vulnerable intelligence judgments that cannot be substantiated at this time and promise almost certainly to lead to even graver credibility problems than the current debate over orders of battle." Walsh strenuously objected to the "unbelievably cavalier and shocking consignment of the thousands of militia and self-defense forces into the realm of fellow-travelers and sympathizers." This reasoning was a "complete and wanton scuttling" of the Order of Battle process.[15]

Carver agreed with Walsh and quickly informed Philip Goulding, assistant secretary of defense for public affairs, that the CIA had serious substantive and procedural problems with MACV's version of the proposed briefing and hence could not support it or concur in its use. Carver argued that the press was too sophisticated to fall for the new OB statistics. "The whole proposed treatment of the old irregular and new guerrilla figure will be torn apart by the Saigon press corps."[16] The CIA feared that MACV's intelligence judgments could not be substantiated and would compound credibility problems if presented in the proposed form.

Rostow's preference for MACV's new numbers was evident, and he pushed MACV's case to President Johnson. In a memo to the president he maintained that the latest MACV estimates showed that regular and guerrilla strength of VC had been in steady decline. "The truth is that on latest MACV estimates, the VC/North Vietnamese Army regulars reached a peak strength of 127,000 in September 1966; and have declined to 118,000 regular forces now. The guerrilla strength of the VC has almost certainly declined by an even larger figure over this period of time. Further, the peak in VC/NVA incidents came as early as the end of 1965: November-December 1965–January 1966, 2,845 per month average; the average for June-July-August 1967 is 1,769. In short, the picture is of a war which has reached a peak and is beginning to decelerate slowly."[17]

On October 14, 1967, Supreme Court Justice Abe Fortas sent LBJ a lengthy handwritten note on the subject of Vietnam, recommending that "we must get off the defensive in the propaganda battle," and outlining an aggressive campaign for turning the tide of public opinion. Fortas had been an old friend and confidant since 1948 when he defended Johnson in legal proceedings involving irregularities in Johnson's Texas primary election. The first phone call to LBJ following Kennedy's assassination had come from Fortas, who was then a partner in the prestigious Washington law firm of Arnold, Fortas and Porter. When Justice Arthur Goldberg resigned from the Supreme Court in order to become ambassador to the United Nations, Fortas was nominated to fill the vacancy. Ironically, the nomination was made on July 28, 1965—the same day Johnson announced the Americanization of the war.

In his unofficial capacity as friend, counsellor, and strategist, Fortas supported an unrestrained policy for stepping up the war.

> We can't sustain a shooting war on a non-emotional basis. Our support in this country seems to be slipping with respect to the war. Young people, subject to draft, need some stirring up. We should shift emphasis as to the reasons for our involvement—away from helping South

Vietnam to helping ourselves and the free world to combat the "new" Communist technique of conquest by infiltration and subversion. We should take or make an early opportunity to state, emphatically, that we're going to see this through to a successful conclusion. Nothing, I think, is as destructive as the notion that we may quit. This is harmful inside the country and its effect on the enemy's disposition to come to terms. We must sound this theme soon, so we can state it as collaboration with the South Vietnamese. . . . Success means an end to the overthrow of governments by infiltration and subversion from sources outside of their borders. We hope it will come quickly and at the conference table. But come it will—and come it must. We cannot and will not permit South Vietnam to be a monument to freedom's defeat—or a franchise to infiltration and subversion. Our resistance in South Vietnam has given courage to the people of Asia, Africa and Latin America to resist the efforts of Communism to take over. Our retreat would be a mortal and savage blow to them. This country has never left the field of battle in abject surrender of cause for which it fought. We shall not do so now. We shall apply the minimum of the tremendous force available to us—the minimum necessary to protect freedom—to resist a Communist victory—to obtain the modest goal that we seek and must obtain. But obtain it, we shall."[18]

Mid-October also brought a series of new proposals from the Joint Chiefs for accelerating the rate of progress in the war. Fortified by the Stennis subcommittee's recommendation for removal of target restrictions, General Wheeler (recovered and back at the helm) charged that the rate of progress had been and continued to be slow, largely because U.S. military power had been restrained in a manner that had reduced significantly its effectiveness. The chiefs believed that U.S. objectives could still be achieved but only by removing present limitations on military operations.[19]

Johnson was being pushed into the hawks' corner. The crisis brought a thoughtful memo from McGeorge Bundy, who recommended that the president distance himself from the political hawks. "They are overwhelmingly wrong, on all the evidence, and the belief that you are gradually giving in to them is the most serious single fear of reasonable men in all parts of the country." Knowing Johnson as he did, Bundy warned that it would be a major mistake to marshall "any elaborate effort to show by new facts and figures that we are 'winning' the war in Vietnam." The credibility gap was hurting LBJ politically and "we do not gain with the mass of the people by what we report of progress in Vietnam."

Bundy returned to the distinctions he had drawn in earlier memos between tactical and strategic bombing. "Dick Helms told me solemnly today that every single member of the intelligence staff agrees with the view that bombing in the Hanoi-Haiphong area has no significant effect whatever on the level of supplies that reaches the southern battlefields. Nor does any intelligence officer of standing believe that strategic bombing will break the will of Hanoi in the foreseeable future. This strategic air war engages our pilots and the pride of our air commanders; it also has a military life of its own, with its own claimed imperatives. But it does not affect the real contest, which is in the south. Its political costs are rising every week. We have everything to gain politically and almost nothing to lose militarily if we will firmly hold our bombing to demonstrably useful target areas."[20]

At the conclusion of an October 23, 1967, meeting with the Democratic leadership, LBJ asked all members of the White House staff to leave in order to hold "a confidential discussion on Vietnam." Attending the meeting with McNamara, Rusk, and Helms were the following members of Congress: Senators Everett Dirksen, Bert Hickenlooper, Robert Byrd, Margaret Chase Smith, John Sparkman, Russell B. Long, and Mike Mansfield and Congressmen Carl Hayden, John Mahon, and Carl Albert. Discussion first focused on whether one more bombing pause might lead to negotiations. The president opened the discussion with a lengthy overview: "Unfortunately, it is my conclusion, and that of all of my principal advisers, that a total cessation of bombing at this time would not in fact lead to productive negotiations. I want to review with you the reasons why we have come to that conclusion. Hanoi has applied serious military pressure south of the DMZ. General Westmoreland's forces beat this back in late September but the threat now seems to be building again. Several North Vietnamese in private conversations have referred to Hanoi's expectation that it will achieve a significant military victory—probably meaning in the DMZ area—in the near future. There has even been talk by North Vietnamese representatives of 'another Dien Bien Phu.' "

Johnson then turned to questions of military policy. He had decided that war, not peace, was what Hanoi wanted. They had outlasted the French, they would outlast the United States. "I recognize that there will continue to be people who will urge—despite the evidence—that a change in our bombing policy could lead us toward peace. But I am not prepared to act simply on hope."

Few at the meeting voiced opposition to Johnson, but Secretary McNamara came precariously close: "We cannot win the war with bombing in the north. We need action in South Vietnam supplemented by bombing in the north with limited objectives. Bombing is a supplement to not a substitute. The great danger is to lead our people to think we can win the war overnight with bombing. We cannot." The president shot back at McNamara: "We do have differences of opinion."

The difficulties in maintaining the president's congressional coalition emerged during the meeting. Congressman John Mahon urged, "You should keep the pressure on. Continue the bombing." Senator Long added, "Don't stop the bombing. If anything, step it up. Anytime you want to lose a war you can. If we lose Vietnam we lose influence in this entire area of the world. We must make a stand here." Senator Robert Byrd interjected, "You can't do more than you've done. If anything, you have been overly eager. . . . These people have every reason to believe they should hold out until the next election. I hope you continue to be firm. I hope you try to work through the U.N. If you feel what you are doing is right I hope you continue to do it. You may lose next year's election because of it, but I believe that history will vindicate you."

As the meeting drew to a close Senator Mike Mansfield took issue with the majority of those present. "I am not in accord on the matter of the effectiveness of the bombing. We could bomb North Vietnam into the stone age if we wanted to. I do not believe we have reached the objective which was stopping the flow of men and material into the South. We have lost many planes and we are flying within 24 seconds of China. We should think of contact between the NLF and Saigon to try to cut them out from North Vietnam." But Mansfield found little support among his colleagues. Congressman Carl Albert closed the meeting by saying, "I would tell them to jump in the lake. We must continue to do what we have to do."

"Doing what we have to" involved a dual-pronged effort in military initiatives from the field and a public-relations campaign at home. During the final week of October a blue-ribbon, non-partisan committee for Peace and Freedom in Vietnam (organized with active White House prodding and supervision) was announced. The committee, with two former presidents as members, gave strong endorsement to U.S. policy in Vietnam. Democratic Senator Paul Douglas denied charges that the committee was being formed as part of an administration counterattack against critics of Vietnam policy. "Our objective is to make sure that the voice of America is heard—loud and clear—so that Peking and Hanoi will not mistake the strident voices of some dissenters for American discouragement and a weakening of will."

On October 27, 1967, Harry McPherson joined the growing chorus of doubters. Although he had never openly opposed bombing and "never will," McPherson explained to Johnson, "I get the impression that a lot of Harry McPhersons out in private life—middle-road-Democrats who've supported American foreign policy decisions since 1948 and who believe we have to stay in Vietnam for one reason or another—have grown increasingly edgy about the bombing program. Indeed, I think it is one of the main causes of disaffection with our Vietnam policy. To a great many people, it doesn't look as if it will get the North to the conference table or otherwise out of the south. It doesn't look as if it is hurting the enemy much."

Bombing had become the war in the eyes of the press and in the minds of the public. "Yet we know it is not the war," McPherson wrote to Johnson. "The war is the tough frustrating slow struggle in the south, on the ground, in the villages, and in the Saigon government. If we can't win that war and can bomb the North into rubble, we won't have won a thing. The air war, in a sense, diverts our attention from the real tasks we face in Vietnam." McPherson warned the president that as things now stood, "we are a big mechanized white nation obliterating a small agricultural brown nation."

Bombing had become the greatest obstacle to negotiations because it was the only pressure the United States could apply, McPherson argued. But it was also the one kind of pressure the North was most effective at proving itself capable of resisting. President Johnson was very close to being forced into accepting population bombing—the kind of war that created the greatest kind of moral unease in people. McPherson urged Johnson not to cave into the political hawks and military leaders. "You are the Commander in Chief. If you think a policy is wrong, you should not follow it just to quiet the generals and admirals. Generals and admirals like to bomb. People trust their judgment when it is a question of this or that military tactic; but when it is a question of this or that policy, they mistrust the military. It appears to some people that the military are blackmailing you into following their policy toward North Vietnam."[21]

The Beginning and an End

President Thieu and Vice-President Ky were inaugurated in Saigon on October 31, 1967. Representing the United States at the inauguration, Vice-President Hubert Humphrey said, "I came as a witness for those millions of Americans who trust in the steady progress being made in Vietnam as symbolized by this inauguration."

During lunch in the White House on the same day, Secretary of Defense McNamara told President Johnson that the "continuation of our present course of action in Southeast Asia would be dangerous, costly in lives, and unsatisfactory to the American people." As Thieu and Ky were being sworn in, Secretary McNamara spent the evening in Washington preparing a memorandum identifying the failure of U.S. policy in Vietnam.

McNamara's position was a major break within the ranks of the best of the brightest. It had been one thing for college professors, nervous-nellies, and hippy demonstrators to challenge the war's progress, but one of the principal architects of that policy was now confronting its inevitable contradictions. President Johnson had always feared that Hanoi could win by the breaking of American resolve what it could not achieve on the battlefield, and now, with the secretary of defense questioning policy, that resolve appeared to be weakening.

VII

The Progress Report of November 1967

There are ways of guiding the press to show light at the end of the tunnel.

Walt Rostow, Remarks at a meeting of the Wise Men, November 2, 1967.

On November 1, 1967 Secretary of Defense Robert McNamara forwarded President Johnson a memorandum containing his "personal views" on the direction of U.S. policy in Vietnam which "may be incompatible with your own." (Johnson later acknowledged that McNamara's memo raised "fundamental questions of policy with reference to the conduct of the war in Vietnam."[1]) In this memorandum McNamara warned the president that "continuing our present course of action will not bring us by the end of 1968 enough closer to success, in the eyes of the American public, to prevent the continued erosion of popular support for our involvement in Vietnam." The impending presidential election would force Johnson either to defend a stalemated policy or to escalate the war in order to avoid the politically motivated charge by Republicans and conservative Democrats that LBJ's policy was not achieving its goal and that American soldiers had become the ante for continued stalemate. The

93

secretary again proposed a policy of stabilization in the U.S. military effort that included a halt to increases in force levels and no further expansion of air operations against North Vietnam.

Secretary McNamara's argument was that progress in the war had been and would continue to be so slow that "this progress will not be readily visible to the general public either in the United States or abroad." Although Johnson's other advisors, particularly Generals Wheeler and Westmoreland, Ambassador Bunker, and Special Assistant Walt Rostow, had repeatedly been assuring the president for months that the crossover point had been reached or was very close, McNamara argued that bombing had not interrupted the flow of supplies and men to the South, nor had it helped create conditions for stabilizing the political situation in South Vietnam. Instead, bombing had become an empty trump card for negotiations that were not going to be held. Air bombardment had not broken the will of the North Vietnamese or the Viet Cong: "Nothing can be expected to break this will other than the conviction that they cannot succeed. This conviction will not be created unless and until they come to the conclusion that the US is prepared to remain in Vietnam for whatever period of time is necessary to assure the independent choice of the South Vietnamese people. The enemy cannot be expected to arrive at that conclusion in advance of the American public. And the American public, frustrated by the slow rate of progress, fearing continued escalation, and doubting that all approaches to peace have been sincerely probed, does not give the appearance of having the will to persist."

McNamara's argument in favor of a bombing halt was based on the premise that American air attacks on North Vietnam were what kept the war going and prevented a political settlement. McNamara believed that a bombing halt would lead to a suspension of enemy operations across the DMZ, and he recommended that during this period of stabilization, the United States should make every effort to restrict the war and not increase its forces above authorized levels, not call up Reserves, and not expand ground actions in the North. No president wanted to defend a war with no end in sight, he wrote LBJ, and while there was always the danger that Hanoi might use the talks as a propaganda tool, the internal dynamics of the situation could result in productive discussions moving toward a settlement. "No other course affords any hope of these results in the next 15 months," he warned.

The war was indeed stalemated; 525,000 troops had not been enough. Moreover, any additional combat troops would produce an increase of between 700–1000 casualties per month without producing any significant change in the nature of military operations. "But neither the additional troops now scheduled nor augmentation of our forces by a much greater amount holds great promise of bringing the North Vietnamese and Viet Cong forces visibly closer to collapse during the next 15 months. Nonetheless we will be faced with requests for additional ground forces requiring an increased draft and/or a call-up of reserves."

McNamara reminded the president that the Joint Chiefs could only counsel additional operations against North Vietnam, Laos, and Cambodia. The military's creativity involved mining the ports and waterways, attacking shipping and aircraft, expanding bombing, and covert programs. "I do not," McNamara urged, "think adoption of any or all of the proposals would bring us significantly closer to victory in the next 15 months."

Progress in the "other war" of pacification revealed that "the chances of dramatic impact by any measurement of security were slim. The pacification program is moving forward but progress is slow and likely to remain slow." Despite some encouraging advances, the political situation would not be sufficiently improved by 1968. "It is not at all clear that the image or performance of this government over the next 15 months will make it appear to the US public to be a government worthy of continued US support in blood and treasure."

According to McNamara's memorandum then, public opinion would force two choices on the administration for ending the stalemate in Vietnam: escalate the air war in the North and expand the ground war in the South; or, on the other hand, withdraw from Vietnam. In order to avoid this polarization in U.S. public opinion, McNamara concluded that it was necessary to stabilize the war and actively seek negotiations.[2]

The Wise Men

On the same night that Secretary McNamara handed LBJ his proposal for stabilizing the U.S. military program, a remarkable meeting of President Johnson's senior foreign policy advisory group was held. Some members of this informal group of former and present government officials had played important roles in implementing the doctrine of containment in the 1940s and in shaping U.S. foreign policy ever since. As a result of their periodic visits and counsels with the president they were later dubbed "the wise men."[3]

In addition to the president's principal advisors on foreign policy, these distinguished senior advisors included: Dean Acheson, secretary of state under President Truman; George Ball, under-secretary of state in the Kennedy-Johnson period; McGeorge Bundy, special assistant to Presidents Kennedy and Johnson; Douglas Dillon, ambassador to France under President Eisenhower and secretary of the treasury under President Kennedy; Cyrus Vance, deputy secretary of defense under McNamara and a diplomatic troubleshooter for President Johnson; Arthur Dean, chief Korean War negotiator; John J. McCloy, high commissioner to West Germany under President Truman and assistant secretary of war during World War II; General Omar Bradley, World War II commander and the first JCS chairman; General Matthew Ridgway, Korean War commander and later NATO commander; General Maxwell Taylor, JCS chairman under President Kennedy and later ambassador to Saigon; Robert Murphy, a senior career ambassador of the Truman-Eisenhower period; Henry Cabot Lodge, former U.S. senator and twice ambassador to Saigon; Abe Fortas, a sitting associate justice of the Supreme Court and a personal adviser to President Johnson; and Arthur Goldberg, ambassador to the United Nations and a former secretary of labor and Supreme Court justice.

The meeting was organized by Walt Rostow and Clark Clifford. In a recently declassified document Rostow had explained to Johnson that he and Clifford "would propose to invite them to join the President and the senior officers of the government for 'a periodic review of our whole posture in Southeast Asia.'" In scripting the scene,

Rostow suggested that the president might then come over to the State Department where the advisors would hold their primary briefing, "so that the story would be, if it came out, that Secretary Rusk had these men in for general consultation and you joined them for informal talks." Clifford and Rostow did not "wish to develop either a sense of crisis—if the gathering should leak—or an implication that you were dissatisfied with the advice of your senior advisers."[4] The group convened for an evening session on November 1 that did not include the president, but a lengthy morning session the following day had LBJ at the helm.

During the evening session,* Secretary McNamara candidly admitted that "perhaps he and Rusk's efforts since 1961 have been a failure." But the wise men did not intend to dwell on failure; instead, they listened to briefings from General Wheeler and George Carver that reported great progress since 1965, but insufficient to collapse the enemy within the next fifteen months. Carver reported that Hanoi would end the war only when "they had decided the U.S. would not behave like the French did in 1954 and when a viable state structure seemed on the way to emerging in Saigon."

All those present agreed that bombing did not prevent the present level of infiltration of men and arms from North to South but opinions varied with respect to strategy. George Ball and Dean Acheson urged that the United States "use bombing as a negotiating chip against pressure across the DMZ." Acheson said that "bombing should be stopped only when Hanoi did not press across the DMZ." Secretary Rusk pointed out that "the United States had tried to establish that connection but had failed." Robert Murphy and General Bradley, in particular, said "they were sure that the bombing was having some effect on operations in the South, although it could not be precisely measured. In this discussion it emerged that while Helms agreed with McNamara that the present level of bombing would not have a demonstrable effect on flows to the South, he disagreed with the judgment that a stoppage of bombing would not result in increased flows to the South. It might."

Arthur Dean made the point that "an excessive eagerness to negotiate or a broad humanitarian gesture to the Communists is interpre-

*The quotes from these meetings are from notes taken by Tom Johnson, Jim Jones, and Walt Rostow, each of whom kept a record of the meetings.

ted as a sign of weakness by Communists." At the close Secretary Rusk urged the advisors to put their minds to this question: "In the face of the situation, as it was outlined to them, what would they do if they were President?"[5]

With the evening session behind them, Rostow composed a "thinking agenda" for the next day's meeting with the president. Rostow also suggested that deputy press secretary Tom Johnson be present and keep a tally sheet on each man with respect to each question.

President Johnson opened the November 2 morning meeting with the excessively flattering statement, "I have a peculiar confidence in you as patriots and that is why I have picked you." The president then asked, "Is our course in Vietnam right?" If so, what could be done about "the deterioration of public support and the lack of editorial support for our policies. . . . How do we unite the country?" Johnson placed five questions on the table. (1) What could we do that we are not doing in South Vietnam? (2) Concerning the North, should we continue what we are doing, or should we mine the ports and take out the dikes, or should we eliminate the bombing of the North? (3) On negotiations—should we adopt a passive policy of willingness to negotiate, or should we be more aggressive, or should we bow out? (4) Should we get out of Vietnam? (5) What positive steps should the administration take to unite the American people and to communicate with the nation better?

Secretary of State Dean Rusk responded to the president's agenda by reading Ambassador Bunker's cable summarizing his first six months in Saigon. The cable emphasized that "steady progress is being made." Admitting that "in the past we have been overly optimistic and have become prisoners of this optimism," Bunker was now "enthusiastic about the progress being made." Bunker reported that "the civil side of the war is proceeding well with the constitutional process and the pacification process equalling in importance the military improvements. . . . The newly elected government, especially Thieu and Ky, know that they must show progress in order to gain the support of the people. Steady progress is being made. Much still needs to be done, however, such as a vigorous processing of the war, elimination of corruption, improvement of the standard of living, especially in the rural areas."

The frustrations of those who had helped shape U.S. foreign policy in Vietnam were evident in this meeting. The president described himself as feeling "like the steering wheel of a car out of control"; McNamara and Rusk felt "worthless about their efforts since 1961." When Robert Murphy said that the bombing should be left in the hands of the Joint Chiefs, LBJ (showing immediate recall of McNamara's memo) responded, "The JCS came up with 10 proposals, all of which involved the North. I sent it back to them to focus on the South and they reported we can't do anything more than we are doing in the South now."

Douglas Dillon believed that both the doves and hawks viewed the situation as hopeless. "We must show some progress. To talk of 15 years seems like forever." General Omar Bradley charged that "our troubles can be blamed on the communications media. . . . If it wasn't for all the protesters, the North Vietnamese would give up. . . ." When the president asked General Bradley (who had just returned from Vietnam) to review the competence of allied troops, Bradley replied, "They get ice cream about three times a week. Only two out of a thousand that I and my wife visited disliked being there or did not understand why they were there." General Bradley concluded, "We need to raise patriotism. We never had a war without patriotic slogans. 'Patience,' 100 years means nothing to a Chinaman, but we do not have their same patience." Robert Murphy recommended that the administration orchestrate "a hate complex directed at Ho Chi Minh similar to Hitler."

Dean Acheson soothed Johnson with the observation, "The cross you have to bear is a lousy Senate Foreign Relations Committee. You have a dilettante fool [J. William Fulbright] at the head of the committee." Acheson also warned President Johnson that negotiations were not going to happen. "The bombing has no effect on negotiations. When these fellows decide they can't defeat the South, then they will give up. This is the way it was in Korea. This is the way the Communists operate."

McGeorge Bundy urged LBJ, "Don't let communications people in New York set the tone of the debate. Emphasize the 'light at the end of the tunnel' instead of the battles, deaths and danger." Bundy shared Acheson's view that negotiations were no longer viable. "I suppose we can't say that publicly because the judges of public opinion in the nation won't believe it. But I think it is logical to say that we in the Administration do not expect negotiations in the next year. Public support is eroded because people see dying with no picture of result in sight. If we can permeate to the public that we are seeing the results at the end of the road, this will be helpful." Walt Rostow added that while the war was not popular, it was necessary to show progress. "There are ways of guiding the press to show light at the end of the tunnel," Rostow insisted.

Johnson then called on Supreme Court Associate Justice Abe Fortas who repeated the strident thoughts of his earlier memo to the president. "I believe there is a good deal of over-reaction to what appears to be the public attitude of the United States. This opposition exists in only a small group of the community, primarily the intellectuals or so-called intellectuals and the press." Fortas shared Dean Acheson's view that "negotiations are symbolic rather than a real thing. . . . We've been fortunate so far that NVN has rejected our offer. . . . To continue to talk about negotiations only signals to the communists that they are succeeding in winning over American public opinion."

Clark Clifford (who would soon replace McNamara at the Pentagon and then lead a searching reexamination of policy) followed Fortas and encouraged President Johnson not to cave in to public opinion. "One of the measures of the success that history will look very favorably upon is that both Presidents Kennedy and Johnson didn't wait for public opinion to catch up with them. They went ahead with what was right, and because of that the war is a success today."

Perhaps the most absurd aspect of the meeting occurred at 1:45 when the president's daughter brought Patrick Lyndon Nugent into the meeting. Grandson "Lyn" stayed in his grandpa's arms for the remainder of the luncheon, while the president of the United States reviewed the consensus of opinions given at the meeting.

As the meeting moved to a close, Secretary McNamara thanked the group for their support. LBJ interjected that "no nation has been more enlightenedly served than under Secretaries Rusk and McNamara." He went on to say that they represented the "highest type of manhood that this country can produce" and "their only test is what is good for their country." The president concluded by saying that he, Rusk, and McNamara could hold out, "but he didn't know about the resoluteness of the American people."

The meeting ended with almost unanimous agreement amongst the senior advisors on the question of getting out of Vietnam. "Absolutely not," said Acheson. "As impossible as it is undesirable," said Bundy. "Definitely not," said Dillon. "Unthinkable," said Lodge, "we are trying to divert a change in the balance of power." "The public would be outraged if we got out," said Fortas. As the advisors were leaving the room, George Ball, who had been unusually quiet during the dialogue, confronted Acheson and his colleagues: "I've been watching you across the table. You're like a flock of buzzards sitting on a fence, sending the young men off to be killed. You ought to be ashamed of yourselves."[6]

But Ball was out of tune with this meeting. Shame belonged with those opposing the war, not with these patriots. Yet, within a day, dissent within the group manifested itself. Averill Harriman wrote privately to the president concerning his disagreement with certain opinions made by members of the senior advisory group during the November 2 meeting. Appointed by President Johnson in 1965 as ambassador-at-large with primary responsibility for Southeast Asian Affairs, Harriman disagreed with the opinion that proposals for negotiation by the United States only encouraged Hanoi to hold out. "There is no evidence whatever supporting this contention. On the other hand, it seems clear that the President's position has been materially strengthened both at home and abroad by the statements and efforts he has made or authorized to bring about talks."[7] (Johnson later named Harriman to lead the U.S. negotiation in the Paris Peace talks.)

McGeorge Bundy also wrote to LBJ that the November 1–2 discussions were "enormously interesting and [I] have found my own mind stretched to some new thoughts as a result." Johnson's former national security advisor reaffirmed the group's "strong and unanimous negative" on pulling out of Vietnam. "I suspect that George Ball would be inclined to settle for a deal which might eventually turn sour in the South. I think the rest of us would wish to stay there until there is a viable non-Communist South Vietnam. This difference is not currently critical."

Bundy noted that bombing North Vietnam had dominated discussion at the meeting, just as the differences between McNamara and the Joint Chiefs had dominated public discussion. The president needed to get his advisory team harmonized for the long haul: "There is no doubt that the public airing of differences between McNamara and the top brass has created some confusion, especially when followed by air operations which seemed inconsistent with one or another of the McNamara arguments. And on their side, the top brass have given the impression that they could have done things much better if they had been allowed to do them their own way. This pulling and hauling has been natural, and to some degree inevitable, but the discussion of November 2 suggests that we may be reaching a point where you can find a solid position from which to put a stop to it."

Bundy urged Johnson to draw on his account of straight loyalty from the top military men. "My impression is that they still feel cut off from you and somehow think they really do not get your ear as much as they should. (Naturally it never occurs to them that their real trouble may be simply that they have not got a very good case, and that you may find them as tiresome as any other powerful but narrow-minded pressure group.)" Bundy recommended that a compromise be forged between McNamara and the chiefs and that McNamara be required to join in a rationale for the bombing that would be broader than what he had told the Stennis subcommittee.

Bundy also warned Johnson that few advisors were really knowledgeable about events in South Vietnam. The two men who knew the most, Lodge and Taylor, had raised the toughest questions about the military tactics now being followed. General Taylor had questioned Westmoreland's strategy of digging in and holding ground with forces in the DMZ and in the highlands; Ambassador Lodge questioned the wisdom of large-scale, search-and-destroy operations. It seemed evident, Bundy argued, that increased casualties should be expected from these strategies. Moreover, "the prospect of endless inconclusive fighting is the most serious single cause of domestic disquiet about the war."

Bundy urged Johnson to question General Westmoreland's military strategy. Questioning the tactical judgment of the commander in the field was obviously a highly sensitive matter, but the president had every reason to satisfy himself about questions as important as those raised by Lodge and Taylor. Bundy urged the president to do something which had not yet been done in this war: "For extremely good reasons the top men in Washington have kept their hands off the tactical conduct of the war, and most discussions have been directed rather to questions of force levels in the South and bombing limits in the North. (Even in Saigon the successive Ambassadors have been careful to keep out of military matters.) But now that the principal battleground is in domestic opinion, I believe the Commander-in-Chief has both the right and the duty to go further."

This war was more political than any in U.S. history except the Civil War, Bundy argued, and the visible exercise of presidential authority was necessary for the war and public opinion, but "also best for the internal confidence of the Government. Briefings which cite the latest statistics have lost their power to persuade. So have spectacular summits. These things are not worth one-quarter of what would be gained by the gradual emergence of the fact that the President himself—in his capacity as political leader and Commander-in-Chief—is shaping a campaign which is gradually increasing in its success and gradually decreasing in its cost in American lives and money."

Bundy concluded with a warning that the administration's preoccupation with statistical demonstrations of progress had backfired on them. "I think we have tried too hard to convert public opinion by statistics and by spectacular visits of all sorts. I do have to say also that I think public discontent with the war is now wide and deep. One of the few things that helps us right now is public distaste for the violent doves—but I think people are getting fed up with the endlessness of the fighting. What really hurts, then, is not the arguments of the doves but the cost of the war in lives and money, coupled with the lack of light at the end of the tunnel."[8]

Johnson instructed Rostow to compare the McNamara and Bundy positions. In a "Literally Eyes Only for The President," Rostow explained that where Secretary McNamara favored an announced new policy of stabilization, Bundy accepted the new posture outlined within the president's San Antonio speech. On bombing, McNamara was ready to move ahead with a unilateral stand-down and await Hanoi's reaction; Bundy was against any unconditional pause, any extended pause for sake of appearances, and any major headline-making intensification of bombing. Neither Bundy nor McNamara supported troop reinforcements beyond those already approved.

Rostow informed Johnson that Bundy had not explicitly addressed other issues but presumably he would agree that there would be no call-up of Reserves; no expansion of ground action into North Vietnam, Laos, or Cambodia; no attempt to deny sea imports into North Vietnam; no effort to break the will of the North by an air campaign

on the dikes, locks, or populated targets; and that the United States
would gradually transfer the major burden of the fighting to the
South Vietnamese forces.[9]

The Debate on Stabilization

The McNamara proposal for a stabilized military program became
the lightening rod for private debate among the advisors. President
Johnson seemed determined to give McNamara's memorandum a
complete airing, and it was circulated amongst his principal advisors.
Walt Rostow was the first to respond to the memorandum, writing
the next day to President Johnson that any cessation of bombing
would push the president off his "middle ground at home." Citing a
Gallup poll that showed that 67 percent of the American people
favored continuing the bombing of the North, Rostow warned LBJ
that the Republicans would use a bombing halt against the president
during the upcoming campaign. "Acknowledging my limitations as
a judge of domestic politics, I am extremely skeptical of any change
in strategy that would take you away from your present middle
position; that is, using rationally all the power available, but avoiding
actions likely to engage the Soviet Union and Communist China. If
we shift unilaterally towards de-escalation, the Republicans will
move in and crystallize a majority around a stronger policy."

Rostow remained optimistic in regards to U.S. military prospects.
"If I felt Bob's strategy would measurably increase the chances of a
true settlement, I believe the risk might be worth taking. But both
a unilateral bombing cessation and an announced policy of 'stabilization' would, in my view, be judged in Hanoi as a mark of weakness
rather than evidence of increased U.S. capacity to sweat out the war.
. . . Although I certainly will not predict for you an early end for the
war, I believe that, with a little luck and reasonable performance by
the South Vietnamese under the new government, the evidence of
solid progress will become increasingly clear to one and all."

Rostow argued that McNamara's strategy would actually ease the
Communists' negotiating position at a time when intelligence
showed an increase in Soviet influence in Hanoi and a shift in Hanoi
"to the view that they cannot directly take over the South now" and

"within this framework, a probing for what the status of the Communists would be within South Vietnam in a time of peace." The next day Rostow buttressed this point by sending LBJ data from Long An province in South Vietnam that showed "the process of erosion which, for old professional guerrilla warriors, indicates the clock is ticking slowly against them."[10]

Rostow speculated that the war had already entered a stage during which Communist military operations were designed merely to improve their negotiating position. Increasing pressure on the North was necessary for preserving future U.S. negotiating options. Distinguishing his position from McNamara's, Rostow said, "I believe Bob's strategy would ease their problem and permit them rationally to protract the negotiation—unless Bob is correct on domestic politics and I am wrong. That is, if the country settled down for the long pull comfortably with Bob's program, he could be right. If his policy opened up a debate between united Republicans claiming he had gone soft and a Democratic Administration, with the JCS in disagreement if not open revolt, then my view is correct."

Ambassador Ellsworth Bunker's first cable of November contrasted sharply with McNamara's perspective. Bunker acknowledged the difficult road ahead, but thought it was one worth traveling. "It is obvious, I think, that the effort to establish a functioning representative democracy in Vietnam will encounter many problems. Some of them will be difficult for us to live with. . . . Yet, I think we can take considerable pride in the fact that a functioning constitutional government is being established, especially in what seems to me to be a new feeling of confidence and pride on the part of the Vietnamese, and in their determination to increase their efforts and to do more than they have been doing in carrying their share of the burden."[11]

General Maxwell Taylor weighed in strongly against the proposed stabilization policy. "Of the alternatives (pull-out, pull-back, all-out, stick-it-out), this is one form of the pull-back alternative which would probably degenerate into pull-out." While the proposal might allay the fears of those concerned over an expansion of the conflict, it would "provide fresh ammunition for the numerically larger number of critics who say that we are embarked on an endless and hopeless struggle or that we are really not trying to win." Curtailment of the bombing would discourage the South Vietnamese as well as our allies, jeopardize our in-country forces, and mobilize "the large majority of our citizens who believe in the bombing but who thus far have been silent." The enemy would undoubtedly interpret any such move as a retreat and a sign of weakness.

Writing directly to the president, Justice Abe Fortas derided McNamara's proposal, describing it as "an invitation to slaughter." McNamara's analysis and recommendations were based "almost entirely, upon an assessment of U.S. public opinion and an unspoken assumption as to the effect that should be given to it." Fortas rejected the premise that the American people were "unwilling to sustain an indefinitely prolonged war." Moreover, "our duty is to do what we consider right . . . not what we consider (on a highly dubious basis with which I do not agree) the 'American people' want." Military decisions could not be made in response to a volatile public opinion that could not define the national interest.

McNamara's program of stabilization would, according to Fortas, produce demands in this country to withdraw from Vietnam—and, in fact, "it must be appraised for what it is: a step in the process of withdrawal." Fortas rephrased the issue for LBJ: "The American people . . . do not want us to achieve less than our objectives— namely, to prevent North Vietnamese domination of South Vietnam by military force or subversion; and to continue to exert such influence as we reasonably can in Asia to prevent an ultimate Communist take-over." Fortas endorsed a strategy that included increasing pressure on the North Vietnamese and destruction of the Viet Cong. Negotiation should not be considered an objective or a target. "It is a propaganda symbol that we should keep alive."

Fortas then suggested that perhaps it was time to clean house. "I must frankly state again that I am not convinced that our military program in South Vietnam is as flexible or ingenious as it could be. I know that new proposals have been sought from our military. Perhaps a new and fresh look, including new people—civilian as well as military—might be warranted."[12]

Clark Clifford's critical response to McNamara's memorandum echoed Fortas's. Clifford disagreed with the recommendations and believed that stabilization would "retard the possibility of concluding the conflict rather than accelerating it." The proposed policy would play directly into Hanoi's hands because it validated Hanoi's strategy for weakening the will of the United States to carry on the war.

"Their previous experience with the French has convinced them that the same result will occur again insofar as the United States is concerned. It is my opinion that Hanoi will never seek a cessation of the conflict if they think our determination is lessening. On the one hand, if our pressure is unremitting and their losses continue to grow, and hope fades for any sign of weakening on our part, then some day they will conclude that the game is not worth the candle."

Clifford rejected the very premise for a bombing halt. "I am at a loss to understand this logic. Would the unconditional suspension of the bombing, without any effort to extract a quid pro quo persuade Hanoi that we were firm and unyielding in our conviction to force them to desist from their aggressive designs? The answer is a loud and resounding 'no.' " Hanoi would interpret the action as (a) evidence of discouragement and frustration, (b) an admission of the wrongness and immorality of bombing the North, and (c) the first step in ultimate total disengagement from the conflict. "It would give an enormous lift to the spirits and morale of the North, and an equally grave setback to the will and determination of the South Vietnamese and our other allies fighting with us."

With respect to stabilizing the military effort in the South, Clifford asked, "Can there be any doubt as to the North Vietnamese reaction to such an announcement? The chortles of unholy glee issuing from Hanoi would be audible in every capital in the world. Is this evidence of our zeal and courage to stay the course? Of course not! It would be interpreted to be exactly what it is. A resigned and discouraged effort to find a way out of a conflict for which we had lost our will and dedication. And what of our bargaining position? It would have been utterly destroyed. Hanoi would be secure in the comforting thought that we had informed the world that we would refrain from practically all activities that would be damaging to North Vietnam. It would be tantamount to turning over our hole card and showing Hanoi that it was a deuce."

No war had ever been successfully terminated by such a program, Clifford argued. Pressure needed to be constantly increased until the enemy found it intolerable and capitulated. "The President and every man around him wants to end the war. But the future of our children and grandchildren require that it be ended by accomplishing our purpose, i.e., the thwarting of the aggression by North Vietnam, aided by China and Russia. . . . Because of the unique position we occupy in the world today, we cannot expect other countries and other peoples to love us, but with courage and determination, and the help of God, we can make them respect us. It is clear to me that the course of action offered in the memorandum does not accomplish this purpose."[13]

Bunker and Westmoreland each responded to Secretary McNamara's memorandum. Westmoreland opposed any bombing halt in North Vietnam and believed it would be "foolish" to announce a stabilized policy. Ambassador Bunker also weighed in against a bombing stand-down but was attracted to announcing a troop ceiling. "We are fighting a limited war for limited objectives and . . . we will not need more than 525,000 U.S. forces."[14]

Secretary of State Rusk also forwarded LBJ "a digest of my personal reactions to Secretary McNamara's memorandum of November 1 on Vietnam." Rusk said he possessed a fundamental disagreement with McNamara's forecast: "I accept, as realistic, the prospect that U.S. forces will reach 525,000, other free world forces will reach 59–75,000, and that South Vietnamese forces can be increased by 60,000. I do not agree that these increased forces cannot bring the North Vietnamese and Viet Cong forces visibly closer to collapse during the next 15 months. The indicators point in the other direction."

Rusk sided with Ambassador Bunker in the opinion that progress "will accelerate," but he warned LBJ that "we must resist pressures to take direct action against foreign shipping entering Haiphong or to bomb irrigation dikes." The secretary strongly supported intensive bombing of infiltration routes in North Vietnam and Laos and sectors of the battlefield such as the DMZ and areas north of the DMZ. But Rusk recognized the fallacy inherent in those who argued that "continuous escalation of the bombing will break the will of Hanoi."

Rusk concluded with the assessment, "I am more optimistic than Secretary McNamara about whether progress will be 'visible to the general public in the months ahead.' General Westmoreland's estimate that only 60% of enemy battalions are combat effective is significant. Success is cumulative—and so is failure. The enemy has problems which are growing."

Rusk did strongly agree with McNamara that ground operations should not be extended into North Vietnam, Laos, and Cambodia.

"There are large forces in North Vietnam which have not been committed to South Vietnam. If we cannot deal satisfactorily with forces now in South Vietnam, I do not see how we could improve the position by taking on more than 300,000 additional forces in North Vietnam. No one knows just where the "flash point" is which would change the present rules insofar as Peking and Moscow are concerned. There is a very high risk that ground action against North Vietnam would cross the 'flash point.' "

With respect to stabilization of the military effort, Rusk said he "generally agreed with the concept of stabilization—but I would not announce it." Over time, stabilization would become apparent, and it would come without giving guarantees to Hanoi. "I would use the bombing of the North as a central card to play in connection with some interest on the part of Hanoi in a peaceful settlement. It would take some of the drama, and the losses, out of our present bombing effort in the Hanoi-Haiphong area. I would be prepared to build upon cease fires at Christmas, New Year's, and Tet if the enemy shows any interest."[15]

Special National Intelligence Estimate 14.3-67 Is Submitted

On November 13 CIA Director Helms finally submitted to President Johnson SNIE 14.3–67, "Capabilities of the Vietnamese Communists for Fighting in South Vietnam." Helms wrote to LBJ that the SNIE "is sensitive and potentially controversial primarily because the new strength figures are at variance with our former holdings." Helms had considered not issuing the SNIE but decided that "too many people are aware that the exercise to get agreed figures has been going on. In short, the charge of bad faith or unwillingness to face the facts would be more generally damaging than the issuance of this document which can stand on its own feet."

In a covering memorandum to Helms's memo, Rostow distilled the SNIE for President Johnson. "It comes to this," wrote Rostow. "Manpower is the major problem confronting the Communists; there has been a substantial reduction in guerrillas since an estimated peak in early 1966; there has been a slight reduction in main force units in the past year, but this has been possible only by using more North Vietnamese replacements in Viet Cong units; there is a 'fairly good chance' that the Communist military strength and political infrastructure will continue to decline; Communist strategy is to sustain protracted war of attrition and to persuade the United States that it must pull out or settle on Hanoi's terms. Their judgment is that the 'Communists still retain adequate capabilities to support this strategy for at least another year.' "

Rostow informed Johnson that "the memo to you and the introductory note reflect a considerable debate in the intelligence community. The debate centers on the fact that they now know more from captured documents than they did about guerrillas, village defense forces, etc. What they know indicates that guerrilla strength was probably underestimated last year, but has declined substantially since. . . . In general, this is a conservative estimate; but it is not a bad thing to build our plans on conservative estimates."[16]

A special Cabinet meeting was called in order to brief the president's team on the new data charted from figures supplied by Ambassador Bunker and General Westmoreland. Rostow began the briefing by recalling CIA Director Helms's previous statements bearing on "the complexity of any statistical analysis on 'who is doing what to whom in Vietnam.' " The president interjected, "Nevertheless, Bunker and Westmoreland have stayed up nights working up these figures and I would like to keep them all off the record for now."

CIA Director Helms reviewed the new intelligence findings. Alluding to the difficulty involved in answering questions like "How is the war going?" Helms emphasized, "It has always been difficult to answer with any statistical certainty." The new study addressed "the perplexing question of force levels and the numbers of people involved. . . . The new intelligence estimate allows for these and other variables. But statistical uncertainties remain. The findings must be closely held. . . . 'We can't let the press in on this. We must still be careful in talking about the number of people in the game.' "

The Cabinet meeting was filled with restrained optimism. Helms explained that, "The war is in no sense over. . . . There won't be any collapse. . . . But U.S. and South Vietnamese forces are doing well . . . the war is going in our favor." The president said that he needed "to see things in perspective. I can see that our curve is better than the first hundred days of President Kennedy, or Eisenhower's eight

years and the way it is going now, better than our first three years."
Following the meeting, Rostow told those assembled, "Statistics can't
give you everything 100%, but they can and do confirm progress."

Did Westmoreland Deceive Anyone?

Was General Westmoreland conspiring against President Johnson by
altering the categories, and thus the numbers, used in the SNIE and
MACV's Order of Battle? Was Johnson the victim of mendacious
intelligence? If so, MACV, not the president, bore responsibility for
America's failure in Vietnam. As *New Yorker* writer Reneta Adler
explained in her analysis of the CBS-Westmoreland trial some twenty
years later, "If CBS was right, for example, and Westmoreland had
lost the war by deceiving his military superiors and his civilian Commander-in-Chief, then the Commander-in-Chief, President Johnson,
was inescapably exonerated from responsibility both for the escalation of the war and for its loss."[17]

The CBS documentary "The Uncounted Enemy" charged that
intelligence estimates were dishonest rather than incorrect. By accepting General Westmoreland's reduced OB as presented in the
CIA's estimate, the unsuspecting president was led to believe that
the crossover point had been reached—enemy losses could not be
replaced at their rate of attrition. Having been lulled into this false
sense of security, LBJ and the nation were unprepared for the size
of the enemy onslaught during the Tet offensive of January 31, 1968.

Could MACV intelligence officers have deliberately downgraded
and then successfully hid from the president and his advisors the
strength of enemy forces? Could the CIA actually "cave in" to
MACV's official estimates? And could this conspiracy have been kept
from the Lyndon Johnson who has been described by the director of
the White House military office, William Gulley, as "big ears"?[18]

Johnson's preoccupation with gathering information was legend-
ary. His White House office resembled an information command
center—three television sets ran simultaneously, their channels
changed by the click of a presidential remote control, their only
competing sound was the tickers spewing forth information from
Vietnam. All of this reflected Lyndon Johnson's commitment to the

dictum that a man's judgement was no better than his information.

The available documents show that LBJ was receiving a voluminous amount of statistical material on Vietnam. It is inconceivable that MACV could have hidden something of this magnitude from the president. Moreover, both sides of the debate had bureaucratic advocates who were in the business of slanting data towards their perspective. The raw intelligence from which MACV derived its estimates was disseminated throughout the intelligence community. A conspiracy would have had to involve Admiral Sharp, General Wheeler, the State Department, and even the White House Situation Room. Westmoreland would have needed literally hundreds of accomplices in the State Department, Defense Department, CIA, and the White House in order to suppress reports of North Vietnamese regular army infiltration of 25,000 a month between August and January 1968.

Nor could there have been a conspiracy when it was in the national news. During a November 22 MACV press briefing, Westmoreland told reporters that over the past six months the "fighting efficiency" of the VC/NVA had "progressively deteriorated." Since May 1967 the enemy had lost 40,000 troops killed-in-action. That this 40,000 could not be replaced was evidenced in MACV's new Order of Battle which now dropped enemy strength from 285,000 to 242,000. Westmoreland then admitted to the press that the new figures "do not include the political infrastructure." The Order of Battle debate was well known and well worn amongst decision makers and the press. On November 30, 1967, Jack Anderson's syndicated column titled "Vietnam Intelligence Experts Disagree" had even focused on the great OB debate.

Why would Westmoreland conspire against his president? The dictionary defines conspiracy as "an evil, unlawful plot." CBS explained that Westmoreland was under extraordinary pressure to show progress in the war because attrition had been his only strategy. How could he have gone to LBJ with news that the enemy was twice as large as currently reported? The press would crucify the administration once it learned that 525,000 U.S. troops were not nearly enough strength to force the enemy to the conference table. Thus, CBS claimed, when confronted with a disintegrating military strategy, and sensitive to its domestic repercussions, Westmoreland cooked the books.

Westmoreland was certainly under pressure to show progress; attriting the enemy was MACV's only strategy for winning the war, and LBJ wanted results. Nevertheless, Westmoreland did not try to deceive his Commander in Chief. The National Intelligence Estimate was an honest one and it was only a single input into LBJ's daily intelligence menu.

The problem of defining who was and was not an enemy soldier was part of the problem of the war itself. Counting the size of the enemy forces and the rate of infiltration was an inexact process. That's why an NIE is called an estimate! Estimating guerrilla forces was tantamount to "trying to estimate roaches in your kitchen," as General Westmoreland testified in the libel trial. While the CIA believed that every Vietnamese who stuck a pungi stake (a bambo stake used as a booby trap) in the ground belonged on the Order of Battle, Westmoreland did not, even though two percent of U.S. combat wounds occurred from these traps.

In retrospect, the intelligence process was corrupted from above by an excessively paranoid president. It *was* Lyndon Johnson's war. Yes, the numbers were often contrived, but not by Westmoreland on an unsuspecting president, but by the White House on an unsuspecting public. By the end of 1967, virtually every unit of American government was involved in selling the war's progress. The documents show that LBJ was briefed on the bureaucratic dispute between CIA-MACV concerning the size of enemy forces. LBJ placed extraordinary pressure on MACV for demonstrations of military progress in order to buttress Johnson's political fortunes at home. That pressure might have made Westmoreland feel uncomfortable, but he could hardly have led a bureaucratic conspiracy.

Why would LBJ act as he did? Politics did not stop at the water's edge for Johnson. General Westmoreland was a pawn of a president fighting for his political life. November 1967 was a few months prior to the first presidential primary and only a year before the 1968 presidential election. President Johnson needed to get his house in order before proceeding with the campaign. When Westmoreland spoke optimistically of progress in Vietnam, he did so at the president's urging.

VIII

The Big Sell: The Tortoise of Progress vs. the Hare of Dissent

> We have a story in Texas about Ford automobiles carrying a slogan on the trunk of each car that said, "Made in Texas by Texans for Texans." My motto now is, "Peace in South Vietnam for South Vietnam and by South Vietnamese."
>
> President Lyndon Johnson's private remarks to the Pope, December 22, 1967. The Vatican

The events of mid-November help cast Johnson's political strategies in their proper light. After McNamara's November 1 memorandum, and the responses from his advisors following it, it was evident to Johnson that Secretary McNamara could no longer adequately represent the president's policy and that key changes needed to be made in the composition of the principals. Heeding the counsel of Bundy, Fortas, and Clifford, the president took control of the campaign to dramatize progress to the American public but in ways that grossly exaggerated future military prospects. This campaign to accentuate the positive became a massive administration effort to exaggerate U.S. prospects for a favorable outcome in the war. This campaign was more than just self-deception by the principal players involved in policy making; it was an active effort by the government to convince the American Congress and the American people that progress was being made in the war in Vietnam beyond what actually was the case.

Richard Moose, who worked as Walt Rostow's assistant in the west wing from late 1966 until March 1968, later confessed that he "resigned quietly, but in frustration and dismay." He came to realize that there were many games going on with numbers during the war—one set was presented to the public via the press and "the second set of numbers were what some of us worried about."[1]

Westmoreland, Bunker, and Wheeler returned to Washington in November to help squash any public pessimism concerning progress in Vietnam. At a November 13 press conference, Ambassador Bunker told newsmen that he had just told the president, "In my view we are making steady progress in Vietnam, not only militarily, but in other ways as well: In the evolution of the constitutional process, in the pacification program, which is, in my view, equally as important as the military situation." Bunker projected that, "There is every prospect, too, that the progress will accelerate."

For the next two weeks virtually every official statement bearing on the war was framed optimistically in a concerted effort to stabilize public support for U.S. policy in Vietnam. During a November 17 press conference, President Johnson was asked to assess U.S. progress and prospects in Vietnam. He used the opportunity to take direct aim at the administration's number one target: "Our American people, when we get in a contest of any kind—whether it is in a war, an election, a football game, or whatever it is—want it decided and decided quickly; get in or get out. They like that curve to rise like this (indicating a sharp rise) and they like the opposition to go down like this (indicating a sharply declining line). That is not the kind of war we are fighting in Vietnam. . . . We don't march out and have a big battle each day in a guerrilla war. It is a new kind of war for us. So it doesn't move that fast. . . . We are making progress. We are pleased with the results that we are getting. We are inflicting greater losses than we are taking." Rostow wrote the president that the press conference "made big strides" in its "projection of confidence, moderate progress, and a will to sustain the efforts."

In an address to the National Press Club, General Westmoreland continued to emphasize that VC strength was "declining at a steady rate." The general noted that the war had entered a new phase "when the end begins to come into view." Westmoreland's remarks received wide circulation. "In the past two and one-half years I have seen the progressive commitment of United States troops in support of the Vietnamese. I am absolutely certain that whereas in 1965 the enemy was winning, today he is certainly losing. There are indications that the Vietcong and even Hanoi know this. . . . It is significant that the enemy has not won a major battle in more than a year."

On November 19, Westmoreland and Bunker appeared jointly on "Meet the Press." Ambassador Bunker again emphasized, "We are making steady not spectacular, progress. . . . We are at the point now not only of being able to continue, but to accelerate the rate of progress." Westmoreland explained that the United States was "winning a war of attrition now," basing his claim on MACV's new Order of Battle. Westmoreland stated that it was "conceivable that within 2 years or less the enemy will be so weakened that the Vietnamese will be able to cope with a greater share of the war burden. We will be able to phase down the level of our military effort, withdraw some troops . . ."

General Westmoreland's public comments were questioned during a meeting of the Joint Chiefs the next day. General Westmoreland first reviewed the impact of U.S. military strategy on enemy activity in the South and emphasized that the guerrilla forces had undergone serious attrition. Enemy recruits were hard to come by. "We estimate that a year ago he recruited 7,000 a month and that he is now down to 3,500." Future prospects looked even better. "The present trends should continue at an accelerated rate, providing we keep up the pressure, to include the bombing of the north. I might say parenthetically that I know of no better way to prolong the war than to stop the bombing of the north. In approximately two years or less the Vietnamese Armed Forces should be ready to take over an increasing share of our effort."

Westmoreland's briefing of the JCS was interrupted when General James L. Holloway interjected, "By when?" General Westmoreland repeated, "In approximately two years or less the Vietnamese Armed Forces should be ready to take over an increasing share of the war thereby permitting us to start phasing down the level of our effort. . . . In summary, we have the capacity to progressively weaken the

enemy and strengthen GVN so that our commitment can be gradually reduced in time."[2] Following the meeting Rostow wrote the
president that he was buoyed "by Westmoreland's vision of a U.S.
troop withdrawal within two years as the ARVN build up."[3]

Amidst this optimism arrived a rather distressing assessment from
Under-Secretary of State Nicholas Katzenbach who shared
McNamara's and Bundy's reservations that the bombing program
exacted too great a price at home and abroad with very little to show
for it in South Vietnam. "Indeed, the very fact that those who have
access to all relevant intelligence continually disagree about its value
should be proof at least that its value is dubious. . . . Nobody really
believes that the war can be won with bombs in the North."

In retrospect, Katzenbach's memo was one of the most cogent
analyses made of a stalemated military situation. "Hanoi uses time
the way Russians used terrain before Napoleon's advance on Moscow, always retreating, losing every battle, but eventually creating
conditions in which the enemy can no longer function. For Napoleon
it was his long supply lines and the cold Russian winter; Hanoi hopes
that for us it will be the mounting dissension, impatience, and frustration caused by a protracted war without fronts or other visible signs
of success; a growing need to choose between guns and butter; and
an increasing American repugnance of finding, for the first time,
their country cast as 'the heavy' with massive fire power brought to
bear against a 'small Asian nation.' "

Katzenbach proposed two strategic options available to Johnson.
The president could reduce restrictions on the military and go for a
quick knock-out of enemy forces. But Katzenbach knew the president did not believe military power could destroy the enemy's
forces, eliminate its infrastructure, or destroy its will to persist. The
alternative to an all-out military assault would be to pursue a strategy
with the principal purpose of restoring the political center in the
United States. Devising a strategy for strengthening the center at
home meant making a precise statement of U.S. objectives in Vietnam; the very objectives for which Secretary McNamara had long
maintained there was no consensus among the advisors. "Our objective should be to provide the military cover and non-military assistance needed to enable the GVN to grow in capacity and popular
support to the point where it can survive and, over a period of years,
deal with what will be a continuing and very serious communist

problem." Katzenbach pointed out that "We must make clear to the American people that our objective is defined in a way that can be attained without massive destruction of North Viet-Nam, without significant ground operations in any of the present sanctuary areas, and without any further increase in troop strength."

Katzenbach imaginatively phrased an important problem facing the administration: "Can the tortoise of progress in Vietnam stay ahead of the hare of dissent at home?" The rate of U.S. disenchantment with the war was growing rapidly, and Katzenbach warned Johnson that "even a rapid acceleration of progress would not bring the light at the end of the tunnel." The principal battle for the war was being waged with the minds of the American people, and escalation would bring rejection of the war.[4]

The administration's game plan for swaying public opinion had only mixed results with the press. The *New York Times* of November 19 referred to a "new chorus of official optimism, apparently designed to refute the spreading wave of national pessimism over the prospects in Vietnam." On November 24, Hedrick Smith, in his *Times* article "Accounts by Bunker and Westmoreland Stirring Unease" reported, "For the last 10 days or so, the American people have heard the most optimistic reports in years about the progress of the war in Vietnam from the ranking American officials in the field." In the *Washington Post*, Don Oberdorfer, using the headline "Statistics on War Fail to Prove Real Progress," concluded that "in no case is there a clear, direct or broadly-accepted relationship between the statistical progress and the end of the war. Government analysts concede that most of the progress curves could climb right off the charts and still leave half-a-million or more U.S. troops in Vietnam, bloody fighting continuing and no end to that in sight. In almost every chart and column of figures, the trend is favorable. This upward trend in the statistics is almost universally accepted. It is the sweeping conclusions being drawn from the figures that are in doubt."

A November 26, 1967, *Washington Post* article by Ward Just reported that the high-level review of the war "ended up being a high-level campaign to convince the American people that the war was being won and that the United States had reached the point where, as General William C. Westmoreland put it, the end 'comes into view.' "

Despite the misgivings in the press, the end of November brought excellent, if not dramatic, results in the presidential approval index. For the first time in months the polls in both Gallup and Harris indexes showed dramatic increases for Johnson's handling of the war. The improvement was so marked that for the first time since July 1967 (and the summer riots) the president's approval ratings were higher than disapproval. Johnson concluded that the hard sell had been successful. The American people had rallied behind their president who seemed visibly to be taking charge of the war.

Yet, the signs of strategic and political discontent were mounting. On November 28, former-president Eisenhower publicly called for a limited invasion of North Vietnam, and on November 30, Senator Eugene McCarthy of Minnesota announced his intent to challenge President Johnson in several Democratic primaries.

Order of Battle, Again

On November 21 Rostow provided LBJ with a list of issues likely to confront the administration in the weeks ahead; included on the list was the problem of "How we present order of battle statistics." The president was reminded that "MACV is completing retroactive estimate, including previous understatement of guerilla forces." Rostow warned that "the danger is press will latch on to previous underestimate and revive credibility gap talk. My recommendation is that Gen. Westmoreland present new order of battle statistics in context of year-end review in Saigon by changing course of the war in 1967 as opposed to 1966—removing emphasis from statistics themselves."

During a November 22 press briefing at the Pentagon, General Westmoreland could not escape questions on the new and old statistics. Westmoreland listed enemy strength at 242,000—about 55,000 below the 297,000 figure used in previous MACV estimates. When questioned about the drop Westmoreland explained, "Well, what I have on this strength is armed strength. The political infrastructure is not included. Now, if you include the political infrastructure, that figure is still a good one. I might say that this matter is under constant study. It's been studied during the last several months actually in considerable depth and there may be some readjustment in this in due time, but there's no inconsistency in the figures because I have talked about armed strength. I have excluded the political infrastructure." Westmoreland emphasized that the new figures on enemy strength in all areas except regular forces "must not be considered increases or decreases from old figures. Since they are based on new data, they logically cannot be used in conjunction with old data for any firm comparisons of past and present enemy strengths."[5] A *New York Times* headline the next day quoted Westmoreland as being "Sure of Victory," calling the battle at Dakto a "Great Defeat for Foe."

On November 26, 1967, Westmoreland cabled his deputy commander, General Creighton W. Abrams, Jr., with a distillation of what he had told the president, nationwide television programs, the National Press Club, and the on-the-record press conference in the Pentagon. "On each occasion, I presented in full or in part the following concept: We are grinding down the Communist enemy in South Vietnam, and there is evidence that manpower problems are emerging in North Vietnam. Our forces are growing stronger and becoming more proficient in the environment. The Vietnamese armed forces are getting stronger and becoming more effective on the battlefield. The Vietnamese armed forces are being provided with more modern equipment. These trends should continue, with the enemy becoming weaker and the GVN becoming stronger to the point where conceivably in two years or less the Vietnamese can shoulder a larger share of the war and thereby permit the US to begin phasing down the level of its commitment." Westmoreland then explained that this concept was "compatible with the evolution of the war since our initial commitment and portrays to the American people 'some light at the end of the tunnel.'" Of equal importance, "the concept straddles the presidential election of November 1968, implying that the election is not a bench mark from a military point of view."[6] Thus, if LBJ needed more time, he would not get it from the military.

McNamara Resigns

On November 29, 1967, after seven years as secretary of defense, Secretary McNamara announced his decision to accept the presidency of the World Bank. A Harris poll taken at the time of McNamara's resignation revealed that 45 percent of the population gave the secretary a negative rating for his handling of the job compared to 42 percent positive rating. In contrast, General Westmoreland received a 68 percent positive to a 16 percent negative rating for his job as commanding general in Vietnam. Writing on the front page of the *Washington Post*, pollster Louis Harris reported that it "is clear from the results that the American people are not particularly concerned at this juncture over keeping a strong civilian authority in the Pentagon." Harris reported his key results as: By 53 to 36 percent, the public felt that in wartime "civilian government leaders should let the military take over running the war." By a decisive 73 to 10 percent, Americans believed that "when civilians tell the military what to do, too often politics rather than military action results." By 65 to 10 percent, Americans felt "in Vietnam the military has been handicapped by civilians who won't let them go all out."

The secretary's resignation reflected the end of his long personal battle to get the president to stabilize the military commitment. McNamara later recalled, "I didn't believe we had reached a crossover point. I didn't believe the strength would decline. I didn't believe that the bombing would prevent North Vietnam from supplying the forces in South Vietnam with whatever strength North Vietnam wished to have there."

McNamara also held in his possession a secret study which revealed why the bombing of North Vietnam had played such a negligible role in Hanoi's ability to support operations in the South. The top-secret study conducted by the Jason division of the Washington-based think-tank, Institute for Defense Analysis (IDA),* charged that those who expected bombing to erode the determination of Hanoi and its people had clearly "overestimated the persuasive and disruptive effects of the bombing and, correspondingly, underestimated the tenacity and recuperative capabilities of the North Vietnamese." Moreover, bombing had not achieved its anticipated goals because

---

*This was the second Jason study. In 1966 McNamara sought an independent assessment of Rolling Thunder from America's most prominent scientists. Meeting throughout the summer of 1966 under the auspices of IDA, the Jason report charged that the bombing "had no measurable direct effect" on the enemy's capability to sustain the war effort. A year later, the next Jason study was similarly critical and added to McNamara's doubts on the war's progress.

its advocates failed to appreciate the fact, "well-documented in the historical and social scientific literature, that a direct, frontal attack on society tends to strengthen the social fabric of the nation, to increase popular support of the existing government, to improve the determination of both the leadership and the populace to fight back, to induce a variety of protective measures that reduce the society's vulnerability to future attack and to develop an increased capacity for quick repairs and restoration of essential functions." In their examination of alternate campaigns and optimal attack strategies the ad hoc group was "unable to devise a bombing campaign in the North to reduce the flow of infiltrating personnel into SVN."[7]

Lyndon Johnson's Private Doubts

President Johnson was now having personal doubts and contemplating not seeking reelection. During his Washington visit in November, General Westmoreland learned that Secretary McNamara would be leaving the Defense Department and would be replaced by Clark Clifford. Westmoreland spent an evening in the White House, and alone with the president, he soon realized that LBJ had already decided on the exit. "The President suddenly became intensely serious," Westmoreland later wrote. " 'What would my men in Vietnam think,' he asked, if he failed to run for re-election in 1968? Would they consider that their Commander in Chief had let them down? Although taken aback, I responded that if the troops knew why he made such a decision, I was certain they would understand. His health, he said, was 'not good,' and he was weary. Lady Bird and his two daughters wanted him to retire. They had discussed the possibility of four more years in the White House at length and were against it. Noting that the Constitution made no provision for an invalid president, he alluded to the illnesses of Presidents Woodrow Wilson and Eisenhower. Those were not the words of a man feeling his way, using his companion as a sounding board before making his decision, as some who would claim to have driven him from the White House would later profess. The President was tired; his wife was tired; he was concerned about his health. He had obviously made up his mind."[8]

Around the World with LBJ

In December 1967 President Johnson's personal friend and staunch ally, Australia's prime minister Harold Holt, disappeared while swimming off the coast of Australia. The president decided to personally attend the memorial services which were scheduled for December 23. President Johnson travelled to Australia's capital, Canberra, where he first held a series of meetings, the most important with South Vietnam President Nguyen Van Thieu, who used the memorial services to meet with Johnson on the question of the Government of South Vietnam's negotiations with the National Liberation Front (NLF)—the political arm of the Viet Cong. President Johnson and Ambassador Bunker had been urging Thieu to open discussions with "representatives" of the NLF, but Thieu had publicly rejected the idea, stating he would only talk with "defectors" from the NLF. A December 21 front-page headline in the *New York Times* had stated "Thieu, Disputing Johnson, Rejectes Talks with Foe." A Thieu-Johnson rift now threatened the credibility of the U.S. commitment and the two presidents met privately in Canberra to iron out their differences.

Following two hours of discussion, Johnson and Thieu issued a joint communiqúe that endorsed a policy of national reconciliation and stating that the GVN would be willing to talk with anyone, but that it would not be useful to talk with individuals from an organization committed to the destruction of South Vietnam's government. Johnson's hands were apparently tied to Thieu's decision not to negotiate with the NLF.

The president then flew to U.S. bases at Korat in Thailand and Cam Ranh Bay in South Vietnam. The visit to Cam Ranh Bay was the president's second in fourteen months. Dressed in a tan gaberdine shirt and brown trousers and looking relaxed, the president promised his troops that he would remain on course because the enemy had "met their master in the field." The president then declared, "We're not going to yield. And we're not going to shimmy." R.W. Apple of the *New York Times* reported that "the President's lavish embrace" of his military commanders "went far beyond a routine peptalk from a Commander-in-Chief on the war front." In presenting General Westmoreland with the Distinguished Service Medal, the president gave credit for bringing policy "from the valleys and depths of despondence to the cliffs and heights where we know now that the enemy can never win."[9]

Johnson's surprise visit to Cam Ranh Bay had buoyed the troops and sent a clear message—the president was sticking with his military leaders. Just a day earlier Johnson had privately acknowledged to the Australian cabinet, "The enemy is building his forces in the south. We must try very hard to be ready. We may face dark days ahead." In his book *Diffusion of Power,* Rostow wrote that the president felt that "Hanoi was under extreme pressure to achieve some tactical victory. Northern forces were being infiltrated into the South. He foresaw Kamikaze attacks in the months ahead. That is one reason he is pressing so hard for additional power."[10]

The president then flew to Rome for a private Vatican meeting with Pope Paul VI. The meeting occurred on the day before Christmas—a better day could not have been manufactured. President Johnson even presented Pope Paul with a foot-high bust of LBJ. During their private meeting in the pope's library, the president talked bluntly. "Hanoi has great problems but they believe the U.S. will tire and fail just like France did—and then they can win by default what they lost on the battlefield," LBJ told the pope. "We are being extremely careful not to widen the war by bringing in China and Russia. Over half of our people want to do more. Twenty percent of our people want to pull out. Thirty percent follow the moderate course of the President—thus 80% of the U.S. either follows the President or wants to do more. Twenty percent make all the noise and mislead Hanoi into believing we will give up. So I have this problem of keeping the pressure on without widening a war. My right hand keeps the pressure steady and with my left hand we seek negotiations."

LBJ confided to the pope that direct U.S.-Hanoi negotiations would probably not work. Johnson then revealed the cleavage between President Thieu and himself. "Hanoi is simply not going to the conference table because Hanoi believes they will win this war in Washington. It will take a long time to prove but I am convinced the best avenue available to us now is in the South—talks informally between the Thieu government and representatives of the NLF." LBJ implored the pope to intervene with President Thieu on behalf of peace. The declassified transcripts make for fascinating reading:

PRESIDENT: We must begin. It would be very useful if the Pope through his sources in South Vietnam could persuade Thieu and others to talk to the NLF informally. Anything the Holy Father can do to encourage this will be very beneficial. This would be one effective way of disengaging the NLF from Hanoi—and South Vietnam from us. I am also very hopeful the Pope will send a representative to see our prisoners in North Vietnam and to see the prisoners being held in South Vietnam. Hanoi is ignoring and violating the Geneva convention prisoner rules. If the Pope can call on both sides to accord just and humane treatment to prisoners and ask for permission to visit both sides, we would be willing to open our doors immediately. What I would hope that the Pope would do is this: Through your Apostolic Delegate or other effective channels tell Thieu and the Senate President to talk to representatives of the NLF and to do it in their own way. If the Pope would do this, I strongly believe it would offer some chance of peace.

POPE: I think I can do something.

PRESIDENT: You can say that President Thieu is willing to have informal discussions, why not you?

POPE: Is it possible that the truce at Christmas could be extended by a day or two? Could you not show the world that on the day of peace January 1, you will also make this a day of truce?

PRESIDENT: My problem is this: My military leaders tell me that the North Vietnamese have trucks lined up bumper to bumper and as soon as the truce begins they start them moving and those supplies and those men kill our soldiers. On August 25 I told Hanoi we would draw a circle around it of three hundred miles and if we stopped bombing there could talks begin? On September 10 at San Antonio I made my speech which publicized a portion of this. I held back until October 25—and during that time they kept coming and they kept killing. Archbishop Lucey went to South Vietnam as one of my observers during the election. He told me that every time we quieted down they increase their pressure. In the 37 day bombing pause, they built up a seven months supply.

The president's 1968 tax bill "chalk talk" to congressional leaders.

President Johnson recovering from surgery—business as usual. November 1966.

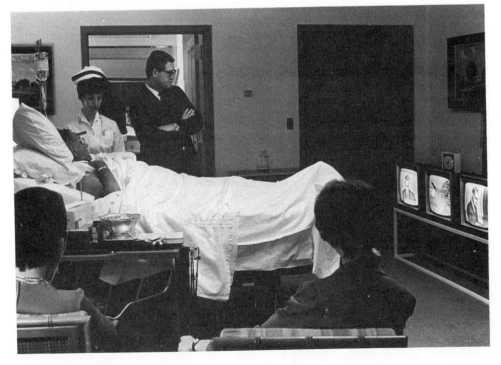

The president reviewing his press conference. November 1967.

The president and Lady Bird reviewing a presidential address. November 1968.

President Johnson meeting in the White House with Senator Eugene McCarthy.

The president meeting with Senator Robert Kennedy.

The president with Richard Nixon.

A meeting of the Tuesday lunch group. January 1968.

Arthur Dean.

John McCloy.

Dean Acheson.

General Omar Bradley.

Clark Clifford and Abe Fortas.

General Creighton Abrams briefing Johnson and Humphrey. March 1968.

General Creighton Abrams briefing Johnson on the implications of a bombing halt. October 1968.

LBJ reading his political obituary. March 1968.

General Earle Wheeler issuing the order to stop bombing North Vietnam. October 1968.

President Johnson with Walt Rostow, McGeorge Bundy, and former president Eisenhower on Air Force 1. *April 1968.*

The president with his senior advisors at Camp David. April 1968.

President Johnson with the Paris Peace negotiators: Philip Habib, Andrew Goodpaster, Averell Harriman, and William Jorden.

The president's final day in the White House. January 1969.

Lyndon B. Johnson conferring with the next president.
January 1969.

POPE: Where do they get their men, their means, their matériel?

PRESIDENT: By terror they are recruiting in the South—and they are now down to 14-year-old boys. They are getting desperate and we are certain that we are hurting them very very much. They are using Kamikaze tactics for they desperately want a victory and they are unable to achieve one.

POPE: We shall pray for you and we shall pray for your efforts for peace.

PRESIDENT: I don't want to press the point but I did want to know if I can assume that the Pope will try to bring the South Vietnamese to informal talks—and will immediately help out the prisoner problem.
   (The pope nodded.)

PRESIDENT: Would you have any objection to receiving an aide memoir from me which would set forth my views? I want you to know that we will follow the same theme as we have before. I assure you of my loyalty and devotion to the ideals that the U.S. stands for.[11]

In the aide memoir to the pope, Johnson conveyed his deep sense of frustration concerning the search for peace in Vietnam. He could not stop the bombing because "in every case in the past, cessation of the bombing has been used by the other side to accelerate the movement of supplies and men to the South." Johnson again alluded to a possible massive buildup by the NVN. "Your Holiness, I have just today come from Vietnam. My responsible commanders in the field tell me that the North Vietnamese are at this moment taking steps to exploit even the very short pause agreed to for Christmas, New Year's end and Tet. Our experience and current intelligence tell me an increased price will be paid in the blood of my men."

Following his private meeting with the pope, President Johnson returned to the United States in time to deliver a Christmas message from the White House. The 27,000-mile, 4-day journey had been the ultimate experience in presidential tourism. As the *New York Times* reported, "Those who would belittle or even condemn the haste, the extravagance or the corn of some of Mr. Johnson's performance, had best begin therefore with the new signs last week that he remains one of the most formidable political showmen in American history." He would need these skills for the events which lay ahead.

Ambassador Bunker's final cable of 1967 reviewed the president's recent activities. "Your visit to Cam Ranh on December 23rd was an encouragement to all of us; that you should have added many thousands of miles to your journey to come here and to speak generous words of appreciation and support has been an inspiration to all of us who are engaged in this great task on the soil of Viet Nam. And your working session with President Thieu and other free world leaders in Canberra served to reassure the Vietnamese of our commitment here."

Johnson's big sell throughout November and December had raised the stakes in the game of winning public support for the war by manipulating the press and the SNIE in order to present optimistic scenarios to the public in an election year. Following Tet, the administration blamed the press for not reporting the battle as a devastating defeat of the enemy, yet to most members of the media, Tet juxtaposed with the optimism of November showed up LBJ's public relations campaign for what it was. Although the administration and the military were aware that North Vietnam was planning a major offensive, LBJ took a gamble by distorting U.S. military prospects in the war. He had everything to lose politically, and when Hanoi called his hand it would be Johnson who was holding only "one aces."

IX

The Tet Offensive

War is an ugly thing, but not the ugliest: the decayed and degraded state of moral and patriotic feeling which thinks nothing worth a war is worse. . . . A man who has nothing which he cares about more than his personal safety is a miserable creature who has no chance of being free, unless made and kept so by the exertions of better men than himself.

On February 8, 1968 President Johnson sent this quotation from John Stuart Mill to Dean Rusk, Robert McNamara, Clark Clifford, and the Joint Chiefs.

I just don't understand it. Am I that far off? Am I wrong? Has something happened to me? My wife said, I think so. But she said you don't know what year you are living in. This is '68.

Remarks by President Lyndon Johnson to a Congressional delegation in the White House, January 30, 1968.

Khe Sanh

On January 11, 1968, U.S. intelligence detected a buildup of forces in the Laotian panhandle west of the demilitarized zone, threatening the Marine base at Khe Sanh in western Quang Tri province of South Vietnam. Khe Sanh was located eight miles east of Laos and eighteen miles south of the DMZ. The base occupied a strategically important

139

location for the purposes of hindering enemy infiltration down the Ho Chi Minh Trail as well as providing a staging post for possible operations into Laos.

The enemy force buildup of two additional North Vietnamese divisions was incontrovertible; but Hanoi's motives were wildly disputed. Prisoner reports and captured documents revealed that a massive winter-spring offensive was being planned. Truck traffic down the Ho Chi Minh Trail had reached massive proportions and major North Vietnamese troop reinforcements were in the border areas. Was Hanoi merely setting the stage for negotiations or was the offensive intended to topple the government of South Vietnam? What was the enemy up to? General Westmoreland believed a maximum military effort was underway, possibly to improve chances of achieving an end to the war through negotiations that would lead to a coalition government involving the NLF. A major offensive by Hanoi might also be aimed at achieving one major psychological victory in the United States prior to the start of the presidential campaign.

The enemy was finally coming to Westmoreland for battle. This would not be search and destroy in the jungle. Years of waiting for the enemy were almost over, and even though U.S. forces were significantly out-numbered, Westmoreland cabled Wheeler on January 12 that a withdrawal from Khe Sanh was unthinkable. "I consider this area critical to us from a tactical standpoint as a launch base for Special Operations Group teams and as flank security for the strong point obstacle system; it is even more critical from a psychological viewpoint. To relinquish this area would be a major propaganda victory for the enemy. Its loss would seriously affect Vietnamese and US morale. In short, withdrawal would be a tremendous step backwards."

With 15–20,000 North Vietnamese reinforcements circling Khe Sanh, Westmoreland bit the lure by ordering the 6000 Marine troops to defend the garrison. General Westmoreland also set in motion plans for implementing Operation Niagara (evoking an image of cascading bombs and shells), which became the most intense and successful application of aerial firepower yet seen in the war.

During the predawn hours of January 21, 1968, Khe Sanh came under constant rocket and mortar fire from the North Vietnamese. The battle was on, and it appeared to President Johnson and his

principal advisors that the North Vietnamese envisioned Khe Sanh
as a potential Dien Bien Phu. During a January 23 White House
meeting with members of the Democratic leadership, the president
reported that "intelligence reports show a great similarity between
what is happening at Khe Sanh and what happened at Dien Bien
Phu." Johnson became preoccupied with the analogy and had a table
model made of sand of the Khe Sanh plateau constructed in the
bunker-like Situation Room of the White House. He feared that Khe
Sanh would be his "Dinbinphoo," as LBJ was prone to pronounce it.

The Khe Sanh–Dien Bien Phu analogy was fraught with historical
misapplication. The actual siege by the Viet Minh of Dien Bien Phu
in 1954 had lasted 56 days. The French forces included Montagnards,
North Africans, Vietnamese, and Foreign Legionnaires. The total
force was about 13,000 and casualties amounted to 1100 killed, 1600
missing, and 4400 wounded. The Viet Minh totaled 49,500 combat
troops plus 55,000 support troops. At Khe Sanh, U.S. forces num-
bered 6000 against an enemy strength of about 20,000. The enemy's
advantage was less than 4 to 1 rather than 8 to 1 (including support
troops) as it had been at Dien Bien Phu. Moreover, usable supplies
parachuted into Dien Bien Phu had averaged about 100 tons per day;
General Westmoreland had a capability of 600 tons per day. The
French had possessed 75 combat aircraft and 100 supply and reconnaissance aircraft. By comparison, the United States had more than
2000 aircraft and 3300 helicopters.

Uncertainty about the military situation at Khe Sanh led LBJ to
question the Joint Chiefs. At a meeting on January 29, the president
requested that each member submit "his views concerning the validity of the strategy now pursued in South Vietnam by the Free World
Forces." The declassified meeting notes show that LBJ had asked the
chiefs "if they were completely in agreement that everything has
been done to assure that General Westmoreland can take care of the
expected enemy offensive against Khesanh." General Wheeler and
the Joint Chiefs "agreed that everything which had been asked for
had been granted and that they were confident that General Westmoreland and the troops were prepared to cope with any contingency."

It was during this period that Johnson, finding it difficult to sleep,
would walk the halls of the White House or call down to the Situation
Room for a report on Khe Sanh. Secretary of State Dean Rusk re-

called that, "We couldn't break him of the habit, even for health reasons, of getting up at 4:30 or 5:00 every morning to go down to the operations room and check on the casualties from Vietnam, each one of which took a little piece out of him."[1]

NSC staff assistant, Colonel Robert Ginsburgh, frequently found himself on night watch at the Situation Room in the basement of the White House. The Situation Room was actually two rooms—one a windowless room with a long table for private meetings; the other an active hub of communications with AP, UPI, and Reuter tele-types. Four clocks were mounted on the wall—Washington, GMT, Saigon, and the official presidential time which was set to follow LBJ's travels. The room also contained three television sets and other forms of technology befitting a White House communications cen-ter—especially a telephone. Ginsburgh recalled that during the bat-tle for Khe Sanh, "I had the night-time watch. And so, every two hours I was either in touch with the President on the phone, that is, he would call me or I would have sent him a message, a little memo to try and preclude his calling. He wanted to know, 'How is it going, what is happening?' "[2]

Johnson wanted to know how things were going because he was running out of trust for those who had brought him to this point. Johnson later denied pressuring the chiefs, but the declassified re-cord contradicts his position. Meeting on February 2 with White House correspondents, the president discussed the JCS assurances about Khe Sanh. In the meeting notes he is recorded as saying, "I asked the JCS to give me a letter saying that they were ready for the offensive at Khesanh." Yet, when reporters wrote that Johnson had obtained these letters from the chiefs, the president vehemently denied the claim.

The president then asked his assistant Tom Johnson to review all meeting notes to see whether there was any proof to the press re-ports. Tom Johnson wrote the president, "I have reviewed all of the notes of meetings held during the past two weeks. In addition, I have searched my memory thoroughly . . . At no time do my notes show, or my memory recall, an incident when the President said: 'I do not want any Damn Dien Bien Phu.' The President said we wanted to make sure we had done everything here and the JCS had done everything to make certain there is not another Dien Bien Phu. The word "damn" was not used in any meeting I attended in this context.

Never did the President say he had "made each chief sign a paper stating that he believed Khe Sanh could be defended." LBJ could thus claim that he had not said either "damn" or "each chief"; but he had made the Dien Bien Phu analogy and he had at least told members of Congress that the chiefs had signed a paper.[3]

During a particularly contentious morning meeting on January 30 with the Democratic congressional leaders, Senator Robert Byrd remarked, "I am very concerned about the buildup at Khesanh. I have been told that we have 5,000 troops there compared with 40,000 enemy troops. Are we prepared for this attack?" The president responded, "This has been a matter of great concern to me. I met with the Joint Chiefs yesterday. I went around the table and got their answer to these questions. In addition, I have it in writing that they are prepared. I asked, 'Have we done all we should do?' They said yes. I asked, 'Are we convinced our forces are adequate?' They said yes. I asked, 'Should we withdraw [troops to be used in Vietnam] from Korea?' They said no, that Khesanh is important to us militarily and psychologically. . . ."

General Wheeler, who was also at the meeting, sought to provide clarification for Byrd's queries: "On the matter of your question, Senator Byrd, about 5,000 U.S. troops versus 40,000 enemy troops. Khesanh is in very rugged areas. There are 5,900 U.S. troops in the Khesanh Garrison. There are support troops including 26th Marines and a battalion of the ARVN. . . . There are 39,968 friendly forces versus 38,590 enemy forces. Roughly, there are 40,000 allied troops to match the 40,000 enemy. We think we are ready to take on any contingency. In addition, there are 40 B-52 sorties and 500 tactical air sorties in the area Niagara each day hitting the enemy. . . . General Westmoreland is confident he can hold the position. To abandon it would be to step backward. The Joint Chiefs agree with General Westmoreland. The Joint Chiefs believe that he can hold and that he should hold. General Westmoreland considers it an opportunity to inflict heavy casualties on North Vietnam. We have 6,000 men there, and 34,000 available. It is 40,000 versus 40,000."

A week later during a White House meeting of the principals the president again asked Wheeler, "Are you as confident today as you were yesterday that we can handle the situation at Khesanh? General Wheeler answered, "I do not think the enemy is capable of doing what they have set out to do. General Westmoreland has strengthened his position. He has contingency plans and can meet any contingency. There is nothing he has asked for that he has not been given. Khesanh is important to us militarily and psychologically. It is the anchor of our defensive situation along the DMZ." Johnson again asked General Wheeler, "Are you sure that you have everything that is needed to take care of the situation in Khesanh?" Wheeler responded, "Yes, we are. General Westmoreland has been given everything he has requested."

Prometheus Bound

The enemy build up at Khe Sanh was followed on January 23, 1968, by North Korea's capture of the U.S. Navy Intelligence ship *Pueblo* on grounds of espionage. Seized in international waters some 26 miles off the coast of Japan, the 906-ton USS *Pueblo* was on its first electronic surveillance mission. The crew of 83, captained by Lloyd Bucher, was forced into the North Korean port at Wonsan, the first U.S. naval vessel captured since the USS *Chesepeake* in 1807—during the Napoleonic wars.

Had the seizure been a pre-planned effort to provoke a U.S. response and to exert pressure on the United States in Vietnam? Were the North Koreans supporting their Communist allies in North Vietnam and trying to create fear in South Korea? "Prometheus Bound," proclaimed a *Newsweek* article in describing how "a tenth-rate country" had "abruptly confronted Lyndon B. Johnson with one of the most delicate and intractable emergencies of his crisis-wracked Administration."[4] Secretary of State Dean Rusk declared publicly, "I would not object to designating this an act of war in terms of the category of actions to be so construed. My strong advice to North Korea is to cool it." But North Korea had no intention of cooling it; instead, it released a confession signed by the *Pueblo*'s skipper, Commander Bucher, obviously obtained under duress, which contained alleged admissions of CIA contacts and proposed aggression against Korea.

Ironically, the seizure allowed Johnson to mobilize 15,000 Air Force and Navy Reservists as well as 370 inactive aircraft. Johnson also convened a "crisis" meeting of an informal planning committee which included all of the principal advisors to the president, somewhat like President Kennedy's Executive Committee (ExComm) during the Cuban Missile Crisis of 1962. The president was determined not to act hastily and to do everything possible diplomatically to get the crew returned safely. (Which succeeded only after a protracted period of eleven months.)

The seizure raised difficult problems for Johnson's political leadership. The president could hardly afford a second war front in Asia, yet he was being pressured at home to retaliate against what Massachusetts congressman William Bates, senior Republican on the House Armed Services Committee, called, "a dastardly act of piracy." Hawks were not the only ones pressuring Johnson. Democratic senator Frank Church of Idaho, one of the Senate's most outspoken doves on Vietnam, derided the *Pueblo*'s seizure as "an act of war," in which the honor of the United States was at stake.

Tet: Move Forward to Achieve Final Victory

During the early morning hours of January 31 (the Vietnamese New Year, Tet) approximately 80,000 North Vietnamese regulars and guerrillas attacked over 100 cities throughout South Vietnam. Tet involved enemy attacks on 35 of 44 province capitals, 36 district towns and many villages and hamlets. For weeks prior to the offensive, enemy forces had been infiltrating into Saigon in civilian clothes in preparation for a well-planned campaign of terror. The goal was to achieve a popular uprising against the GVN and to show the American public that the very notion of security in the South was null and void.

Communist forces had been given the general order "Move forward to achieve final victory." Combat orders had urged the assaulters to do everything possible to completely liberate the people of South Vietnam. The orders found on captured guerrillas described the Tet strategy as one that would be "the greatest battle ever fought throughout the history of our country." The infiltrators were exhorted to "move forward aggressively to carry out decisive and repeated attacks in order to annihilate as many American, Satellite and Puppet troops as possible in conjunction with political struggles and military proselyting activities. . . . Display to the utmost your revolutionary heroism by surmounting all hardships and difficulties and making sacrifices as to be able to fight continually and aggressively. Be prepared to smash all enemy counter attacks and maintain your revolutionary standpoint under all circumstances. Be resolute in achieving continuous victories and secure the final victory at all costs."

While the attack itself did not surprise the principals, its timing during the Tet holiday phase-down did. In Washington, Walt Rostow was called away from a foreign-affairs advisors' luncheon to receive news of the offensive. Rostow quickly returned to report, "We have just been informed we are being heavily mortared in Saigon. The Presidential Palace, . . . the Embassy and the city itself have been hit." General Wheeler did not seem very alarmed: "It was the same type of thing before. You will remember that during the inauguration that the MACV headquarters was hit. In a city like Saigon people can infiltrate easily. They carry in rounds of ammunition and mortars. They fire and run. It is impossible to stop this in its entirety. This is about as tough to stop as it is to protect against an individual mugging in Washington, D.C. We have got to pacify all of this area and get rid of the Viet Cong infrastructure. They are making a major effort to mount a series of these actions to make a big splurge at TET."[5]

But General Westmoreland quickly cabled Admiral Sharp that the enemy attacks constituted more than a D.C. mugging. The enemy "appears to be [using] desperation tactics, using NVA troops to terrorize populated areas. He attempted to achieve surprise by attacking during the truce period. The reaction of Vietnamese, US and Free World Forces to the situation has been generally good. Since the enemy has exposed himself, he has suffered many casualties. As of now, they add up to almost 700. When the dust settles, there will probably be more. All my subordinate commanders report the situation well in hand."

From a military assessment, the VC suffered a major defeat at Tet. Over half of their committed force was lost and perhaps a quarter of their whole regular force. Moreover, the Communists failed to bring about the diversion of U.S. forces from Khe Sanh or elsewhere. Nevertheless, the psychological impact of Tet was demoralizing to the American public. The enemy had demonstrated a capability to enter and attack cities and towns and had employed terrorism for doing vast damage. Bunker cabled Johnson on February 8, "Hanoi may well have reasoned that in the event that the TET attacks did not bring the outright victory they hoped for, they could still hope for political and psychological gains of such dimensions that they could come to the negotiating table with a greatly strengthened hand. They may have very well estimated that the impact of the TET attacks would at the very least greatly discourage the United States and cause other countries to put more pressure on us to negotiate on Hanoi's terms."

The impact on the American public was indeed great. A front-page photograph on the *New York Times* February 1 edition showed three military policemen, rifles in hand, seeking protection behind a wall outside the consular section of the U.S. Embassy in Saigon. The bodies of two American soldiers slain by guerrillas who had raided the compound, lay nearby. All 19 guerrillas had been killed, but not until they had blasted their way into the embassy and had held part of the grounds for six hours. Four MPs, a Marine Guard, and a South Vietnamese employee were killed in the attack. President Thieu declared a state of martial law, yet during a news conference from the Cabinet room, President Johnson likened Tet to the Detroit riots, asserting "a few bandits can do that in any city."

Meeting with key congressional leaders in the evening of January 31, LBJ reviewed the events preceding Tet as well as Khe Sanh. "The Joint Chiefs, and all the Joint Chiefs, met with me the day before yesterday and assured me that they had reviewed the plans and they thought they were adequate. I told them I thought I almost had to have them sign up in blood because if my poll goes where it has gone, with all the victories, I imagine what it would do if we had a good major defeat. So General Westmoreland and the Joint Chiefs of Staff are sure that we are not anticipating some major activity there that we have not heard about."

General Wheeler then explained that Hanoi's military purpose in the Tet offensive had been to draw forces away from the Khe Sanh area. The second objective seemed to have been more political, to demonstrate to the South Vietnamese people and the world, that the Communists still possessed a considerable strength in the country and thereby shake the confidence of the Vietnamese people in the ability of their government to provide them security, even when they were within areas held by government and U.S. troops. "A significant thing about this attack," Wheeler said, "is that in many areas, particularly in Saigon, and at Bien Hoa, the attackers were dressed in one of three types of clothing: Civilian clothes, military, ARVN military police uniforms, or national police uniforms. Apparently, they gave no attention at all to whether or not they killed civilians. This is a sort of an unusual action for them because they have posed as the protectors of the civilian populace. Apparently this is the effort to reestablish by terror a degree of control over the population."

The meeting of congressional leaders was followed by a Cabinet meeting which Johnson opened by acknowledging, "There is a lot of stress and plenty of overtime for us all." President Johnson then engaged in a series of free-flowing remarks in which he came close to blaming the pope for Tet:

> I think I admired President Kennedy most during the Bay of Pigs when he said 'no one is to blame but me.' I know that wasn't true. . . . We went into Rome at night and we could have been faced with two million Red demonstrators. The Pope appealed to me. We had no differences, no quarrels. He said 'I want to do something, anything for peace—can't you give us one extra day of the holiday truce?' General Westmoreland told me how many American lives it would cost, but we did give the Pope his extra day. Now it's hard not to regret the number of boys who were killed. It is now so much worse after the Tet truce. Westmoreland cancelled the Tet truce because the house was on fire. So you look at *Pueblo,* Khe Sanh, Saigon and you see them all as part of the Communist effort to defeat us out there. We can dodge it by being weak-kneed if we want to. I said at San Antonio that we have gone as far as we could—farther, I might add, than the military wanted. We made it clear how much we want to talk and not bomb, just so long as there is some prompt and productive response. But if you sneak in the night and hit us, we can't stop bombing. Now we have their answer with this new offensive. It just should satisfy every dove who loves peace as much as any mother does.

The president then read excerpts from a memorandum received from Ambassador Bunker, calling particular attention to a passage recalling Thomas Paine's remark, "These are the times that try men's souls. . . . What we attain too cheaply, we esteem too lightly."

Attending the annual presidential prayer breakfast at the Shoreham Hotel, the president sounded weary and burdened by events. "The nights are very long. The winds are very chill. Our spirits grow weary and restive as the springtime of man seems farther and farther away. I can, and I do, tell you that in these long nights your President prays." Indeed, as these personal pressures grew, LBJ sought private solace in late-night prayer at St. Dominic's Church, in southwest Washington. Accompanied only by the secret service, the president and his "little monks" would read scriptures, psalms, and sing hymns.[6]

On February 1, Wheeler cabled Sharp and Westmoreland raising the possibility of "whether tactical nuclear weapons should be used if the situation in Khe Sanh should become that desperate." While Wheeler considered that eventuality unlikely, he requested a list of susceptible targets in the areas "which lend themselves to nuclear strikes, whether some contingency nuclear planning would be in order, and what you would consider to be some of the more significant pros and cons of using tac [tactical] nukes in such a contingency."

Westmoreland responded, "The use of tactical nuclear weapons should not be required in the present situation." However, should the situation change, "I visualize that either tactical nuclear weapons or chemical agents would be active candidates for employment." During an emotional February 16 news conference, Johnson vehemently denied that nuclear weapons had ever been considered, adding even more fuel to the credibility gap fire. LBJ stated that it was "against the national interest to carry on discussions about the employment of nuclear weapons with respect to Khesanh."

While Wheeler and Westmoreland privately discussed tactical nukes, Walt Rostow privately drew charts for his wife Elspeth. "Responding to a question from Elspeth last night," Rostow wrote Johnson, "I explained events in Vietnam as follows. The war had been proceeding in 1967 on an attritional basis with our side gradually improving its position, the Communists gradually running down. [See Figure 1.] Behind these curves were pools of military forces and fire power which represented the working capital available to the two sides. As the documents forecast, the Communists decided to take a large part of their capital and put it into: an attack on the cities; a frontier attack at Khe Sanh and elsewhere. In the one case their

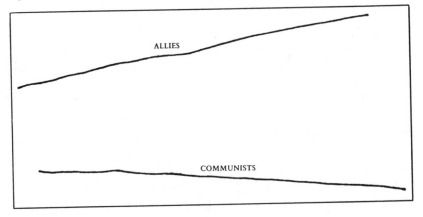

Figure 1

objective was the believed vulnerability of the GVN and the believed latent popular support for the Viet Cong. In the other case, the believed vulnerability of the U.S. public opinion to discouragement about the war. So the curves actually moved like this [see Figure 2].

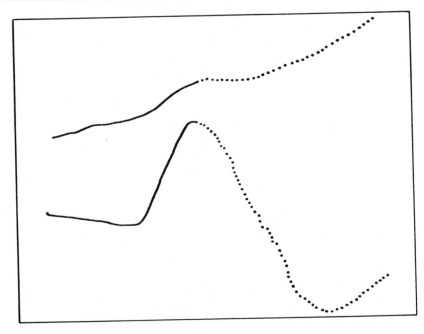

Figure 2

The dotted portions indicate the potentiality if: the cities are cleared up and held against possible follow-on attacks; the GVN demonstrate effective political and relief capacity; we hold Khe Sanh; we keep U.S. opinion steady on course. In short, if all on our side do their job well, the net effect could be a shortening of the war."

But administration critics weren't convinced. Satirist Art Buchwald likened administration optimism to another historical event: " 'We have the enemy on the run,' says General Custer at Big Horn. 'It's a desperation move on the part of Sitting Bull and his last death rattle.' " Senator George Aiken wryly remarked, "If this is a failure, I hope the Viet Cong never have a major success." Yet Rostow again wrote Johnson that the degree of Communist terrorism during the Tet period would actually strengthen the South Vietnamese resolve to get even with these terrorists. "There is a chance that South Viet Nam will emerge in the weeks and months ahead with stronger political institutions and a greater sense of nationhood and common destiny than before."

More Troops

General Wheeler understood the severity of Westmoreland's military position. Allied forces were stretched to their maximum extent and effectiveness. On February 3, Wheeler cabled Westmoreland, "The President asks me if there is any reinforcement or help that we can give you?" Receiving no answer, Wheeler tried again on February 8: "Query: Do you need reinforcements? Our capabilities are limited. . . . However, if you consider reinforcements imperative, you should not be bound by earlier agreements. . . . United States government is not prepared to accept defeat in Vietnam. In summary, if you need more troops, ask for them."

Westmoreland now cabled Wheeler that there was cause for alarm. "From a realistic point of view we must accept the fact that the enemy has dealt the GVN a severe blow. He has brought the war to the towns and the cities and has inflicted damage and casualities on the population. Homes have been destroyed, distribution of the necessities of life has been interrupted. Damage has been inflicted to the LOC's [Lines of communication] and the economy has been decimated. Martial law has been invoked, with stringent curfews in the cities. The people have felt directly the impact of the war."

While U.S. forces had repelled the Communist onslaught and inflicted major losses on the enemy manpower pool, Tet revealed the enemy's great skill in planning, coordination, and courage. The enemy had infiltrated previously secure population centers and exploited the GVN claim of security from attack. But there had been no general uprising, and the enemy did not hold a single city, although enemy units had waged a fierce three-week battle at the ancient city of Hué where they had occupied the Citadel—a nineteenth-century fortress which shielded the nation's historic imperial palace. Hué, a city of 100,000, was also the traditional center of religious and intellectual life in Vietnam. After weeks of fighting, U.S. and ARVN forces secured Hué, but not until some of the worst carnage of the war had been unleashed on its civilian inhabitants.

Westmoreland cabled Wheeler that enemy activity at Hué and elsewhere had helped Hanoi to score "a psychological blow, possibly greater in Washington than in South Vietnam, since there are tentative signs that the populace is turning against the Viet Cong as a result of these attacks." The enemy had also succeeded in temporarily disrupting South Vietnam's economy, and Westmoreland believed the enemy would continue to strain the will of the people by maintaining pressure on the populated areas with his forces already committed. The general also expected another major offensive in the Saigon area, commencing in mid-February.

Meeting with the Democratic congressional leadership at breakfast on February 6, 1968, the president once again faced tough questions from Senator Robert Byrd. "I am concerned about: 1. That we had poor intelligence; 2. That we were not prepared for these attacks; 3. We underestimated the morale and vitality of the Viet Cong; 4. We over-estimated the support of the South Vietnamese government and its people." Johnson shot back at Byrd: "I don't agree with any of that. We knew that they planned a general uprising around TET. Our intelligence showed there was a winter-spring offensive planned. We did not know the precise places that were going to be hit. General Abrams said the Vietnamese are doing their best. There was no military victory for the Communists. Just look at the casualties and the killed in action."

The discussion then moved to a more general level of political analysis:

SENATOR BYRD: I have never caused you any trouble in this matter on the Hill. But I do have very serious concerns about Vietnam. I think this is the place to raise these questions, here in the family.

CONGRESSMAN HALE BOGGS: What about Bob Byrd's charge that we are under-estimating the strength of the VC? I personally do not agree with that.

THE PRESIDENT: I have never under-estimated the Viet Cong. They are not push-overs. I do not think we have bad intelligence or have under-estimated the Viet Cong morale.

SENATOR BYRD: Something is wrong over there.

THE PRESIDENT: The intelligence wasn't bad.

SENATOR BYRD: That does not mean the Viet Cong did not succeed in their efforts. Their objective was to show that they could attack all over the country and they did.

THE PRESIDENT: That was not their objective at all.

SENATOR BYRD: You have been saying the situation with the Viet Cong was one of diminishing morale. When I say you, I mean the Administration.

THE PRESIDENT: I personally never said anything of the sort. I am not aware that anyone else has been saying that. What do you think the American people would have done if we had sent in troops and had lost 21,000 of them as the enemy has?

SENATOR RUSSELL LONG: If we had planned to have an up-rising in Cuba and you had caused 21,000 men to be lost as the Viet Cong did, I am sure you would have been impeached.

THE PRESIDENT: I am of the opinion that criticism is not worth much. I look at all these speeches that are in the [congressional] Record. I look at all the people who are going around the country saying our policy is wrong. Where do they get us? Nowhere. The popular thing now is to stress the mis-management to Vietnam. I think there has been very little. I wish Mike (Senator Mansfield) would make a speech on Ho Chi Minh. Nothing is as dirty as to violate a truce during the holidays. But nobody says anything bad about Ho. They call me a murderer. But Ho has a great image.

SENATOR BYRD: I don't want the President to think that I oppose you. I am just raising these matters.

THE PRESIDENT: I don't agree with what you say.

SENATOR LONG: I am happy you raised the point, Bob.

THE PRESIDENT: Everybody should say and do what they want to. But we have put our very best men that we have out there. I believe that our military and diplomatic men in the field know more than many of our Congressmen and Senators back here. Anybody can kick a barn down. It takes a good carpenter to build one. I just wish all of you would expose the Viet Cong and Ho. We have got some very crucial decisions coming up. Personally, I think they suffered a severe defeat. But we knew there would be a general uprising, and they did not win any victory. It seems to be an American trait to ask why. I just hope that we don't divert our energies and our talents by criticizing unnecessarily. We've got all we can of this "What's wrong with our country?" Fulbright, Young and Gruening haven't helped one bit.

SENATOR BYRD: I do not want to argue with the President. But I am going to stick by my convictions.

The Tuesday luncheon following Tet revealed frustration amongst the advisors. For the departing Secretary of Defense Robert McNamara, the Tet offensive demonstrated that Hanoi had "more power than we credit them with. I do not think it was a 'last-gasp' action. I do think that it represents a maximum effort in the sense that they poured on all of their assets and my guess is that we will inflict a very heavy loss both in terms of personnel and material and this will set them back some but that after they absorb the losses they will remain a substantial force. I do not anticipate that we will hit them so hard that they will be knocked out for an extended period or forced to drop way back in level of effort against us. I do think that it is such a well-coordinated, such an obviously advanced planned operation, that it probably relates to negotiations in some way. I would expect that were they successful here they would then move forward more forcibly on the negotiation front and they are thinking they have a stronger position from which to bargain."

Johnson wanted to know what should be done militarily to punish the enemy? McNamara argued that the Joint Chiefs had no answer. "I have talked to the Chiefs about some kind of a reciprocal action—retaliation for their attack on our Embassy or in retaliation for their attack across the country. There just isn't anything the Chiefs have come up with that is worth trying. They talk about an area-bombing attack over Hanoi but the weather is terrible. You can't get in there with pinpoint targeting. The only way you could bomb it at all at the present time is area bombing and I would not recommend that to you under any circumstances. They have just not been able to think of retaliation that means anything. My own feeling is that we ought to be able to depend upon our ability to inflict very heavy casualties on them as our proper response and as the message we give to our people."

But the chiefs did have an answer. In a meeting with the president on February 5, they proposed removing the restrictions around Hanoi and Haiphong, reducing the circles to three miles around Hanoi and one-and-one-half miles around Haiphong. Secretary of State Rusk feared that the proposed action "opens up the possibility of large civilian casualties and leads to extensive devastation of the area. From what we have seen in other areas this leads to almost total devastation. What to hit is up to the pilot." Wheeler responded, "We do not advocate attacking the population centers. We never have before, and we don't ask for that now. I admit there will be more civilian destruction, but we will be going after trucks and water craft. They are secure now, but represent genuine military targets."

Secretary McNamara challenged Wheeler's logic. "Any attack of this type is very expensive both in the number of U.S. aircraft lost and in civilian destruction. I do not recommend this. The military effect is small and our night time attack capability is small. Civilian casualties will be high. In my judgment, the price is high and the gain is low. The military commanders will dispute all the points I have made except aircraft loss."

Wheeler directly contradicted Secretary McNamara: "I do not

think the effects on the civilian population will be that high. As you know, they have an excellent warning system and most of them go to shelters and tunnels. From that standpoint, civilian loss could be lower than it is in other areas. We have had nothing like the civilian destruction that took place in World War II and Korea. But the targets which are there are military targets of military value. Frankly, this (civilian casualties which might result) does not bother me when I compare it with the organized death and butchery by the North Vietnamese and the Viet Cong during the last two weeks in South Vietnam. All of this relates to the matter of pressure."

Choices had to be made. The president told the chiefs, "I believe somebody in government should say something. I do not share the view that many people have that we took a great defeat. Our version is not being put to the American people properly. . . . What are we going to do now on these bombing targets?" It was the incoming secretary of defense, Clark Clifford, who recommended accepting the chiefs' proposal. Clifford believed that the Tet offensive was Hanoi's answer to the San Antonio formula. "I am inclined to resume the bombing in North Vietnam and go ahead with the suggested three-mile and one-and-a-half mile limits. As long as the enemy has demonstrated that they are not going to respond positively we should go ahead with this."

When Rusk and McNamara warned about the need to distinguish restricted from authorized targets, Wheeler showed his discontent: "I am fed up to the teeth with the activities of the North Vietnamese and the Viet Cong. We apply rigid restrictions to ourselves and try to operate in a humanitarian manner with concern for civilians at all times. They apply a double standard. Look at what they did in South Vietnam last week. In addition, they place their munitions inside of populated areas because they think they are safe there."

The discussion between the principals in the February 7 National Security Council meeting reveals their continuing uncertainty concerning enemy capabilities and U.S. military strategy:

> SECRETARY RUSK: What about the possibility of the MIGs attacking a carrier?

> GENERAL WHEELER: No, I do not think this is likely. The carriers do have air caps and are distant from the MIG bases.

THE PRESIDENT: Go in and get those MIGs at Phuc Yen.

GENERAL WHEELER: We will as soon as the weather permits.

SECRETARY MCNAMARA: The MIGs would have negligible military effects but they would have spectacular psychological impact. We do get the feeling that something big is ahead. We do not exactly know what it is, but our commanders are on alert.

THE PRESIDENT: I want all of you to make whatever preparations are necessary. Let's know where we can get more people if we need to move additional ones in.

GENERAL WHEELER: I have a preliminary list on my desk. I am not satisfied with it.

SECRETARY MCNAMARA: This would include Army, Navy, Air Force and Marine units.

THE PRESIDENT: What about the allies?

GENERAL WHEELER: The Australians are incapable of providing more troops. The problems in Korea are such that it will be hard to get the South Koreans to even send the light division they had promised. The Thai troops are in training and to move them in now would be more detrimental than helpful.

THE PRESIDENT: So it would be only Americans? Well, I want you to know exactly where you could get them, where they are located now and what we need to do. Get whatever emergency actions ready that will be necessary.

SECRETARY MCNAMARA: All we would recommend at this time are the three items we had discussed earlier. There may be some increase in draft calls but this would have no immediate effect.

THE PRESIDENT: Do we have adequate hospitals and medical personnel?

GENERAL WHEELER: We have ample space, ample supplies, and enough doctors for the present.

SECRETARY MCNAMARA: There are 6,400 military beds. Of that, 2900 are occupied by U.S. troops and 1100 by Vietnamese civilians. So we have an additional capacity of about 2400.

THE PRESIDENT: Look at this situation carefully. If we have another week like this one, you may need more.

SECRETARY RUSK: How do you interpret their use of tanks?

GENERAL WHEELER: They had to bring them all the way from Hanoi. This shows that this plan has been in staging since September. It represents a real logistic feat. They want to create maximum disruption.

USIA DIRECTOR LEONARD MARKS: Could they do anything at Cam Ranh Bay?

GENERAL WHEELER: They could. On this last attack, we caught frogmen in there. They could put rockets in the hills and fire on to the base.

THE PRESIDENT: How many of the 25,000 killed were North Vietnamese Regulars?

GENERAL WHEELER: Approximately 18,000 were of a mixed variety of South Vietnamese enemy. Approximately 6,000 to 7,000 were North Vietnamese.

THE PRESIDENT: How do things look at Khesanh? Would you expect to have to move out of Lang Vie?

GENERAL WHEELER: It was not planned that we would hole some of these outposts. We may have to move back that company on Hill 861.

THE PRESIDENT: Bob, are you worried?

SECRETARY MCNAMARA: I am not worried about a true military defeat.

GENERAL WHEELER: Mr. President, this is not a situation to take lightly. This is of great military concern to us. I do think that Khesanh is an important position which can and should be defended. It is important to us tactically and it is very important to us psychologically. But the fighting will be very heavy, and the losses may be high. General Westmoreland will set up the forward field headquarters as quickly as possible. He told me this morning that he has his cables and his communications gear in. He is sending a list of his needs, including light aircraft. We are responding to this request.

THE PRESIDENT: Let's get everybody involved on this as quickly as possible. Everything he wants, let's get it to him.

Senator Clark's Report

In early February the Senate Committee on Foreign Relations published Senator Joseph Clark's report based on a recent study mission to South Vietnam. "Stalemate in Vietnam" was a singularly powerful indictment of U.S. policy. The report concluded, "The war in Vietnam is at a stalemate which neither side can convert into a military victory without leaving the country—and perhaps the world—in ruins." America's national unity was threatened by the divisiveness of convictions on the war creating a condition whereby "the political fabric of our society is at the tearing point." Senator Clark believed that Vietnam had become "a cancer" which threatened to destroy the country. "Never, never again," concluded the Senator, "should we commit a ground army on the mainland of Asia."

In his analysis of the effect Tet could have on the polls, and thus, on the election, Rostow warned the president: "There is a widespread assumption in the country, even among those who support our policy, that peace requires only that the right button can be found to push—the right gimmick discovered. This is, of course, naive. But it furnishes the basis for what will probably be a growing issue as the year proceeds. The serious opposition will not call for a pull-out from Vietnam. They will, instead, promise to do it better. They will say you cannot find the right button—and they will imply they can. We can defuse this issue by saying plainly that there can be no peace because the enemy still wants war. And those who talk of peace only cause the enemy to redouble his attacks on our men in Vietnam."

The president, now fearing he could lose both Vietnam and his political credibility, confronted his advisors, "Well, it looks as if all of you have counseled, advised, consulted and then—as usual—placed the monkey on my back again. . . . I do not like what I am smelling from those cables from Vietnam and my discussions with outside advisers. We know the enemy is likely to hit the cities again. They will likely have another big attack and there undoubtedly will be surprises. I want you to lay out for me what we should do in the minimum time to meet a crisis request from Vietnam if one comes. Let's assume we have to have more troops. I think we should now tell the allies that we could lose Southeast Asia without their help."

The president's meeting on February 8 with the Joint Chiefs revealed perceptions of a deteriorating military situation. Westmoreland needed an immediate deployment of 45,000 men to meet a similar increase in enemy strength. The president first asked, "What is the ARVN strength?" General Wheeler responded, "Approximately 360,000 men now. Total forces about 600,000." The discussion then turned to the enemy's strength since it appeared that few North Vietnamese regular forces had been utilized for the Tet attack, the question now raised was how many guerrillas and irregulars (recently removed from the OB) were still available as reserves or replacements.

LBJ instructed the chiefs to "work up all the options and let's review them together. I want you to hope for the best and plan for the worst. Let's consider the extensions, call ups, and use of specialists. Dean, should we have more than the Tonkin Gulf resolution in going into this? Should we ask for a declaration of war?" The secretary answered, "Congressional action on individual items would avoid the problems inherent in a generalized declaration. I do not recommend a declaration of war. I will see what items we might ask the Congress to look at." President Johnson persisted, "What would be the impact internationally on a declaration of war?" Rusk responded, "It might be a direct challenge to Moscow and Peking in a way we have never challenged them before. There would be very severe international effects."

At this point in the meeting, Clark Clifford interjected with a series of troubling questions: "There is a very strong contradiction in what we are saying and doing. On one hand, we are saying that we have known of this build up. We now know the North Vietnamese and Viet Cong launched this type of effort in the cities. We have publicly told the American people that the communist offensive was (a) not a victory, (b) produced no uprising among the Vietnamese in support of the enemy, and (c) cost the enemy between 20,000 and 25,000 of his combat troops. Now our reaction to all of that is to say that the situation is more dangerous today than it was before all of this. We are saying that we need more troops, that we need more ammunition and that we need to call up the reserves. I think we should give some very serious thought to how we explain saying on one hand the enemy did not take a victory and yet we are in need of many more troops and possibly an emergency call up."

The president was shaken by Clifford's remarks and offered the following observation, "The only explanation I can see is that the enemy has changed its tactics. They are putting all of their stack in now. We have to be prepared for all that we might face. Our front structure is based on estimates of their front structure. Our intelligence shows that they have changed and added about 15,000 men. In response to that, we must do likewise. That is the only explanation I see."

The meeting ended with Secretary Rusk pointing out another contradiction in U.S. strategy. "In the past, we have said the problem really was finding the enemy. Now the enemy has come to us. I am sure many will ask why aren't we doing better under these circumstances, now that we know where they are."

Johnson's own frustrations were evident during his next meeting with the Joint Chiefs. In this instance LBJ appears close to the caricature of an embattled and unyielding president:

THE PRESIDENT: All last week I asked two questions. The first was "Did Westmoreland have what he needed?" (You answered yes.) The second question was, "Can Westmoreland take care of the situation with what he has there now?" The answer was yes. Tell me what has happened to change the situation between then and now?

GENERAL WHEELER: I have a chart which was completed today based on a very complete intelligence analysis. It relates to all of South Vietnam, Laos and the area around the DMZ. It shows the following: Since December the North Vietnamese infantry has increased from 78 battalions to 105 battalions. Estimating there are 600 men per battalion that is approximately 15,000 men. This represents a substantial change in the combat ratios of U.S. troops to enemy troops. This ratio was 1.7 to 1 in December. It is 1.4 to 1 today. In the DMZ and I Corps area, there is a 1 to 1 ratio. There are 79 enemy battalions in the 1st Corps area (60 North

Vietnamese and 19 Viet Cong). In the same area there are 82 Free World battalions (42 U.S.; 4 Free World; and 36 ARVN). This is about 1 to 1.

THE PRESIDENT: What you are saying is this. Since last week we have information we did not know about earlier. This is the addition of 15,000 North Vietnamese in the northern part of the country. Because of that, do we need 15 U.S. battalions?

GENERAL WHEELER: General Westmoreland told me what he was going to put in tonight's telegram. This is the first time he has addressed the matter of additional troops. . . . The last report was that there was approximately 15,000 enemy near and around Khesanh. As of today, our estimates range between 16,000 and 25,000. Their infantry has been built up.

During a February 10 meeting of foreign policy advisors, Secretary Rusk was still puzzled about enemy strength. "I can't find out where they say those 15,000 extra enemy troops came from. They say that these battalions came in between December and January," Rusk noted to the group. The president responded, "The chiefs see a basic change in the strategy of the war. They say the enemy has escalated from guerrilla tactics to more conventional warfare." Clark Clifford added another perspective, "All we have heard is about the preparation the North Vietnamese have made for the attack at Khesanh. I have a feeling that the North Vietnamese are going to do something different. I believe our people were surprised by the 24 attacks on the cities last week. God knows the South Vietnamese were surprised with half of their men on holiday. There may be a feint and a surprise coming up for us."

Order of Battle, Again

Westmoreland cabled Wheeler and Sharp concerning the high number of enemy casualties during Tet. The high figures had caused a great deal of consternation for MACV. How, for example, could the enemy have absorbed such a high number in light of their manpower shortages? "The enemy committed virtually every VC unit in the country regardless of combat effectiveness and regardless of normal area of operations," Westmoreland answered. "They were committed with do-or-die orders, forbidden to retreat, and with no withdrawal or rallying plans. The enemy attacks might be described as a country-wide series of 'Loc Ninhs.' The very high casualties are not strange in this light. We cannot, of course, provide a very precise breakdown of casualties by type of enemy force." Westmoreland then tried to deflect any insinuation that irregulars might have been involved. "I do not doubt that some of the enemy's casualties were guerrillas, porters, and such, but the percentage will probably be small. Thus, the enemy obviously banked heavily on surprise in its TET offensive. This may account for minimal participation by guerrillas."

In a chilling analysis of the enemy manpower situation, Major General W.E. DePuy wrote to Wheeler: "It seems that [the enemy] is pushing all his chips into the middle of the table. Ours are there also. It is not credible to think in terms of a peak of effort followed by subsidence and a return to the status quo ante. Vietnam will never be the same again."

On February 11, 1968, Rostow forwarded the most recent Order of Battle estimates to President Johnson. MACV's figures for the December-January period reflected "no significant change" in the confirmed strength of main-force and local-force combat units. Rostow explained to LBJ that changes had occurred in the listing of noncombat elements such as combat support and administrative support which involved "a bookkeeping character which do not really reflect changes in the enemy's combat potential."

Once again, MACV's statistics proved the United States was winning the war. At this time Sam Adams wrote George Carver requesting a transfer from the department of Southeast Asia–Vietnamese Affairs (SAVA). "I do not feel that SAVA has been sufficiently diligent in bringing to the attention of the intelligence community the numerical and organizational strength of our adversaries in Vietnam. . . . I feel we (the CIA in general and SAVA in particular) have basically misinformed policy-makers of the strength of the enemy. The pressures on the CIA and on SAVA, I realize, have been enormous. Many of the pressures—but not all—have originated from MACV, whose Order of Battle is a monument of deceit. The Agency's and the office's failing concerning Viet Cong manpower, I feel, has been its acquiescence to MACV half-truths, distortions, and some-times outright falsehoods. We have occasionally protested, but nei-ther long enough, nor loud enough."[7]

Carver shared Adams's viewpoint, and he now recommended re-opening the OB debate in order to realistically reassess the enemy's over-all capabilities. Excluding main and local force, administrative service, and guerillas from the numerical military order of battle had been an error. CIA analysts strongly suspected that many of the Communist forces at Tet were drawn from secret self-defense com-ponents, perhaps the assault youth, and other elements written out of the Order of Battle because they were thought to have no military significance by MACV.

A CIA Directorate of Intelligence memorandum of February 21, which analyzed the Communist units participating in attacks during the Tet offensive, concluded that if MACV's latest estimates were correct, the enemy would have committed over 50 percent of their regular force to battle. "If the reported losses of 32,500 killed in action and 5,500 detained applied solely to the VC/NVA regular forces, the commands would have lost more than 65% of the forces committed to the Tet offensive. This would have been a devastating blow. However, there are a number of pieces of evidence which suggest that such an interpretation would overstate the Communist manpower drain." According to the CIA, the VC/NVA forces partici-pating at Tet were augmented by large numbers of guerrillas operat-ing in independent units or integrated into local-force units. More-over, prior to Tet, the VC had actively recruited additional laborers and civilians who almost certainly constituted the higher proportion of casualties during the offensive.

Wheeler's Ploy for More Troops and Mobilization

In the wake of Tet, Wheeler had twice asked Westmoreland if he needed more troops. On February 12, 1968, Westmoreland cabled Sharp and Wheeler with his assessment of the military situation and force requirements in Vietnam. Westmoreland emphasized that the enemy "had launched a major campaign signaling a change of strat-egy of protracted war to one of quick military/political victory during the American election year." Yet the enemy had failed to secure the border areas or to initiate a public uprising.

Westmoreland now argued that since the enemy has changed his strategy, "We are now in a new ball game where we face a determined, highly disciplined enemy, fully mobilized to achieve a quick victory. He is in the process of throwing in all his 'military chips to go for broke.' We cannot permit this. . . . I have approximately 500,000 US troops and 60,981 free world military assistance troops. Further contributions from the Thais and Koreans are months away. I have been promised 525,000 troops, which according to present programs will not materialize until 1969. I need these 525,000 troops now. It should be noted that this ceiling assumed the substantial replacement of military by civilians, which now appears impractical. I need reinforcements in terms of combat elements. . . . Time is of the essence. . . . I must stress equally that we face a situation of great opportunity as well as heightened risk. However, time is of the essence here, too. I do not see how the enemy can long sustain the heavy losses which his new strategy is enabling us to inflict on him. Therefore, adequate reinforcements should permit me not only to contain his I Corps offensive but also to capitalize on his losses by seizing the initiative in other areas. Exploiting this opportunity could materially shorten the war."

In addition to the previously authorized 525,000, Westmoreland requested an additional six battalions (10,500) for resuming offensive operations against a weakened enemy. Wheeler wrote to President Johnson that Westmoreland "does not know how sacrosanct that (525,000) figure is. . . . He does not anticipate 'defeat,' but he desperately needs the troop elements requested in order to capitalize on opportunities available to him. . . . If requested troops are not made available, he would have to undertake an unacceptably risky course of drawing additional forces from elsewhere in South Vietnam."

As Chairman of the JCS, Wheeler was required to take a broad look at the war's impact on world-wide U.S. military capabilities. For nearly three years Wheeler had pushed unsuccessfully for a mobilization of the strategic Reserve so that the United States could meet these commitments. By forcing Westmoreland to make his troop request Wheeler knew a priori that acceptance would be harmful to U.S. deployments throughout the world. Wheeler hoped that the rejection would wake LBJ up to the necessity for mobilization.

The Joint Chiefs rejected Westmoreland's request for the additional 10,500 on grounds that United States military manpower requirements were at its limit; any further authorizations without a mobilization of Reserves might erase even minimal levels of readiness for other military contingencies. Wheeler had hoped to use the Tet crisis as a justification for reconstituting the strategic reserve. The 10,500 was a minor issued compared to mobilization. Having encouraged Westmoreland to make the request, Wheeler then rejected it on grounds that U.S. forces were already pushed to their limits. Johnson would now be forced into accepting a Reserve call-up. Wheeler's plan backfired; the Commander in Chief rejected the JCS recommendation for mobilizing the Reserves and directed the deployment of the 10,500 troops to South Vietnam.

President Johnson was very worried about the political costs of mobilizing the Reserves. Would the new units be used as reinforcements in Vietnam; for contingencies outside Vietnam; or to reassure NATO allies that the United States would meet its military commitments? Johnson worried about the size of the call-up and whether it could be diminished by reducing overseas garrisons in Europe or Korea? What were the budgetary implications of these actions? Before making any decisions, the president ordered Wheeler to Vietnam for an on-the-spot report of Westmoreland's manpower needs, but the general's visit was delayed one week because the Senate Foreign Relations Committee was holding hearings on the 1964 Tonkin Gulf incident, and Wheeler was needed in Washington.

President Johnson's political standing was now plummeting. A Gallup poll conducted in early February showed that only 41 percent of the nation's adults approved of the president's handling of his job. This represented a seven point decline from the January survey and the first such decline in the three months since November's big sell.

Explaining the Unacceptable

Rostow tried to nudge Johnson towards a positive decision to use the Reserves. The enemy had shaken U.S. and world opinion with its offensive and the government of Vietnam was tottering on the brink of insolvency. "Only you can make the political assessment of what it would cost to call up the reserves," Rostow advised the president, "but that would be the most impressive demonstration to Hanoi and its friends." Rostow believed that the issue needed to be handled carefully, particularly with respect to explaining mobilization in terms of past statements of progress. "We are sending men to assure Westy the reserves he needs; we are calling up reserves to make sure no one gets the idea that we can't handle our other world commitments."

Doubts about military strategy were emerging from all quarters. In a message communicated directly to the president, former president Eisenhower expressed personal support for a Reserve call-up. The fact that Westmoreland was only asking for an additional 10,500 suggested to Eisenhower that MACV did not have enough troops to fight the kind of campaign necessary to win the war and U.S. forces were so scattered and committed that "we cannot hit the enemy when he concentrates, for example, around Khe Sanh." Eisenhower wanted to know, "Has Westmoreland really been given the forces he is asking for; if he has asked for 525,000 men why didn't we send them sooner, and are we going to have enough in the area to provide a 'corps of maneuver'? He said that moving a relatively small force of this size sounds as though we have been on a shoestring, suggests weakness on our part to the enemy, and gives the critics of what we are doing in Vietnam a target."

Ambassador Taylor also possessed grave doubts on the military situation in South Vietnam, and he endorsed the Joint Chiefs' proposal to mobilize the Reserves on grounds that the possibilities of an unpleasant surprise in Korea or elsewhere in the Far East were sufficiently acute "that it is an act of prudence to move additional ground forces to the area as rapidly as possible." Taylor believed a call-up of Reserves was justified by the military requirement and that, in addition, it would have some political-psychological value in demonstrating to the world, including Hanoi, that the United States meant business. "It would also serve as a reminder to our people at home that, while we are not technically at war, we are in a situation of similar emergency which places on our citizens duties and responsibilities analogous to those in a state of declared war."

General Westmoreland's decision to hold Khe Sanh also came under careful scrutiny. The occupation of Khe Sanh had been premised on establishing a forward operating base against infiltration routes in eastern Laos. But, there had been little effect on infiltration from Laos. Moreover, General Westmoreland did not argue strongly for the defense of Khe Sanh because of its present value in relation to impeding infiltration routes or in the defense of major areas of the northern provinces. Instead, his cables stressed the difficulty of getting out of Khe Sanh and the adverse psychological effects of a withdrawal upon South Vietnam and upon the American people. What was the military importance of maintaining Khe Sanh? Why not withdraw and redeploy the troops? Maxwell Taylor wrote LBJ, "Whatever the past value of the position, it is a positive liability now. We are allowing the enemy to arrange at his leisure a set-piece attack on ground and in weather favorable to him and under conditions which will allow us little opportunity to punish him except by our air power."

Taylor urged LBJ to have the Joint Chiefs instruct Westmoreland to pull out. Rostow then weighed in with the opinion "that Khe Sanh probably can be held but that it will be at a heavy price in terms of casualties and in terms of other ground troops necessary to support and reinforce it. I have real doubt that we can afford such a defense in view of the limited reserves which General Westmoreland is likely to have in the time frame during which these events may take place."

It was evident that Westmoreland needed direction from Washington, and Rostow explained to LBJ, "I would feel greatly relieved if the Joint Chiefs of Staff would see fit to send General Westmoreland guidance which would provide Westmoreland with a way out of Khe Sanh." For example, the chiefs might suggest that "it is less clear that its present value now justifies the cost of an all-out defense." Perhaps Westmoreland could be persuaded to reassess the feasibility or desirability of withdrawing from Khe Sanh.

The president decided to stand by his field commander's judgment. Moreover, the president instructed Clark Clifford to draft a statement of unequivocal support to General Westmoreland—but support which left Westmoreland a way out of a possible no-win situation.

The President wants General Westmoreland to know that he has freedom of action to conduct his military operations as he thinks wise from a military point of view without being inhibited by political or psychological factors originating in the United States. To the extent that such factors in South Vietnam itself are an important part of the struggle, General Westmoreland should take those into account in close consultation with Ambassador Bunker and President Thieu.

Specifically with regard to Khe Sanh, the President does not wish to inhibit General Westmoreland's judgment as to when, where and under what circumstances he wishes to fight his battles. When the President became convinced that General Westmoreland intended to defend Khe Sanh, the President threw himself into the task of insuring that General Westmoreland had the means to do so successfully. He further sought the judgment of the Joint Chiefs of Staff both as to the desirability and capability of defending Khe Sanh. This interest on the part of the President should not be interpreted, however, as a directive from the Commander in Chief to defend Khe Sanh under all circumstances if, in General Westmoreland's judgment, it is better to have his battle somewhere else. The purpose of this message is not to export to General Westmoreland the responsibility for events which are inherent in the responsibilities of the Commander in Chief. The President just wants General Westmoreland to know the General has his fullest confidence and does not want his hands tied by the build up of irrelevant factors on the home front in a way that would cause General Westmoreland to make military judgments which are contrary to his best thinking. If General Westmoreland wishes to defend Khe Sanh he will be supported; if he wishes to avoid a major engagement in a fixed position which does not utilize the peculiar mobility of U.S. forces, he will also be supported.

With the Senate Foreign Relations inquiry on Tonkin done, Wheeler flew from Washington to Vietnam on February 23. In anticipation of the visit, Maxwell Taylor wrote the president, "Reflecting on the possible objectives of General Wheeler's visit, I would hope that he would obtain answers to some of the fundamental questions which are troubling us, derived from detailed private discussions with General Westmoreland and his staff." Taylor wanted Westmoreland to answer questions on his operational plans, force requirements, and force availabilities. In particular, "What enemy units have been identified in the attacks on the cities? What uncommitted units are available for a second cycle? What grounds are there for the allegation of an 'intelligence failure' at the time of the first wave of attacks on the cities? How does General Westmoreland feel about the functioning of his own and the Vietnamese intelligence services in connection with this situation? What has been the nature of our psychological warfare activities directed at North Vietnam and the VC since January 30? These are all hard questions for which there are probably no final answers at this time but whatever [Wheeler] can bring back will be most helpful."

On February 24, Rostow wrote LBJ that the enemy was preparing to make a total effort, "with all their capital soon. They will then try to lock us into a negotiation at their peak position before we can counter-attack." Rostow and Taylor both agreed "with Napoleon that Providence is on the other side with the last reserves. Therefore, right now we should be moving out to Westy all the ready forces we have and calling up reserves for: A Vietnam counter-attack; Korean contingency; General purposes, for our world posture." Rostow believed, "We face the decisive battle of the war. They will try to dissipate Westy's reserves by simultaneous attacks at a number of places and take Khe Sanh if possible. I am uncertain about timing; but they are so obsessed with memories of 1954 I suspect they will hit soon, get a maximum position, and then force a negotiation, perhaps via the San Antonio formula before the weather opens up for us in I Corps and at Hanoi-Haiphong. The Geneva Conference of 1954 opened on April 26. Dien Bien Phu fell on May 7/8."

While in Vietnam General Wheeler concluded that the last three years had adversely impacted the U.S. worldwide military posture. Something had to be done about the attrition of U.S. forces and the lack of progress in the military area. Wheeler cabled LBJ at his ranch with the tentative conclusions from his trip to Vietnam. The cable must have ruined Johnson's day. Wheeler wrote that, had Westmoreland not re-deployed some of his troops from border areas to urban centers in mid-January, severe setbacks would have occurred. "I will have on my return examples of how narrow the margin was between victory and defeat in certain key areas," Wheeler reported. "The enemy has suffered very substantially, but he still has sizeable un-committed reserves. He displays a tenacity which we have not seen before in this war."

Wheeler also believed that "Westy's forces are stretched too thin. . . . I believe that we must reinforce him promptly and substantially." Wheeler's conclusion left Johnson on uncertain ground: "In summary, the military situation continues to be fluid; the enemy is determined and tenacious; troop morale, both US and ARVN, is good; Westy's forces are stretched thin in view of the enemy threat and the courses of action open to the enemy. I do not have any apprehension that we will be run out of the country by military action, but I do believe that to achieve victory we must expand our effort substantially and promptly."

In his memoirs, Westmoreland recalled his meeting with General Wheeler:

> As Bus Wheeler and I conferred, we did so in the expectation that there was to be a reappraisal of American policy on conducting the war, presumably a new and broadened strategy. A change in strategy almost inevitably would involve a sizable call-up of National Guard and Reserves. In view of Secretary McNamara's coming replacement by a presumably hawkish Clark Clifford, that seemed a plausible possibility. The chairman of the House Armed Services Committee, Congressman Mendel Rivers, had publicly advocated a call-up.
>
> Although I had earlier opposed calling the Reserves in the belief that the war would last long beyond the usual one-year tour for reservists and that extended service would produce cries to bring the troops home, the situation had changed. I was in much the same position as any battlefield commander at whatever level who must choose the optimum time to influence the battle by committing his reserve force; the enemy's losses in the Tet offensive had at last presented the right opportunity. I was convinced that with additional strength and removal of the old restrictive policy, we could deal telling blows--physically and psychologically—well within the time frame of the reservists' one-year tour. The time had come to prepare and commit the Reserve.[8]

On February 27, 1968 General Wheeler sent LBJ his report, "Military Solution and Requirements in SVN." The report was based on three days of conferences with Westmoreland and the senior American commander in each of the 4 Corps areas. (Clifford described Johnson to have been "as worried as I have ever seen him," after he had read Wheeler's report.) As Major Andrew Krepinevich later observed in his book *The Army and Vietnam,* "Wheeler's report reflected the bankruptcy of the Army's strategy. Although in the Tet Offensive the Army had destroyed enemy forces in far greater numbers than in any other period in the war, it had had a negligible impact on the United States' prospects for victory." Hanoi had demonstrated its ability to accept extraordinary losses, without reaching its breaking point. Instead, the enemy had both the capability and the will to continue the struggle indefinitely."[9]

Wheeler now asked for more troops. Specifically, MACV needed a total of 206,000 additional troops to regain the strategic initiative. The troops would be allocated in three installments: 108,000 by May 1; 42,000 by September 1; and 55,000 by December 31, 1968. According to Wheeler, "The enemy has undoubtedly been hurt, but he seems determined to pursue his offensive—apparently he has the capability to do so. . . . It is the consensus of responsible commanders that 1968 will be the pivotal year. The war may go on beyond 1968 but it is unlikely that the situation will return to the pre-TET condition. The forces committed and the tactics involved are such that the advantage will probably swing one way or the other, during the current year. . . . In many areas the pacification program has been brought to a halt. The VC are prowling the countryside, and it is now a question of which side moves fastest to gain control. The outcome is not at all clear. I visualize much heavy fighting ahead." Casualties would be high. Equipment losses would continue at a high level. ARVN would prove to be shaky under sustained pressure. "If the enemy synchronizes his expected major attacks with increased pressure throughout the country, General Westmoreland's margin will be paper thin. He does not have a theatre reserve. We can expect some cliff-hangers, and with bad luck on weather or some local RVNAF [Republic of Vietnam Armed Forces] failures he may suffer some reverses. For these reasons he is asking for additional forces as soon as possible during this calendar year."

While LBJ took a respite on his ranch, his advisors met on February 27 at the White House to discuss Westmoreland's still-secret request for the 206,000. Clark Clifford suggested that, instead of proceeding incrementally, they should announce that the United States intends to put in 500,000 to one million men. (The following excerpt from the meeting is from Harry McPherson's notes.)

> Secretary McNamara responded, "That has virtue of clarity. Obviously we would have decided to put in enough men to accomplish the job. That and status quo both have the virtue of clarity. I do not understand what the strategy is to putting in 205,000 men. It is neither enough to do the job, nor an indication that our role must change."

The discussion then focused on what really had happened at Tet:

BUNDY: We must also prepare for the worst. SVN is very weak. Our position may be truly untenable. Contingency planning should proceed toward possibility that we will withdraw with best possible face and defend rest of Asia. We can say truthfully that Asia is stronger because of what we have done in past few years.

Katzenbach took call from Habib in Hawaii. Reports Habib is "less optimistic" about political situation in Saigon than he was when he went out. Reports that there is various disagreement in American circles in Saigon over 205,000 request. Bunker has doubts about this.

RUSK: If we have to call up reserves, we should take some of our troops out of Europe. Europeans will have to put some more in for their defense.

MCNAMARA: Agree, if we call 400,000.

State of Military Situation:

Rusk, Rostow think enemy took beating in TET offensive. Rostow says captured documents show enemy was disappointed, may be unable to mount heavy coordinated attack on cities. Rusk reminds that enemy took 40,000 casualties. No US units out of operation. Rostow says if we can re-enforce Westy now, he should be able to handle situation until good weather comes to I Corps and NVN.

MCNAMARA: What then? Let's not delude ourselves into thinking he cannot maintain pressure after good weather comes.

(Rostow apparently had air attacks in mind. McN: We are dropping ordnance at a higher rate than in last year of WWII in Europe. It has not stopped him.)

BUNDY: SVN forces uncertain, but almost certainly not as strong as were before.

CLIFFORD: Look at situation from point of view of American public and Vietnamese. Despite optimistic reports, our people (and world opinion) believe we have suffered a major setback. Problem is, how do we gain support for major program, defense and economic, if we have told people things are going well? How do we avoid creating feeling that we are pounding troops down rathole? What is our purpose? What is achievable? Before any decision is made, we must re-evaluate our entire posture in SVN. Unfortunately, Pres. has been at ranch with hawks.

MCNAMARA: Agreed. Decision must not be hasty. Will take a week at least to work out defense and economic measures, if we go big. Wheeler, Habib will meet with Secretaries Wednesday morning at breakfast with President. Decision should certainly not be announced that night.

GENERAL IMPRESSION: Prevailing uncertainty. Radically different proposals were offered and debated, more rejected out of hand. We are at a point of crisis. McNamara expressed grave doubts over military, economic, political, diplomatic and moral consequences of a larger force buildup in SVN. Q is whether these profound doubts will be presented to President.

The doubts would be presented to the president but in a circuitous not linear fashion. Back from his ranch, President Johnson warned Cabinet members during a meeting on February 28, 1968, "The big problem is the impression we make with the public. . . . We have to be careful about statements like Westmoreland's when he came back and said that he saw 'light at the end of the tunnel.' Now we have the shock of this Tet Offensive. Ho Chi Minh never got elected to anything. . . . He is like Hitler in many ways. . . . But we, the President and the Cabinet, are called murderers and they never say anything about Mr. Ho. The signs are all over here. They all say 'Stop the War,' but you never see any of them over there. Then he launches the Tet attack, breaks the truce and escalates by firing on 44 cities, all at the time that we are offering bombing pause. It is like the country lawyer who made the greatest speech of his life but they electrocuted the client. We are like that now."

At the end of February, in his first visit to Dallas since President Kennedy's assassination, Johnson announced that the war had reached a critical turning point. "I do not believe we will ever buckle," he stated. Flying from his ranch near Austin to attend a convention of the National Rural Electric Cooperative Association, the president spoke about the war: "There will be blood, sweat and tears shed. The weak will drop from the lines, their feet sore and their voices loud. Persevere in Vietnam we will and we must. There, too, today, we stand at a turning point."

But Johnson had already lost his most critical support: middle America. CBS news anchor Walter Cronkite had told a national television audience on February 27 that the war was stalemated. "We have been too often disappointed by the optimism of the American leaders, both in Vietnam and Washington, to have faith any longer in the silver linings they find in the darkest clouds. . . . For it seems now more certain than ever that the bloody experience of Vietnam is to end in a stalemate. To say that we are mired in stalemate seems the only realistic, yet unsatisfactory, conclusion."

A television anchorman who closely mirrored public opinion had said the war was unwinnable. After watching the broadcast Johnson concluded, "Cronkite was it."[10] The weeks ahead would lead the president's inner circle of advisors and then Lyndon Johnson to the same conclusions as Cronkite's. The initial impetus would be pressure to meet General Westmoreland's troop request. Should the nation's Reserves be mobilized? The president appointed his new secretary of defense, Clark Clifford, to head a task force to evaluate General Westmoreland's request. The president's initial instructions to Clifford were "give me the lesser of evils."

X

The Ides of March

If we stick with it, I am confident we shall come out all right in the end.

Ambassador Ellsworth Bunker to the President, February 29, 1968.

I shall not seek and I will not accept, the nomination of my party for another term as your President.

Lyndon Baines Johnson, March 31, 1968

The Clifford Task Force:
"Give Me the Lesser of Two Evils"

President Johnson had given Clifford only until March 4 to arrive at an acceptable recommendation for meeting Westmoreland's request for troops. "I was directed," Clifford later wrote in his memoirs, "as my first assignment, to chair a task force named by the President to determine how this new requirement could be met. We were not instructed to assess the need for substantial increases in men and matériel; we were to devise the means by which they could be provided."[1]

Clifford was not only new at the helm of defense but he found that those like himself on the periphery of intelligence data and information were at a distinct disadvantage vis-à-vis those individuals with extensive experience on Vietnam's problems. "Thrust into a vigorous, ruthlessly frank assessment of our situation by the men who knew the most about it," Clifford wrote, he proceeded somewhat cautiously.

Among the documents Clifford researched was the study known as *The Pentagon Papers,* which detailed how the civilian officials in the Defense Department sought to discredit the JCS and MACV military analysis. The study had been commissioned by Robert McNamara on June 17, 1967, in an attempt to assess where the U.S. military policy-making process on Vietnam had failed. The task force of 36 civilian and military analysts had had access to virtually all classified material from the Office of the Secretary of Defense, the CIA, and the State Department. The result was a history of over twenty years of deception by the Defense Department to perpetuate U.S. military power in Southeast Asia with total disregard for the effects of that policy on American and Vietnamese citizens.*

One background paper in particular, "Alternative Strategies," authored by the assistant secretary of defense for systems analysis, Alain Enthoven, was a blistering McNamara-like attack from a "whiz kid" turned whistle-blower: "Our strategy of attrition has not worked. . . . We became mesmerized by statistics of known doubtful validity, choosing to place our faith only in the ones that showed progress. We judged the enemy's intentions rather than his capabilities because we trusted captured documents too much. . . . In short, our setbacks were due to wishful thinking compounded by a massive intelligence collection and/or intelligence failure. . . . We have achieved stalemate at a high commitment."[2] Enthoven's paper was supported by the analyses of Deputy Secretary of Defense Paul Nitze and Assistant Secretary of Defense for International Security Affairs (the Pentagon's "Little State" Department) Paul Warnke.

Clifford also questioned the Joint Chiefs and those advisors who knew the most about Vietnam. He recalled his attempts at fact finding in "A Viet Nam Reappraisal": " 'Will 200,000 more men do the job?' I found no assurance that they would. 'If no, how many more

The Pentagon Papers was published by the *New York Times* in June 1971 after Daniel Ellsberg, a former defense department official and critic of the war, leaked the top-secret study.

might be needed—and when?' There was no way of knowing. 'What would be involved in committing 200,000 more men to Viet Nam?' A reserve call-up of approximately 280,000, an increased draft call and an extension of tours of duty of most men then in service. 'Can the enemy respond with a build-up of his own?' He could and he probably would. 'What are the estimated costs of the latest requests?' First calculations were on the order of $2 billion for the remaining four months of that fiscal year, and an increase of $10 to $12 billion for the year beginning July 1, 1968. 'What will be the impact on the economy?' So great that we would face the possibility of credit restrictions, a tax increase and even wage and price controls. The balance of payments would be worsened by at least half a billion dollars a year. 'Can bombing stop the war?' Never by itself. It was inflicting heavy personnel and materiel losses, but bombing by itself would not stop the war. 'Will stepping up the bombing decrease American casualties?' Very little, if at all.' "

The Joint Chiefs had expected the new secretary of defense to be more supportive of the bombing program than his predecessor because of his past hawkish views, but Clifford now requested to see the military plan for attaining victory in Vietnam: "I was told that there was no plan for victory in the historic American sense. Why not? Because our forces were operating under three major political restrictions: The President had forbidden the invasion of North Viet Nam because this could trigger the mutual assistance pact between North Viet Nam and China; the President had forbidden the mining of the harbor at Haiphong, the principal port through which the North received military supplies, because a Soviet vessel might be sunk; the President had forbidden our forces to pursue the enemy into Laos and Cambodia, for to do so would spread the war, politically and geographically, with no discernible advantage. These and other restrictions which precluded an all-out, no-holds-barred military effort were wisely designed to prevent our being drawn into a larger war."

Clifford also asked the Joint Chiefs, "What is the best estimate as to how long this course of action will take? Six months? One year? Two years? Not only was there no agreement, I could find no one willing to express any confidence in his guesses. Certainly, none of us was willing to assert that he could see 'light at the end of the tunnel' or that American troops would be coming home by the end of the year. After days of this type of analysis, my concern had greatly deepened. I could not find out when the war was going to end; I could not find out the manner in which it was going to end; I could not find out whether the new requests for men and equipment were going to be enough, or whether it would take more and, if more, when and how much; I could not find out how soon the South Vietnamese forces would be ready to take over. All I had was the statement, given with too little self-assurance to be comforting, that if we persisted for an indeterminate length of time, the enemy would choose not to go on."

Clifford finally asked, "Does anyone see any diminution in the will of the enemy after four years of our having been there, after enormous casualties and after massive destruction from our bombing?" The answer was that there appeared to be no diminution in the will of the enemy.

Johnson received the Clifford task-force report on March 4. The report recommended meeting Westmoreland's immediate military situation by deploying 22,000 additional personnel (approximately 60 percent of which would be combat and three tactical fighter squadrons). The task force also recommended approval of a 262,000 Reserve call-up in order to help restore the strategic Reserve. But the report contained none of Clifford's private doubts or questions. Instead, it called for a major new study designed to give Westmoreland "strategic guidance" for the future. It was quite possible that an additional 200,000 American troops or double or triple that quantity, would not be enough to accomplish U.S. objectives.

Upon receiving the task-force report, Johnson convened a meeting of the principals. Now, for the first time, the president heard Clifford outline the problems facing the president. "Your senior advisers have conferred on this matter at very great length. There is a deep-seated concern by your advisers. There is a concern that if we say yes, and step up with the addition of 206,000 more men that we might continue down the road as we have been without accomplishing our purpose—which is for a viable South Vietnam which can live in peace. We are not convinced that our present policy will bring us to that objective."

Clifford then turned to the tragic irony of the previous autumn's progress report. "For a while, we thought and had the feeling that we understood the strength of the Viet Cong and the North Vietnamese. You will remember the rather optimistic reports of General Westmoreland and Ambassador Bunker last year. Frankly, it came as a shock that the Vietcong-North Vietnamese had the strength of force and skill to mount the Tet offensive—as they did. They struck 34 cities, made strong inroads in Saigon and in Hué. There have been very definite effects felt in the countryside."

Clifford emphasized that the 206,000 request was not just another call for more troops. The new request brought the president to the clearly defined watershed of going down the same road of "more troops, more guns, more planes, more ships?" And, "do you go on killing more Viet Cong and more North Vietnamese and killing more Vietcong and more North Vietnamese?" Clifford now shattered any illusions the president may have held with respect to military progress. "There are grave doubts that we have made the type of progress we had hoped to have made by this time. As we build up our forces, they build up theirs. We continue to fight at a higher level of intensity. Even were we to meet this full request of 206,000 men, and the pattern continues as it has, it is likely that by March he [General Westmoreland] may want another 200,000 to 300,000 men with no end in sight. The reserve forces in North Vietnam are a cause for concern as well. They have a very substantial population from which to draw. They have no trouble whatever organizing, equipping, and training their forces. We seem to have a sinkhole. We put in more— they match it. We put in more—they match it. I see more and more fighting with more and more casualties on the US side and no end in sight to the action."[3]

The Sinkhole

President Johnson now found himself in a difficult situation. The American people had been told that General Westmoreland would get all he required. Failure to meet the request of his field commander would leave Johnson vulnerable to the charge that he was not supporting soldiers in the field. Yet, to deploy beyond the 525,000 would raise questions on the viability of attrition and claims of progress. The 525,000 figure had been regarded as a lid. Moreover, the administration had claimed that Tet had been a military victory—

what was the emergency? If enemy manpower had been depleted at Tet, why did Westmoreland now need these additional increments? Would a call-up of Reserves be perceived as a tangible sign of failure? Moreover, the domestic political consequences would polarize the country. The doves would charge that Johnson was dragging his country into a miserable and endless war. Hawks would wonder why the president was disrupting lives by mobilizing the Reserves when he could utilize the tactical weapons at his disposal. Bomb Hanoi, Haiphong, the harbors, and the dikes—hit the sanctuaries in Laos and Cambodia. If necessary, invade North Vietnam.

In virtually every respect, General Westmoreland's 205,000 request represented the failure of U.S. strategy. The reinforcements would bring the total American military commitment in ground forces to three-quarters of a million—yet the United States would be no closer to victory than in 1965 at the outset of the Americanization of the war. Progress had been made but the objective of an honorable peace in Vietnam was nowhere in sight. It was becoming increasingly evident that no amount of military power would bring North Vietnam to the conference table—at least not in an American presidential election year. Why should anyone believe that 750,000 would break the enemy's will?

Tet had been, in the words of General Bruce Palmer, who was deputy to General Westmoreland and later served as Vice-Chief of Staff, "an allied intelligence failure ranking with Pearl Harbor in 1941 or the Ardennes Offensive in 1944."[4] George Kennan, former diplomat, presidential advisor, and author of the containment doctrine, now bitterly denounced administration policy as a "massive miscalculation and error of policy, an error for which it is hard to find any parallels in our history." At a campaign dinner for Senator Eugene McCarthy, Kennan charged that the military effort was "grievously unsound, devoid throughout of a plausible, coherent and realistic object."

American public opinion would not tolerate a long drawn-out military campaign with high casualties. Westmoreland's strategy of search and destroy was based on the faulty premise that a military victory was conceivable if U.S. forces just destroyed enough Viet Cong. This was a sound doctrine in World War II, but was not realistic in the Vietnam war. Vietnam could not be won by attriting the enemy alone.

On March 6, Rostow sent LBJ his personal assessment of prospects for the war. "We are clearly in the midst of an unresolved critical battle. The enemy is committed—having taken stock of his immediate post-Tet situation—to continue to throw forces into the battle at a rate almost four times his average for 1967; he is losing about 1,000 KIA per day as opposed to 241 per day in 1967. He did increase his order of battle in the days before Tet—with several additional North Vietnamese divisions, North Vietnamese fillers for VC main force units, plus hasty recruiting for VC units. But there is no evidence he can sustain present rates for more than a matter of a few months."

Rostow was ready to mine the North Vietnamese ports but knew that Johnson would need a trigger point to justify these actions. "The Reserve call-up may not be able to wait until the battle is joined," he wrote, "but the best time to mine the ports—should you decide to do so—would be at the height of battle. Not since the Civil War has quite so much hinged for our country on immediate battlefield events." Mining the ports was now seen as a bone which could be used to placate the American public. Ginsburgh wrote Rostow on March 1, "Mining is the best way of satisfying that part of the US public opposed to sending more of our boys to South Vietnam, without increasing pressure on North Vietnam."

The Strains of Political Skill

By now the strain to Johnson's political ability was showing. As a senator, in the cloakroom of the Senate chamber or face to face with a political adversary, Johnson had been an overpowering force. "Johnson was a legislative pragmatist," wrote Ralph Huitt. "He learned early and never forgot the basic skill of the politician, the ability to divide any number by two and add one."[5] He possessed an uncanny ability to size up his opponent and, through a variety of techniques that ranged from squeezing the thigh, reasoning nose to nose, horse-trading, or—when all civilized forms of negotiation failed—humiliation, usually got what he wanted; and the individual giving it never forgot how LBJ exacted his price. But as a war leader his political technique failed him.

The technique did not work in Vietnam, primarily because Ho Chi

Minh, by Johnson's standards, was essentially nonpragmatic. During a meeting with labor leaders in the State Department dining room on August 7, 1967, LBJ had revealed the personal reservations of a man who had misplayed his hand: "Some people say that we should turn the bombers loose. But I can't do that. Some people say to pull out. But I can't do that either. And some people say stop the bombing, but I can't tie General Westmoreland's right arm behind his back right now. I wish somebody would stop saying what President Johnson should do and spend a little time trying to get Ho to do something. Don't put all the heat on me. I'm doing everything I can."

As his political maneuverings failed to achieve their anticipated goals, Johnson's great personal insecurities manifested themselves. All presidents feel ill-treated by the press, but with Johnson it had become an obsession. In an interview on September 20, 1967, Johnson claimed that "NBC and the *New York Times* are committed to an editorial policy of making us surrender." He argued that Ho Chi Minh received fairer treatment in the U.S. media than did the president of the United States: "But the television doesn't want that story. I can prove that Ho is a son-of-a-bitch if you let me put it on the screen—but they want me to be the son-of-a-bitch. Press coverage of Vietnam is a reflection of broader and deeper public attitudes, a refusal by many Americans 'to see the enemy as the enemy.' " He told Max Frankel of the *New York Times* that the paper "plays a leading part in prejudicing people against [me]. Editors won't use the words 'President Johnson' in anything that is good. Bigotry is born in some of the *New York Times* people." On his overall relationship with the press Johnson once confided to a friend, "I feel like a hound bitch in heat in the country. If you run, they chew your tail off, if you stand still, they slip it to you."

Johnson also lashed out at the mostly anonymous "intellectuals" for what they symbolized—the freedom to dissent without fear of reprisal. It pained him that those he believed had been helped the most by his presidency were leading opposition to the war. "The same groups continue to call [me] 'that lying SOB.' These are the preachers, liberals and professors who are the first to cry discrimination if anybody says anything about them." College students had received loans and scholarships under his administration; now they chanted slogans for Ho Chi Minh. No president had done more for civil rights; now Martin Luther King, Jr. urged blacks to oppose the war.

Johnson labeled those who dissented "nervous nellies," "half-brights," and "knee-jerk liberals." In an August 19, 1967, meeting with Rusk, McNamara, Wheeler, and Rostow, Johnson had bemoaned the lack of congressional support for administration policy. "In war, politics stops at the water's edge," he asserted, noting that as Senate minority and majority leader he had supported President Eisenhower 79 percent of the time on foreign policy. When Secretary McNamara was called to testify on the Hill, Johnson told his staff, "There is something wrong with our system when our leaders are testifying instead of thinking about the war."

During a November 4, 1967, luncheon meeting with Rusk, McNamara, Rostow, and Helms, LBJ expressed worry over his political fortunes: "Gallup and Harris say anyone could beat us. Gallup takes these polls a month old, juggles them a little, and makes it look that way and the public believes them." Referring to the impending selection of a new Marine commander Johnson said, "I'm going to take that man's blood pressure and make sure he's loyal. It doesn't do any good to win the fight over there and lose it over here."

The Genie Is Out

On March 10, Hedrick Smith of the *New York Times* broke the story that Westmoreland had requested 206,000 additional troops. The secret was out, and the political dominoes quickly fell. The dispatch, written by Smith and Neil Sheehan, with the assistance of Max Frankel and Edwin Dale Jr., reported that Westmoreland's request for 206,000 additional troops had "touched off a divisive internal debate within high levels of the Johnson administration." Perhaps more damaging than the headline were comments from "high administration civilian officials" in the Pentagon who now described Vietnam as "a bottomless pit." Smith quoted a Pentagon official with intimate knowledge of the situation: "We know now that we constantly underestimated the enemy's capacity and his will to fight and overestimated our progress. We know now that all we thought we had constructed was built on sand."

Ironically, two days earlier General Wheeler had cabled Westmoreland, "I do not wish to shunt my troubles on you. However, I must tell you frankly that there is strong resistance from all quarters to putting more ground force units into South Vietnam. . . . You should not count on an affirmative decision for such additional forces."

A Gallup poll released on March 10 reported that 49 percent, more Americans than ever before, believed that the United States was wrong to have ever begun its involvement in Vietnam. Only 33 percent believed the United States was making progress in the war, compared to 50 percent in November's survey following the big sell.

On March 12, Abe Fortas, "after a week of exercise, sleep and relaxation," wrote Johnson with his views on Vietnam. Fortas and Rostow were the only remaining civilian hawks in LBJ's camp. Fortas urged LBJ to stop trying to convince North Vietnam that it should negotiate. "This weakens your position in this country. It stirs doubt here and in the world as to our power and resolve. It encourages the enemy, domestic and foreign. It does not help to end the war. You have a good position: 'They know how to reach me.' " Fortas then moved to a lengthy but revealing personal analysis that advocated "winning" the war on grounds that the United States was "the only— the last remaining—non Communist nation whose existence and presumed willingness to fight and whose power operate as a deterrent to aggressive-Communist domination (first) of all Asia and (second) of other parts of the world." Moreover, "unless we "win" in Vietnam, our total national personality will, in my opinion, change— and for the worse. If we do not "win" here, we will not participate elsewhere in the world on a substantial scale. If we do not "win" here, I think that a long period of national self-doubt and timidity will be reflected in our economy, our social programs, etc.; and our nation will be sufficiently shaken so as to be in real danger from a demagogue (who is not likely to have even the virtues of de Gaulle)."[6]

According to Fortas, 'winning' entailed "bringing [the war] home to North Vietnam" by "asking how far we go short of an American invasion of North Vietnam." Moreover, he recommended mounting all-out air campaign strikes against Hanoi and all other targets in North Vietnam. "I would suggest discarding the theory (or even the pretense) of attacking only North Vietnam's supply capability and infiltration potential."

The Political Death Knell

On March 13, Senator Eugene McCarthy startled the nation with his strong showing in the New Hampshire primary. McCarthy's candidacy centered on the tragic consequences of the war. "The administration can no longer have it both ways," McCarthy declared while campaigning. "The new budget makes it clear what most Americans have known for many months: we cannot wage war in Vietnam and at the same time alleviate the hopelessness that leads to riots."

The New Hampshire primary became, in retrospect, the loose thread which, when pulled, unraveled the Johnson presidency. Senator Robert Kennedy had previously announced that he would not challenge LBJ because to do so would split the Democratic party; McCarthy had none of those reservations. Campaigning as an unabashed peace candidate and assisted by thousands of young college students who came to New Hampshire to dump LBJ, McCarthy's grass-roots candidacy came to symbolize hope, the light at the end of the dark tunnel of endless escalation.

The president's name was not on the New Hampshire ballot; he was not a declared candidate; and delegates could not pledge themselves to a noncandidate. Johnson supporters were banking on a heavy write-in campaign. The timing could not have been worse for Johnson. News of Westmoreland's 206,000-man request broke on Sunday, March 10, and the New Hampshire primary was just three days later. Speculation was rampant that the troop request would help McCarthy. When New Hampshire voted on March 13, Johnson received 49.5 percent (27,243 votes) to McCarthy's 42.4 percent (23,280 votes). When all write-ins were tabulated, the president of the United States had won the primary by all of 230 votes, and McCarthy had captured twenty of twenty-six delegate votes.

The McCarthy vote was deceptive—not all was for peace—many self-proclaimed hawks had voted for McCarthy to protest Johnson's handling of the war. Hawks and doves finally found a common ground in their dissatisfaction with Lyndon Johnson's war. The next day Johnson summoned Dean Acheson to the White House. As Truman's secretary of state, Acheson had helped implement the containment policy that had shaped the parameters of the cold war; but he now told Johnson that American interests were not being served in Vietnam. When the president told Acheson that Westmoreland and the Joint Chiefs remained optimistic, Acheson warned, "Mr. President, you are being led down the garden path." (The president had asked Acheson to explain his views to Walt Rostow. "Walt listened to me with the bored patience of a visitor listening to a ten-year-old playing the piano," Acheson later recalled.[7]) Acheson recommended that Johnson reconvene the president's senior foreign policy advisors—"the wise men."

If McCarthy's showing in New Hampshire was a smoke signal to LBJ, it was a wake-up call to Robert Kennedy. Kennedy had not wanted to split the party in a divisive challenge of LBJ. New Hampshire revealed the degree of malcontent with Lyndon Johnson, and following a brief reassessment, Kennedy announced his candidacy for president on March 16. "These are not ordinary times, and this is not an ordinary election," declared Robert Kennedy.

The erosion of public support threatened to overwhelm Johnson. Should he stop the bombing—if not to negotiate then to win the election? Harry McPherson wrote Johnson on March 18, "I think the course we seem to be taking now will lead either to Kennedy's nomination or Nixon's election, or both." President Johnson, as the incumbent, was the "natural defender of the status quo. You represent things as they are—the course we are following, the policies and programs we have chosen. Therefore, you are the most conservative of the six—the man who is not calling for change, but resisting it. That is a tough position today."

With respect to Vietnam, McPherson pointed out two alternatives to LBJ: "Change from today's status quo could mean either escalating to 750,000–1,000,000 men and seeking a military victory, or de-escalating the fighting by changing our tactics, and ultimately even bringing a few Americans home. I pray we choose the latter. It seems to me that we are not going to win a military victory, in the ordinary meaning of that term, with forces we have there now, plus 25–30,000. Just saying we will won't make it so. . . ."

United Nations Ambassador Arthur Goldberg now wrote Johnson in support of a bombing halt. Goldberg had accepted the ambassadorship in hopes that he could forge a negotiated settlement in Vietnam. The March 15 cable represented one of his final attempts; Goldberg would submit his resignation in April. The cable reached LBJ at the Ranch. Goldberg pointed towards "a growing public belief that the war in South Vietnam is increasingly an American war, not a South Vietnamese war which the U.S. is supporting, and, further, that the war cannot be won on this basis without evermounting commitments not worth the costs. . . . It is my considered opinion that the very best way to prevent further erosion of public support from taking place is to make a new and fresh move toward a political solution at this time." Goldberg recommended a total bombing halt in the North: "We would 'stop' the aerial and naval bombardment of North Vietnam for the limited time necessary to determine whether Hanoi will negotiate in good faith."

But Johnson was still not convinced that, as Commander in Chief, he should stop the bombing and endanger the lives of his troops. "Let's get one thing clear," Johnson told his aides. "I'm telling you now I'm not going to stop the bombing. Now I don't want to hear any more about it. Goldberg has written to me about the whole thing, and I've heard every argument. I'm not going to stop. Now is there anybody here who doesn't understand that?"[8]

Minutes from the March 18 meeting of the Joint Chiefs reveals just how closely their private divisions mirrored the public debate on the war. General Harold K. Johnson was the least optimistic, saying, "We'll find ourselves where we are today—even if we build up forces—one year from today." General John P. McConnell favored hot pursuit into Laos and Cambodia and hitting "any target of military worth in North Vietnam." Admiral Thomas H. Moorer favored relaxing bombing restraints in Hanoi and Haiphong and complained that we "have not really gone out to win the war." General Leonard F. Chapman favored expanding the sea and air campaigns as well as "preparing forces to invade North Vietnam. Unless we can expand our efforts north—we cannot hope to achieve our purpose." General Wheeler urged "maximum protection to population areas. Saigon only city that has to be defended at all costs. (Hué has psychological value.) Build up ARVN as rapidly as possible. Beat up NVN from air and sea." General Johnson then suggested trying an "Inchon landing and take and occupy area 30 miles north of DMZ."

Troops and War or Bombing Halt and Negotiations

On March 19, 1968, the principals convened to discuss the parameters of a national presidential address that would presumably focus on Westmoreland's troop request. No one had a good answer to Clark Clifford's question, "Do we have anything to offer except new war?" Hanoi's rejection of the San Antonio formula had badly divided the administration. Secretary of State Rusk acknowledged that the "element of hope has been taken away by TET offensive. People don't think there is likely to be an end." McGeorge Bundy added, "Right. Great fall-off in support. Hell of statement now is 'here they come again, with $30 billion now forever instead of $25 billion.' Can we convey impression that we are ready for peace by saying, 'This is about the US share'? People agree with the objectives, but wonder what it will cost."

If President Johnson really wanted to open negotiations, he would have to stop the bombing. Unless there was a meaningful offer for peace, LBJ should not make it. The only thing which offered the possibility of talks was cessation of bombing. But President Johnson still would not buy into the de-escalation reasoning. He warned those assembled that "standing down bombing gets the hawks furious. Bunker's argument is that any overture would hurt South Vietnam." Support for LBJ came from Abe Fortas who argued that the slightest hint of negotiations would be taken as a sign of weakness. "People's feeling of discontent is over whether the effort is being prosecuted intelligently and firmly. Our combination of war and peace is confusing." Troop reinforcements represented strength and resoluteness.

Now Clark Clifford broke ranks. The secretary of defense took the same position on disengagement that his predecessor had long held. "In World War II 'prevail we will' would work because conditions were right. Now they aren't." Nothing could stop the erosion of public confidence. The meeting ended abruptly when Johnson interjected, "We are mixing two things when we include peace initiatives. Let's make it troops and war. Later we can revive and extend our peace initiatives."

The fact that President Johnson was heading towards "troops and war" soon became apparent in the strident hawkishness of his public rhetoric. At the National Farmers' Union convention LBJ declared, "We hope to achieve an honorable peace and a just peace at the negotiating table. But wanting peace, praying for peace, and desiring peace, as Chamberlain found out, doesn't always give you peace. If the enemy continues to insist—as he does now, when he refuses to sit down and accept the fair proposition we made, that we would stop our bombing if he would sit down and talk promptly and productively—if he continues to insist, as he does now, that the outcome must be determined on the battlefield, then we will win peace on the battlefield by supporting our men who are doing that job there now."

The speech drew a quick response from McGeorge Bundy who warned LBJ, "If we get tagged as mindless hawks, we can lose both the election and the war. . . . This damned war really is much tougher than—and very different from—World War II and Korea, and I just don't think the country can be held together much longer by determination and patriotism alone. We have skillful and ruthless opponents—and we have just got to do more than give them an easy target. (And that's what I found dead wrong in Abe Fortas's advice on Wednesday—although he was dead right about the need to avoid empty peace gestures right now.)"

Bundy then discussed the deep divisions between Johnson's principal advisors. "And I have to admit that Arthur Goldberg is right when he says the only [choice] that the whole world—and Kennedy and McCarthy too—will call serious is a bombing halt. I know that is what McNamara and Vance also think. I've been against them all up to now—but no longer. . . . A full halt in the bombing—one which ends only by the evident fault of Hanoi—seems to me the indispensable missing ingredient in our package for 1968."

As an unofficial senior foreign policy advisor within the inner circle, Bundy wrote to Johnson, "I'll be with you in whatever decision you make. Until those decisions are final you can count on me to tell you what I think as you asked us to yesterday."

General William Westmoreland: Army Chief of Staff

During a March 23 news conference, President Johnson announced that General Westmoreland would replace General Harold K. Johnson as Army Chief of Staff. While touted as a promotion for Westmoreland, those most knowledgeable described the surprise reassignment as being "kicked upstairs." Westmoreland had first learned of the possibility of reassignment during his visit to Washington in November 1967 when General Wheeler informed Westmoreland that he was "the obvious candidate" to replace General Johnson, whose term was about to expire. But Westmoreland had heard nothing more until March 23, 1968, when Wheeler called to report that LBJ had just announced the reassignment at a news conference. Westmoreland later wrote, "I received news of the appointment with mixed emotions. I had hoped to remain in Vietnam until the fighting ended, yet I was honored by the selection. In my own counsel I knew that with the decision against my proposed new strategy, the war was likely to go on for a long time."[9]

Westmoreland's reassignment was the first tangible signal that Johnson had accepted the failure of his administration's military strategy in Vietnam. Despite Westmoreland's optimism in November and his statement of "turning the corner" in Vietnam, by March it was evident that he and Johnson had "been cornered" by their optimism. Implicit in the decision to bump Westmoreland upstairs was Johnson's recognition that the strategy of search and destroy and a war of attrition had failed.

Within the White House a battle for the president's mind, or as it would evolve, over the president's next speech, was taking sides. On one side was the secretary of defense, Clark Clifford, joined by presidential counsel and speech writer Harry McPherson, who set out to convince LBJ that he had lost control of the war. Five hundred American deaths a week, a budget crisis, and electoral challenges were signals that a change from earlier optimism would be necessary. On the other side were the Joint Chiefs, Ambassador Bunker, and Walt Rostow, who believed that the president needed to fully commit his country's resources to war.

The president's speechwriters were working on Johnson's major address to the nation. During a luncheon meeting with the principals the president explained that he felt "there has been a dramatic shift in public opinion on the war, that a lot of people are really ready to surrender without knowing they are following a party line." The group then focused on Harry McPherson's most recent speech draft. The dialogue showed just how close to the edge administration policy stood. The president had to leave the room for a few moments, and during his absence, McGeorge Bundy said that extreme care had to be taken in the president's statements to avoid hawkish speeches that "will cost the President the election." According to Secretary Clifford, the president's recent speech to the National Alliance of Businessmen "had caused concern among thoughtful people because the President seemed to be saying that he was going to win the war no matter what the cost in American lives."

When he returned, the president suggested that his advisers should get together on their thinking. "He said he felt that Congress was going to interpret the speech as pressure on the taxpayers and that others would say it was a speech for the campaign year if he made the address before a Joint Session. He said he thought he should make the statement from his office on television, talking about taxes, troops and reserves, negotiations and peace." Secretary Clifford said "the major concern of the people is that they do not see victory ahead. The military has not come up with a plan for victory. The people were discouraged as more men go in and are chewed up in a bottomless pit."

The president now asked the principals to speculate on possible peace moves. Secretary Clifford suggested that de-escalation be started by a limited cessation of bombing above the twentieth parallel, with reciprocal action by the enemy. Secretary Rusk did not believe Hanoi would reciprocate. William Bundy, assistant secretary of state, said that in Bunker's judgment this would cause major difficulties in Saigon, and that he was skeptical of the idea but had no alternative. Walt Rostow said Hanoi would know full well that the U.S. was taking advantage of the bad weather. He said it might have some effect on doves and some effect in Europe, but would not succeed and would cause problems. In Secretary Rusk's opinion, a critical time for a peace offensive was later, after the winter fighting had subsided, but if the administration delayed in offering peace and the enemy hit Saigon, our forces would have to be prepared to hit Hanoi very hard in retaliation. Justice Fortas thought the decision would be criticized as too little, too late, and insincere. In his view the speech lacked an essential ingredient in that it did not explain why the United States was in Vietnam. "If we do not talk in terms of Communism, it is like a production of Hamlet without the prince." He suggested emphasizing in the speech the invasion of Laos by the North Vietnamese and the brutal murders of the civilians during the Tet truce. He did not believe the people would give the president the support the administration needed with the speech in its present form.

McGeorge Bundy had found the briefing papers quite illuminating. Like the secretary of defense, the more he had read, the more skeptical he had become. The link between guns and butter, between the war in Vietnam and domestic programs posed the single greatest political threat to the administration. Bundy wrote Johnson, "I now understand, as I did not when I got here, that the really tough problem you have is the interlock between the bad turn in the war, the critical need for a tax increase, and the crisis of public confidence at home. If I understand the immediate needs correctly, the most important of all may be the tax increase, simply because without it both the dollar and the economy could come apart—and with them everything else. So while you may not be able to say so plainly, what you do and do not do on other fronts has to be effectively related to the incredibly tough business of getting the Congress to act, at very long last, on taxes. I hate this fact, because I hate to see the President so hobbled, but I have no instant way to amend the Constitution, so there it is."

Bundy recommended that the president reject the military recommendation for calling Reserves for Vietnam. "No good military case for them exists, on anything I have seen, and to me what may make this call really necessary is simply that you may not be able to get the tax increase unless you can prove to some people that we need it for a war in which we are backing Westy all the way. I have a feeling that the cost at home of sending more reserves will be very high and the real military return very low—specially because what people most want is to see the Vietnamese do more and us do less. I hate to see my President held to ransom by military men, and their Congressional friends, who really do not know what to do with the troops they are asking for."

Bundy used Clifford's reasoning: "I am much affected by my belief that the sentiment in the country on the war has shifted very heavily since the Tet offensive. This is not because our people are quitters, and McCarthy and Kennedy did not create the shift, though they may benefit from it. What has happened is that a great many people—even very determined and loyal people—have begun to think that Vietnam really is a bottomless pit."

The Wise Men: Who Poisoned the Well?

In response to Dean Acheson's proposal, President Johnson invited the "wise men" to assemble in the State Department on March 25. The group was first briefed by Philip Habib of the State Department, George Carver of the CIA, and Major General DePuy. The briefings stunned the "wise men," because most had not recognized the degree of devastation Tet had inflicted upon the pacification and security program. According to George Ball's recollection of the briefing, "If the North Vietnamese were to be expelled from the South and the country pacified, it would—so our briefers estimated—take at least five to ten years."[10] Clark Clifford asked whether the military victory could be won. "Not under present circumstances," answered Habib. "What would you do?" asked Clifford. "Stop bombing and negotiate," Habib answered. Douglas Dillon quickly noticed the contradictions between public and private views: "In November, we were told that it would take us a year to win. Now it looked like five or ten, if that."[11]

Arthur Goldberg questioned Major General DePuy about the killed-to-wounded ratio. DePuy replied that during Tet the enemy had lost 80,000 troops and the kill-to-wounded ratio was 3 to 1. Goldberg wanted to know "how many" were left in the enemy's overall strength? DePuy cited the official MACV Order of Battle of 230,000. According to Goldberg: "It just did not hold up in my mind. The briefing indicated that the enemy had lost 80,000 men killed in the Tet offensive. I asked the general what the normal ratio of killed to wounded would be. He said, as I recall, ten to one. And I said that that was a big figure and that, assuming that the Vietnamese were not as solicitous about their wounded as we were, and would not treat their slightly wounded or would put them back into combat when we would not, could we consider three to one to be a conservative figure for those rendered ineffective by wounds? And he said yes. And then I asked the question, 'How many effectives do you think they have operating in the field?' And he said something like 230,000. And I said, 'Well, General, I am not a great mathematician, but with 80,000 killed and with a wounded ratio of three to one, or 240,000, for a total of 320,000, who the hell are we fighting?" It didn't make any sense to me, and I didn't think that was a very good briefing. I like facts laid out. I thought there was a great obligation to tell the president the facts."[12]

When the group broke up it was apparent that the next day's scheduled meeting with President Johnson would not be a comfortable one. Johnson had always relied on these distinguished patriots for support. This was not a radical group; its members represented the establishment and believed passionately in supporting their president. In early November 1967 they had counseled against the stabilization policy proposed by Secretary McNamara. By March 26, 1968, they were willing to accept the failure of the war. But would the president?

When the "wise men" assembled the next day at the White House, Johnson asked Clifford, Rusk, and most other government officials to leave. Those who remained included Acheson, Ball, General Bradley, McGeorge Bundy, Dillon, Fortas, Murphy, Ridgway, and Vance. The only government officials in the room were Vice-President Humphrey, Wheeler, Taylor, and Lodge.

Former secretary of state Dean Acheson, the senior person present with respect to service in government, was asked to begin. George Ball said he quickly recognized that something was fundamentally out of synch. "Dean Acheson was the first of our group to acknowledge that he had changed his mind; we could not, he said, achieve our objective through military means. Views were expressed around the table, and I thought to myself, "There's been a mistake in the invitation list; these can't be the same men I saw here last November."[13]

The morning session devastated Johnson. The president listened carefully to the reviews of the situation, but it was not until after lunch that LBJ learned just how much rot had existed in his policy. After lunch McGeorge Bundy took the lead: "There is a very significant shift in our position. When we last met we saw reasons for hope. We hoped then there would be slow but steady progress. Last night and today the picture is not so hopeful particularly in the country-side. Dean Acheson summed up the majority feeling when he said that we can no longer do the job we set out to do in the time we have left and we must begin to take steps to disengage." Bundy explained that this view was shared by George Ball, Arthur Dean, Cy Vance, Douglas Dillon. "We do think we should do everything possible to strengthen in a real and visible way the performance of the Government of South Vietnam."

Three men took a different position: General Bradley, General Taylor, and Bob Murphy all felt that the United States should do what the military commanders wanted done. General Ridgway had a special point of view. He wanted to strengthen the Army of South Vietnam so that the United States could complete the job in two years. With respect to negotiations, Ball, Goldberg, and Vance strongly urged a cessation of the bombing now. Others wanted a halt at some point but not while the military situation was still unresolved in certain corps areas. On troop reinforcements the majority sentiment was that the burden of proof rested with those urging the troop increase. "Most of us think there should not be a substantial escalation. We all felt there should not be an extension of the conflict. This would be against our national interest. The use of atomic weapons is unthinkable."

The dialogue from the afternoon meeting is reprinted below:

> RIDGEWAY: I agree with the summary as presented by McGeorge Bundy.
>
> DEAN: I agree. All of us got the impression that there is no military conclusion in sight. We felt time is running out.
>
> DEAN ACHESON: Agree with Bundy's presentation. Neither the effort of the Government of Vietnam or the effort of the U.S. government can succeed in the time we have left. Time is limited by reactions in this country. We cannot build an independent South Vietnam; therefore, we should do something by no later than late summer to establish something different.

HENRY CABOT LODGE: We should shift from search-and-destroy strategy to a strategy of using our military power as a shield to permit the South Vietnamese society to develop as well as North Vietnamese society has been able to do. We need to organize South Vietnam on a block-by-block, precinct-by-precinct basis.

DOUGLAS DILLON: We should change the emphasis. I agree with Acheson. The briefing last night led me to conclude we cannot achieve a military victory. I would agree with Lodge that we should cease search-and-destroy tactics and head toward an eventual disengagement. I would send only the troops necessary to support those there now.

GEORGE BALL: I share Acheson's view. I have felt that way since 1961—that our objectives are not attainable. In the U.S. there is a sharp division of opinion. In the world, we look very badly because of the bombing. That is the central defect in our position. The disadvantages of bombing outweigh the advantages. We need to stop the bombing in the next six weeks to test the will of the North Vietnamese. As long as we continue to bomb, we alienate ourselves from the civilized world. I would have the Pope or U Thant [Secretary General of the United Nations] suggest the bombing halt. It cannot come from the President. A bombing halt would quiet the situation here at home.

CY VANCE: McGeorge Bundy stated my views. I agree with George Ball. Unless we do something quick, the mood in this country may lead us to withdrawal. On troops, we should send no more than the 13,000 support troops.

GENERAL BRADLEY: People in the country are dissatisfied. We do need to stop the bombing if we can get the suggestion to come from the Pope or U Thant, but let's not show them that we are in any way weakening. We should send only support troops.

BOB MURPHY: I am shaken by the position of my associates. The interpretation given this action by Saigon would be bad. This is a "giveaway" policy. I think it would weaken our position.

GENERAL TAYLOR: I am dismayed. The picture I get is a very different one from that you have. Let's not concede the home front; let's do something about it.

FORTAS: The U.S. has never had in mind winning a military victory out there; we always have wanted to reach an agreement or settle for the status quo between North Vietnam and South Vietnam. I agree with General Taylor and Bob Murphy. This is not the time for an overture on our part. I do not think a cessation of the bombing would do any good at this time. I do not believe in drama for the sake of drama.

ACHESON: The issue is not that stated by Fortas. The issue is can we do what we are trying to do in Vietnam. I do not think we can. Fortas said we are not trying to win a military victory. The issue is can we by military means keep the North Vietnamese off the South Vietnamese. I do not think we can. They can slip around and end-run them and crack them up.

On March 27, Bundy wrote Johnson about the meeting of the "wise men": "My own best judgment is that we did not receive an unduly gloomy briefing. I do think we were given too rosy a picture in November, and it may be that to some degree there was a reaction from that. But on balance I think your people gave us a clear, fair picture, and one which matched with what many of us have learned from all sources over recent weeks."

It would take time for Johnson to accept this verdict. LBJ grumbled to Ball, "Your whole group must have been brainwashed and I'm going to find out what Habib and the others told you." LBJ called Carver and DePuy (Habib was out of town) to the White House for the same briefing. "Tell me what you told them!"[15] After listening to the briefing it was evident that disengagement would be Johnson's only option. General Maxwell Taylor later wrote that the Pentagon doves had succeeded in impregnating the "wise men" with their doubts. Nevertheless, "I had heard Carver and DePuy make similar briefings many times in the past and found nothing unusual in what they said on this occasion. I had heard Habib's views less frequently, but, while he seemed slightly more pessimistic about the political situation than I had expected, he too made a temperate, thoughtful presentation. I make these comments on the briefings because the President was at first inclined to blame them for the unexpected reaction of his guests. Whereas only a few months before they had generally supported his policy and concentrated their attention on ways to obtain better public understanding for it, this time they arrived apparently convinced in advance that the policy was a failure and must be changed."[16]

In *The Vantage Point* Johnson wrote of these elder statesmen, "They were intelligent, experienced men. I had always regarded the majority of them as very steady and balanced. If they had been so deeply influenced by the reports of the Tet offensive, what must the average citizen in the country be thinking?"[14]

Checkmate

During McGeorge Bundy's presentation at the meeting of the "wise men," President Johnson jotted on a pad, "can no longer do the job we set out to do . . . Adjust our course . . . move to disengage." The war had become a sinkhole. The notion of American omnipotence and inevitable victory was shattered during Tet. The Tet offensive had contradicted the president's public pronouncements. "I am convinced I made a mistake," Johnson later wrote, "by not saying more about Vietnam in my State of the Union report on January 17, 1968."[17] Cable traffic and intelligence reports all confirmed a buildup of enemy forces, but after presenting optimistic scenarios in November, President Johnson could hardly have done otherwise. "In retrospect, I think I was too cautious. If I had forecast the possibilities, the American people would have been better prepared for what was soon to come." Tet had revealed that despite over 525,000 men, billions of dollars, and extensive bombing, the United States had not stopped the enemy from replacing his forces. The rate of the war and the capacity to sustain it were controlled not by America's superior technology, but by the enemy.

President Johnson had tried to control public perceptions of the war's progress. He appears to have believed he could utilize the prestige of the presidency to legitimize statistics—as though they could stand alone as proof that there was no policy stalemate. Faith in numbers replaced a visible demonstration of presidential leadership.

Between the final meeting of the "wise men" and President Johnson's March 31 speech, Clifford took control of the speech-drafting process. He informed Rusk and Rostow that the country could not accept a war speech; the president as candidate and as Commander in Chief needed a peace speech. Democracy could not survive without majority support for a nation's war policy. LBJ had lost that link. Clifford assigned responsibility for drafting the speech to Harry McPherson, whose views were well known amongst the principals. Clifford and McPherson have provided lengthy oral-history interviews which describe how they literally set out to save their president from the hawks. "Together we'll get our country and President out of this mess," Clifford decided. "Is he with us," a phrase from the French Revolution, became the secret code for those working for disengagement. The speech became the format for a bombing halt at the twentieth parallel of North Vietnam which would be tied conditionally to Hanoi's favorable response for negotiations.

The president was scheduled to deliver his speech at 9:00 P.M. EST; McPherson was still working on the draft in his White House office when LBJ telephoned: " 'Do you think it is a good speech?' the president asked his aide. McPherson thought it was. 'Do you think it will help?' McPherson thought it would, particularly at home. 'Do you think Hanoi will talk?' The aide was much less certain—the chances seemed to him to be less than 50–50. 'I'm going to have a little ending of my own to add to yours,' the president told his aide and friend. McPherson had heard that it was in the works, and he caught a hint the day before of what Johnson might do. 'Do you know what I'm going to say?' Johnson asked. There was a pause. Yes, he thought so. 'What do you think?' 'I'm very sorry,' said McPherson softly. 'Okay,' responded the President with a Texas lilt in his voice— 'so long, pardner.' "[18]

In his speech on March 31, 1968, Lyndon Johnson announced a partial suspension of the bombing against North Vietnam. "There is no need to delay talks that could bring an end to this long and this bloody war. Tonight, I renew the offer I made last August—to stop the bombardment of North Vietnam. We ask that talks begin promptly, that they be serious talks on the substance of peace. We assume that during those talks Hanoi will not take advantage of our restraint. We are prepared to move immediately toward peace through negotiations. So tonight, in the hope that this action will lead to early talks, I am taking the first step to de-escalate the conflict. We are reducing—substantially reducing—the present level of hostilities. And we are doing so unilaterally, and at once." The president then stunned the nation by announcing, "believing this as I do, I have concluded that I should not permit the Presidency to become involved in the partisan divisions that are developing in this political year. With America's sons in the fields far away, with America's future under challenge right here at home, with our hopes and the world's hopes for peace in the balance every day, I do not believe that I should devote an hour or a day of my time to any personal partisan causes or to any duties other than the awesome duties of this office—the Presidency of your country. Accordingly, I shall not seek, and I will not accept, the nomination of my party for another term as your President."

McNamara, Westmoreland, and Johnson—the architects of U.S. policy in Vietnam had fallen. Their departures reflected a recognition that the idea of military victory had been a "dangerous illusion." Writing to Secretary of Defense Clifford on March 14, under-Secretary of the Air Force Townsend Hoopes had discerned from the history of U.S. involvement in Vietnam "repeated miscalculations as to the force and time required to 'defeat the aggression,' pacify the countryside, and make the GVN and the ARVN viable without massive US support. Each fresh increment of American power has been justified as the last one needed to do the job."*

General Westmoreland's 206,000-troop request forced the principals to confront the reality that 750,000 troops would not alter the conditions of stalemate. A 206,000 augmentation would be matched by only a 50,000 corresponding increase in Communist strength. At Johnson's request, the CIA had taken a fresh look at the data on North Vietnamese Army strength in South Vietnam and the rates of NVA infiltration over recent months. Carver reported, "During the past three or four months there has been a dramatic increase in the movement of regular North Vietnamese Army units into South Vietnam. This Agency now believes that last Fall (1 November) there were over 70,000 North Vietnamese soldiers fighting in South Vietnam. The number has risen rapidly in the past five months and today may be over 100,000. This increase in NVA strength in South Vietnam has been achieved despite the thousands of casualties suffered by the North Vietnamese in the intensified combat of the past two months."

*See Appendix for Hoopes memo in full.

What did the data mean? There were nearly twice as many North Vietnamese regular army soldiers in South Vietnam as there were VC regular soldiers. Between November 1, 1967, and February 1968, 35–40,000 NVA personnel had infiltrated into South Vietnam.

By March 1968, the Gallup Poll reported that 49 percent of the American population believed that the United States was wrong to have gotten involved militarily in Vietnam. While seven in ten doves thought the country was wrong to ever have gotten involved, four in ten hawks thought so as well. When the president uttered his March 31 words, "I will not accept . . ." Johnson's colleagues, friends, and political observers unanimously viewed his decision as a positive, forward, and constructive step for national unity and peace in Vietnam. A Harris survey immediately following Johnson's announcement revealed a complete reversal in the president's job approval rating at the start of March. Approval in April stood at 57 percent, in March it had been 43 percent; disapproval had dropped in one month from 57 percent to 43 percent. Stepping aside brought Johnson more praise than any of his actions in the past year—so much had Vietnam become Lyndon Johnson's war.

In Retrospect

I am reminded of the adage, "Those who write history have the gift of revision; those who make it get only one chance." In looking over the course of American foreign policy between 1965 and 1968 there were many chances for those who shaped Vietnam policy to revise that policy. One of these occurred when Senator George Aiken of Vermont remarked, "Let's declare that we have achieved our objectives in Vietnam and go home." A few days later Leonard Marks, Johnson's director of the United States Information Agency, mentioned Aiken's proposal to the president. "He looked at me—he had a way of staring at you—and finally I blinked. I said, 'What do you think?' He said, 'Get out of here.' I picked up my papers and left. That's the first and only time he'd ever been harsh with me. . . . Several years after he left the White House I was invited to spend a weekend at the ranch. We were by ourselves. It was on my conscience and I said, 'Mr. President, I have to ask you something. In all the years we've been together, only once did you act in a way that I could really complain' and I recalled this experience. 'Why did you do it?' He looked at me and he said, 'Because you and George Aiken were right.' "[19]

Lyndon Johnson chose to Americanize the war in July 1965; he chose to accept General Westmoreland's attrition strategy; he chose not to mobilize his country for war; he chose and encouraged others to paint optimistic scenarios for the American public; he chose to hide the anticipated enemy buildup prior to Tet because, in an election year, he had hoped for a military miracle—perhaps Westmoreland would turn the tide when the enemy began its final desperate assault.

It was left to Clark Clifford as secretary of defense to convince Johnson that Vietnam had become a sinkhole. The irony was that Secretary McNamara had been banished from the administration for the same advocacy. George Ball had been listened to but not heard. Johnson's decision to remove himself from the renomination race represented the ultimate recognition that the Vietnam war had become interwoven with his personality and his presidency. "I shall not accept" was the president's admission that Vietnam had become, against his every desire, Lyndon Johnson's war.

Notes

Unless otherwise noted all references are from the Presidential Papers of Lyndon Baines Johnson, 1963–1969, located in the Lyndon Baines Johnson Library, Austin, Texas. The materials available for research on the war and utilized in this book include the *National Security File* (NSF) which was the working file of President Johnson's special assistants for national security affairs, McGeorge Bundy and Walt Rostow. The NSF file contains several important categories: *Country File*, Vietnam; *Country File*, Cambodia, Laos, Thailand; *Head of State Correspondence; International Meetings and Travel File* (February 1966 Honolulu conference and 1967 Guam conference); *Speech File; Agency File; Name File; Intelligence File; Subject File; National Intelligence Estimates; National Security Action Memorandums; National Security Council Meetings; National Security Council Histories* (especially Honolulu Conference, February 6–8, 1966, Manila Conference and President's Asia Trip, October 17–November 2, 1966 and March 31, 1968 speech); *Memos to the President; Files of McGeorge Bundy; Files of Robert Komer.*

The *White House Central Files* (WHCF) and *White House Central Files-Confidential File* (C.F.) also contain important material in ND

19/CO 312 (National Defense-Vietnam War.) *The Meeting Notes File* and *Tom Johnson's Notes of Meetings* provide detailed transcripts of meetings on Vietnam and Tuesday luncheons.

The collection entitled "Tom Johnson's Notes of Meetings" includes notes for more than 190 White House meetings which were taken by W. Thomas Johnson. Tom Johnson served as deputy press secretary under President Lyndon Johnson from October 1967 through January 1969. He started taking notes at White House meetings on a regular basis in July 1967 and continued to do so through December 1968. President Johnson attended all but one of the meetings for which there are notes in this collection.

Three-fifths of the notes in this collection date from 1968. Of the remaining two-fifths, virtually all were taken at meetings held between July and December 1967, but five sets of notes date from June 1966 through June 1967.

The collection includes notes for more than eighty meetings that President Johnson held with House and Senate leaders, correspondents, his Cabinet, the National Security Council, businessmen, and other groups. These notes have been processed and opened for research, but some are still undergoing declassification review or have been exempted from declassification. This first group of notes is currently located in boxes 1 and 2 of Tom Johnson's notes of meetings.

In addition, the collection includes notes for close to 110 other meetings that President Johnson held with his senior civilian and military foreign policy advisers, including some 45 Tuesday luncheons. These have not yet been processed or opened for research, except for those portions that were released in response to a subpoena issued in 1982 in connection with General William Westmoreland's lawsuit against CBS. Only those portions of Tom Johnson's notes that pertained to enemy strength in South Vietnam and the infiltration of North Vietnamese troops into South Vietnam were released in response to the subpoena. The released portions of this second group of notes are currently located in box 3 of Tom Johnson's notes of meetings.

For notes similar to those included in both the groups described above—but taken by individuals other than Tom Johnson—consult the Meeting Notes File, Boxes 1–3.

Preface

1. "Notes of the president's meeting with Chalmers Roberts," October 13, 1967 (Meeting Notes File). "Notes of meeting with foreign policy advisors," November 1, 1967. See also Rostow, Memo to the president, "Summary of discussion and suggestions for today's meeting," November 2, 1967.

2. "Notes of the president's activities during the Detroit crisis," July 24, 1967.

I. Introduction

1. Lodge to the president, February 1, 1966. (Weekly telegram).

2. Bundy to the president, "Memorandum on Vietnam policy," May 4, 1967.

3. Data released in February 1987 by the Federal Center for Disease Control in Atlanta. The study of 18,000 discharged enlisted men who served tours of duty between 1965 to 1971 as well as a control group who served elsewhere, found that the Vietnam combat veterans had an overall higher death rate of 48 percent.

4. See Ben Franklin, "Scrutiny of Agent Orange Data Allowed," *New York Times,* November 17, 1987. William Welch, "White House Doubts Study Finding 'Agent Orange Risk,' " *Sacramento Bee,* September 15, 1987. Phillip Boffey, "Cancer Deaths High for Some Veterans," *New York Times,* September 4, 1987. p. 6. Phillip Boffey, "U.S. Halting Study on Agent Orange," *New York Times,* September 1, 1967.

5. See Harry G. Summers, Jr., *On Strategy: The Vietnam War in Context* (Carlisle Barracks, Penn: Strategic Studies Institute, U.S. Army War College, 1981); General Bruce Palmer, Jr., *The Twenty-Five-Year War: America's Military Role in Vietnam* (Lexington, Ky: The University Press of Kentucky, 1984); Andrew F. Krepinevich, Jr., *The Army and Vietnam* (Baltimore: The Johns Hopkins University Press, 1986); Timothy Lomperis, *The War Everyone Lost—And Won* (Baton Rouge, LA: Louisiana State University Press, 1984); Admiral U.S. Grant Sharp, *Strategy for Defeat: Vietnam in Retrospect* (San Rafael, CA: Presidio Press, 1978).

II. Setting the Stage

1. Lyndon Baines Johnson, *The Vantage Point: Perspectives on the Presidency, 1963–1969* (New York: Popular Library, 1971), p. 383.

2. See *Time,* February 18, 1966; *Newsweek,* February 18, 1966 and February 11, 1966; Johnson, *The Vantage Point,* p. 244.

3. William Westmoreland, trial testimony and deposition. For insights into McNamara see David Halberstam, *The Best and the Brightest* (New York: Random House, 1969); Henry Trewitt, *McNamara* (New York: Harper

and Row, 1971); William Kaufman, *The McNamara Strategy* (New York: Harper and Row, 1964); Douglas Kinnard, *The War Managers* (Hanover, NH: University Press of New England, 1977); Jonathan Rinehart, "The Man Who Wields Power," *USA.1* (May 1967); Stewart Alsop, "McNamara: The Light that Failed," *Saturday Evening Post* (November 18, 1967); Stewart Alsop, "Vietnam: How Wrong Was McNamara?" *Saturday Evening Post* (March 12, 1966); Neil Sheehan, "You Don't Know Where Johnson Ends and McNamara Begins," *New York Times Magazine* (October 22, 1967); Tom Wicker, "The Awesome Twosome," *New York Times Magazine* (January 30, 1966).

4. See Krepinevich, *The Army and Vietnam*, pp. 168–72.

5. See Sharp, *Strategy for Defeat*, p. 164.

6. General John Paul McConnel, "Oral history transcript" (Johnson Library).

7. Admiral Thomas Moorer, "Oral history transcript" (Johnson Library).

8. McNamara to the president, "Actions recommended for Vietnam," October 14, 1966.

9. Wheeler to McNamara, "Actions recommended for Vietnam," October 14, 1966.

10. For an extended perspective and documentation see the NSC history, in the National Security File, "President's Trip to Manila."

11. Johnson, *The Vantage Point*, p. 249.

12. Carver to Komer, November 22, 1966 (Joint Exhibit 221). Komer to McNamara, "Vietnam prognosis for 1967–68," November 29, 1966.

13. Westmoreland to Sharp and Wheeler, "Year-end assessment of enemy situation and enemy strategy," January 2, 1967.

14. Sharp to Westmoreland and Wheeler, "Operational concept for Vietnam," January 3, 1967.

15. Cited in Rostow to President Johnson, January 19, 1967.

III. The Slippery Slope to Stalemate

1. Johnson, *The Vantage Point*, pp. 441–43.

2. Wheeler to Westmoreland, March 9, 1967 (Joint Exhibit 231). Wheeler to Westmoreland and Sharp, "VC/NVA battalion and larger attacks," March 11, 1967 (Joint Exhibit 233).

3. Text of cable from Lodge to Rusk, March 13, 1967.

4. Johnson, *The Vantage Point*, pp. 259–60.

5. See *Newsweek*, March 27, 1967, p. 29.

6. Rostow to the president, "Major themes for Thieu and Ky," March 18, 1967. See Rostow to the president, "Four major points to be made in private session with Thieu and Ky," March 20, 1967.

7. "Notes from meeting of president with Vietnamese leaders," March 21, 1967 (CBS Subpoena Case #27, Document #258). See Carver to Rostow, "Transmittal of Working Notes," March 23, 1967.

8. Rostow to the president, March 22, 1967. See "North Vietnamese Infiltration Into South Vietnam," March 17, 1967 (CBS Subpoena Case #8,

Document #1). Rostow to the president, "Covering memo to Lodge's weekly telegram: Saigon 22177," April 6, 1967 (CBS Subpoena Case #22, Document #113).

9. See *The Pentagon Papers*, Gravel edition, vol. 4 (Boston: Beacon Press, 1971), pp. 151–53. Meeting notes transcript, April 27, 1967. See General William C. Westmoreland, *A Soldier Reports*, (New York: Doubleday, 1976) p. 227–28.

10. Remarks by General Westmoreland before a Joint Session of Congress, April 28, 1967 (Congressional Record). See Westmoreland, *A Soldier Reports*, p. 228.

11. Memo for secretary of defense, "Increase of SEA forces," May 1, 1967. See Enthoven to McNamara, "Force levels and enemy attention," May 4, 1967.

12. McNamara deposition and trial transcripts in author's possession.

13. Rostow CBS interview transcripts in author's possession.

14. Bundy to the president, May 4, 1967.

15. Wheeler to the president, May 5, 1967 (CM-3218-67).

IV. Choosing Among Imperfect Alternatives

1. McNaughton to McNamara, May 16, 1967. See "Proposed bombing program against North Vietnam," May 9, 1967. See McNaughton draft presidential memo, May 5, 1967. See Rostow memo to the president, May 6, 1967 in which Rostow evaluates options before endorsing bombing in the panhandle regions; see also William Bundy memo of May 8, 1967, in *Pentagon Papers*, vol. 4, p. 155.

2. McNamara to the president, "Future actions in Vietnam," May 19, 1967 (EXH. 955).

3. Wheeler to the president, "Operations Against North Vietnam," May 20, 1967 (JCSM 286-67). See also JCS to secretary of defense, "Future actions in Vietnam," May 29, 1967 (Case #85-151, Doc. #6).

4. Rostow to the president, May 21, 1967.

5. Ibid. See Rostow to the president, May 19, 1967. William Bundy, "Comments on DOD First Rough Draft of May 19–May 30, 1967."

6. Sharp to Westmoreland, June 10, 1967 (Joint Exhibit 242, JX 242, p. 1). See Special National Intelligence Estimate 14.3-67. SAVA to Louis Sandine, Saigon 7423 (Exhibit 239A JX239A).

7. McNamara to the president, June 12, 1967.

8. Bunker to the White House, "Eyes only the president," July 14, 1967.

V. The Summer of Discontent

1. Meeting notes, July 7, 1967.

2. Notes of meeting with Peter Lisagor of *Chicago Daily News*, August 4, 1967. Meeting notes, July 12, 1967.

3. Russel Baker, "Observer: Let's Hear It for a Really Swell Policy," *New York Times*, August 8, 1967.

4. Clark Clifford, "A Viet Nam Reappraisal," *Foreign Affairs* (July 1969), pp. 601–23.

5. Rostow to the president, July 22, 1967 (CBS Subpoena Case #19, Document 20).

6. Rostow to the president, July 27, 1967 (Re. Saigon 1954). Bunker to the president, July 26, 1967 (CBS Subpoena Case #10, Document 63).

7. Westmoreland to Wheeler, Johnson, and Sharp, August 2, 1967.

8. See Hedrick Smith, "Army Chief Sees End of Build-up," *New York Times,* August 13, 1967. Rostow to the president, August 11, 1967 (LBJ wrote over the memo, "Bring him in Saturday if George OK's")

9. See Westmoreland to Wheeler and Sharp, August 12, 1967 (Exhibit 1605A); Wheeler to Westmoreland and Sharp, August 8, 1967 (Exhibit 1607A).

10. Meeting Notes, July 25, 1967.

11. See Senate Hearings Before the Preparedness Investigating Subcommittee of the Committee on Armed Services, *Air War Against North Vietnam,* 90th Congress, August 25, 1967. Douglas Kinnard, *The Secretary of Defense* (Lexington, Ky: University Press of Kentucky, 1981) pp. 104–5. Walter Isaacson and Evan Thomas, *The Wise Men,* (New York: Simon and Schuster, 1987), p. 683. See James Clay Thompson, *Rolling Thunder: Understanding Policy and Program Failure* (Chapel Hill: The University of North Carolina Press, 1980).

12. Komer cable to Carver, "RE: Wide discrepancy between MACV and CIA figures on enemy strength," August 19 (CBS, JE 250). [See also Lawyers' Brief, Bk. I, pp. B195-B196, Bk. II, and Bk. III.] Davidson cable to Godding, "RE: Unacceptability of including SD and SSD forces' strength in any strength figure released to the press," August 19, 1967 (Lawyers' Brief, Bk. I, p. B198, Godding 8/24/67 cable to Davidson, Bk. II, and Bk. III—all JE 251). Ginsburgh memo to Rostow, "Increased estimates on Communist strengths in SVN to be published soon," August 18, 1967 (CBS). Ginsburgh to Rostow, August 23, 1967. See Ginsburgh to Rostow, August 18, 1967, "Recommend that you make the following points with Mr. Helms: Now is the time to 'bite the bullet.' The intelligence community should not attempt to sneak up on the new estimate by adding periodic increments into current figures."

13. Westmoreland cable to Wheeler and Sharp, "RE: To prevent erroneous conclusions from being drawn, SD and SSD strength figures should not be included in overall enemy strength," August 20, 1967 (Lawyers' Brief, Bk. I, p. B204, Bk. II, and Bk. III, JE 253). Abrams cable to Wheeler, Sharp, and Westmoreland, August 20, 1967, "RE: Continuing controversy over possible inclusion of SD and SSD strength figures in estimate of overall enemy strength" (CBS, JE 252) [See also Lawyers' Brief, Bk. I, pp. B200-B202, Bk. II, and Bk. III].

14. Bunker to the president, August 23, 1967. "Notes from meeting with correspondents," August 24, 1967.

15. Westmoreland to Wheeler, August 26, 1967. Westmoreland to Wheeler and Sharp, August 25, 1967 (Joint Exhibit 255).

16. Wheeler, "Summary of meeting of Joint Chiefs of Staff," August 25, 1967.

17. Bunker to Rostow, August 29, 1967.

VI. Signs of Optimism

1. See "Notes of weekly meeting with Secretaries Rusk and McNamara, Walt Rostow, George Christian, Dick Helms and General Harold Johnson," September 15, 1967 and September 12, 1967.

2. Ibid.

3. See R.W. Apple, "Thieu and Ky are Victors," *New York Times,* Sept. 6, 1967. Peter Braestrup, " 'Chicago Politics' Benefited Thieu in Delta Province," *New York Times,* September 4, 1967.

4. Bunker to the president, September 5, 1967. See "Notes of meeting with Vietnam election observers," September 6, 1967.

5. Carver to Helms, September 12, 1967 (JX 258A), p. 1.

6. Carver to Helms, September 13, 1967 (Helms affidavit).

7. Helms affidavit in author's possession.

8. Westmoreland to McConnell and Sharp, September 14, 1967 (Exhibit 1508A).

9. Carver to Helms, September 15, 1967.

10. Rostow to the president, September 20, 1967.

11. Johnson, *The Vantage Point,* pp. 408–11.

12. Notes of the president's meeting, September 20, 1967.

13. Philip Habib to Harold Kaplan, "Statistical Defense of Progress in the War," September 26, 1967.

14. See Rusk to Bunker, October 7, 1967 and Ambassador Locke to the president, October 7, 1967 (Saigon 7867).

15. Paul Walsh to George Carver, "MACV Press Briefing on Enemy Order of Battle," October 11, 1967 (Joint Exhibit 265A). Rostow memo, "Vietnam Data and Progress Indicators," October 13, 1967.

16. Carver to Goulding, October 13, 1967 (JE 266).

17. Rostow to the president, October 14, 1967.

18. Fortas to the president, "Vietnam," October 14, 1967.

19. Wheeler to McNamara, "Inversed Pressure on North Vietnam," October 17, 1967.

20. Bundy to the president, October 18, 1967. See Bundy to the president, "Vietnam—October 1967," October 17, 1967.

21. Harry McPherson to the president, October 27, 1967.

VII. The Progress Report of November 1967

1. See Johnson, *The Vantage Point,* Appendices A.

2. McNamara to the president, "A Fifteen Month Program for Military Operations in Southeast Asia," November 1, 1967.

3. See Isaaccson and Thomas, *The Wise Men;* "Notes of Wise Men Meeting," November 1, 1967.

4. See Rostow to Clifford, November 1, 1967; Rostow to the president, "Summary discussion and suggestions for today's meeting," November 2, 1967.

5. Rostow to the president, November 2, 1967.

6. Quoted in Isaaccson and Thomas, *The Wise Men* p. 683, 646. See George Ball, *The Past Has Another Pattern*, (New York: W.W. Norton, 1982).

7. Averill Harriman to the president and secretary of state, "Negotiations," November 3, 1967.

8. Bundy to the president, "A Commentary on the Vietnam discussion of November 2," November 10, 1967.

9. Rostow to the president, November 4, 1967.

10. Rostow to the president, November 2, 1967. Rostow to the president, November 3, 1967.

11. Bunker to President Johnson, November 2, 1967.

12. Fortas to the president, November 9, 1967.

13. Clifford to the president, November 7, 1967.

14. Rostow to the president, "Summary of responses," November 21, 1967.

15. Rusk to the president, November 20, 1967.

16. Rostow to the president, "Westmoreland's assessment for the month of October," 21 p. (6–84). Helms to the president, "Capabilities of Vietnamese Communists for Fighting in South Vietnam," November 14, 1967. See Special National Intelligence Estimate (SNIE) #14.3-67, (Lawyers' Brief, Bk. I, pp. B243-B272, Bk. II, Plate 12, and Bk. III, JE 273).

17. Renata Adler, *Reckless Disregard* (New York: Knopf, 1986) p. 239.

18. Bill Gulley with Mary Ellen Reese, *Breaking Cover* (New York: Simon and Schuster, 1980), pp. 44–45.

VIII. The Big Sell

1. Richard Moose deposition and affidavit in author's possession.

2. Westmoreland's remarks to the Joint Chiefs, Friday, November 17, 1967.

3. Rostow to the president, November 19, 1967.

4. Nicholas Katzenbach to the president, "Memorandum," November 16, 1967.

5. Carver memo to director, Office of Current Intelligence (for president), "Regarding potentially controversial judgments or data holding changes in NIE 14.3-67," (CBS, E 711) [See also Lawyers' Brief, Bk. I, pp. B386-B392, and Bk. II, Plates 9A, 9B, JE 711]. See Rostow to the president, "Issues you wish to raise a noon meeting with Westmoreland," November 16, 1967. See Helms to the president, "The validity and significance of Viet Cong loss data," November 22, 1967.

6. Westmoreland cable to Abrams. "Regarding attempt to encourage hope that Vietnam war was winnable," (Lawyers' Brief, Bk. II, and Bk. III, JE 285)

7. Jason study in *Pentagon Papers,* Vol. 4, p. 116, 224–25.

8. Westmoreland, *A Soldier Reports,* pp. 233–34.

9. R.W. Apple, "Johnson Backs Military Leaders More Firmly Than Ever in Vietnam Visit," *New York Times,* December 24, 1967.

10. Walt Rostow, *The Diffusion of Power.* (New York: MacMillan, 1972), p. 464–67.

11. Transcript of meeting with the pope, December 23, 1967, (LBJ Library).

IX. The Tet Offensive

For a complete list of documents used in the chapter consult the National Security Council History, "The March 31st Speech" at the LBJ Library. The project traces the events between the 1968 Tet attacks and the presidents' speech on March 31st in which he announced the partial cessation of the bombing and his decision not seek reelection.

1. Quoted in Kenneth Thompson, ed., *The Johnson Presidency* (Lanham, MD: University Press of America, 1987), pp. 89–90, 258.

2. Robert Ginsburgh, deposition for CBS-Westmoreland trial in author's possession.

3. See Tom Johnson's meeting notes.

4. See *Newsweek,* February 2, 1968.

5. See Tom Johnson's meeting notes.

6. See Doris Kearns, *Lyndon Johnson and the American Dream* (New York: Harper and Row, 1976) pp. 360–1.

7. Sam Adams to George Carver, February 1968 (CBS-Westmoreland trial document in author's possession).

8. Westmoreland, *A Soldier Reports,* p. 357.

9. Krepinevich, *The Army and Vietnam,* pp. 192–93.

10. See Daniel Hallin, *The Uncensored War: The Media and Vietnam.* (New York: Oxford University Press, 1986) pp. 169–70.

X. The Ides of March

1. Clifford, "A Vietnam Reappraisal," pp. 608–9.

2. Alain Enthoven, "Alternative Strategies," *Pentagon Papers,* Vol. 4, pp 556–57.

3. Clifford, "A Vietnam Reappraisal," pp. 608–10.

4. Palmer, *The Twenty-Five Year War* pp. 80–81.

5. Ralph Huitt, "Democratic Party Leadership in the Senate," *American Political Science Review,* 55 (June 1961) pp. 336–38.

6. Fortas to the president, March 12, 1968.

7. See Isaaccson and Thomas, *The Wise Men.* p. 638–35.

8. See Don Oberdorf, *TET!* (New York: Doubleday, 1971); Herbert Shandler, *Lyndon Johnson and Vietnam* (Princeton, NJ: Princeton University Press, 1977); Stanley Karnow, *Vietnam* (New York: Viking, 1983); Townsend Hoopes, *The Limits of Intervention* (New York: W.W. Norton, 1987).

9. Westmoreland, *A Soldier Reports,* pp. 361–62.

10. Ball, *The Past Has Another Pattern,* pp. 407–9.

11. Isaacson and Thomas, *The Wise Men,* p. 700.

12. Quoted in Shandler, *Lyndon Johnson and Vietnam,* Chapter 15.

13. Ball, *The Past Has Another Pattern,* p. 409.

14. Johnson, *The Vantage Point,* p. 408–9.

15. Quoted in Schandler, *Lyndon Johnson and Vietnam.* p. 260–61.

16. Quoted in Maxwell Taylor, *Swords and Plowshares* (New York: W.W. Norton, 1972), pp. 390–91.

17. Johnson, *The Vantage Point,* p. 415, see Chapter 18.

18. Quoted in Oberdorf, *TET!* p. 317.

19. Leonard Marks Oral History.

Appendix A
Memo from Townsend Hoopes to Clark Clifford, February 13, 1968

February 13, 1968

Dear Clark:

I have concluded that it would be useful, before you take office, to put before you a certain perspective on aspects of the Vietnam problem. I do so in the belief that these aspects involve critical nuances unlikely to come through clearly in formal briefings or even in supplementary talks. I put them to you with more candor than discretion, believing you would prefer this, but believing in any event that candor and clarity are needed at this juncture of our affairs.

I am concerned with two subjects: (1) the intrinsic value of our bombing in the North; and (2) the relationship of our ground strategy in the South to a pause or cessation of bombing in the North. The bleak events of recent days

215

may have temporarily pushed these subjects into the background, but they will recur, for they are among the central elements of the problem.

Let me acknowledge at the outset several personal premises: first, the idea of a US military victory in Vietnam is a dangerous illusion (primarily because both the Soviets and the Chicoms have the capacity to preclude it—probably by supply operations alone, but if necessary by intervening with their own forces); second, if events in Vietnam are ever to take a turn toward settlement, definitive de-escalation is a prerequisite; and third, admitting all the uncertainty and risk, the most promising approach to negotiations and thus settlement continues to involve a cessation of the US bombing effort against North Vietnam as one of the first steps.

Effectiveness of Bombing the North

When I moved over to the Air Force last October, I asked for the Air Staff's current assessment of the bombing effectiveness. To my surprise, no meaningful assessment existed. Data were in abundance, but they did not constitute a considered assessment. All analytical efforts were going into the bombing operations themselves—that is, how to improve bombing accuracy, how to achieve a higher sortie rate, how to improve electronic measures against stronger NVN air defenses, etc.

I mean to cast no aspersions whatsoever on the professional competence of the Air Staff. In one sense, it is unfair to seek definitive assessment of this kind from the professional operators, for it requires them to examine their own *raison d'etre*. They come to the problem with a built-in predisposition to avoid the question whether air power can be efficacious in the circumstances where its application has been ordered; their tendency is to assume that it is or can be, and they prefer to concentrate their energies on developing the means and techniques that will prove them right. Such a "can-do" attitude is eminently desirable in executive agents of national policy, but it does have its shortcomings. Subsequently, Secretary Brown ordered the organization of a joint Air Staff–RAND study to examine bombing effectiveness; this is now underway, but it is a laborious effort oriented to a complicated mathematical model. No results at all are expected for several months, and it is my impression that in the end we will get a dusty answer.

On the other hand, an increasing number of experienced analysts outside the ambit of direct operational responsibility have addressed the available facts (including in some cases the intelligence reports and the relevant material from our Embassy and military command); they have come to some firm if depressing conclusions. The most recent, and in some respects the most comprehensive, study was done by the Institute for Defense Analyses. It was commissioned by Secretary McNamara in October and completed in December. While some of its source material is secret, its conclusions are not—and indeed some of them found their way into Secretary McNamara's final posture statement to the Congress. In summary, these are the conclusions:

- Since the beginning of the air strikes in early 1965, the flow of men and materiel from NVN to SVN has definitely increased.

- The rate of infiltration is not limited by factors in NVN—i.e., available manpower, LOC capabilities, available transport carriers, or available volume of supplies. Rather, the constraints on infiltration relate to the war situation in the South—i.e., the VC infrastructure and distribution system in the South have a limited capacity to absorb and manage additional materiel and troops.

- The bombing has inflicted heavy damage on North Vietnam's economy and society as a whole ($370 million of measurable damage and the diversion of up to 600,000 people from agriculture to road repair, transport, and air defense). But NVN's allies have provided economic and military aid substantially in excess of the damage, and the cost of the manpower diversions may be quite small, owing to the considerable slack in NVN's underemployed agricultural labor force.

- NVN has gone over to decentralized, dispersed and protected modes of producing and handling essential goods and safeguarding the people. It has made a durable adjustment to the bombing.

- The NVN regular army, the VC main forces, and the VC local forces now have better equipment and more effective weapons than in 1965, and the Soviet Union could provide them with even more sophisticated weapons. Only a moderate fraction of the 1.2 million fit males in the prime age groups (17-35) have as yet been inducted into the armed forces.

- On balance, NVN is a stronger military power today than before the bombing began.

Without by any means accepting every point in the IDA analysis, I believe its conclusions are as essentially undeniable as they are unpalatable. Bombing targets in the North did not prevent the current buildup at Khe Sanh, nor notably hinder the recent coordinated VC attacks on the cities. The air war over Hanoi and Haiphong in particular seems increasingly a techno-electronic contest between the US and the Soviet Union with diminishing relevance to the struggle in the South. We seem to have in the bombing campaign an instrument of some modest, but indeterminate, value which plays an essentially psychological role in the struggle and whose most useful service to us may be as a counter to be traded away in a serious bargaining.

This conclusion appears compatible with the San Antonio formula which—if I read it correctly—means that the bombing of the North is something we are prepared to give up while accepting a continuation of the enemy's "normal" activity, provided that our cessation leads promptly to talks.

The Ground Strategy of Attrition

We are pursuing an aggressive ground strategy of attrition in South Vietnam which often involves US troops fighting search-and-destroy battles in totally uninhabited places, in the worst possible terrain for American forces, at the time of the enemy's choosing, and with inconclusive results. This is a strategy devised and executed by the Field Commander with remarkably little detailed guidance from either the JCS or higher civilian authority. Certainly the degree of Washington's critical interest in the way in which the ground war is fought has been in striking contrast to the detailed control which Washington has exercised over the bombing campaign. This strategy generates an increasing rate of US casualties—about 9,500 killed and 20,000 wounded in 1967, as compared to 6,500 killed and 11,000 wounded during the previous seven years.

As indicated by discussion of the bombing, there is only a tenuous military link between our bombing in the North and the casualties we suffer in the South. If we should stop bombing North Vietnam, but continue to pursue the present ground strategy, our casualties are not likely to go down and might go up. But it is doubtful whether a rise would be attributable, in military fact, to a bombing halt. Present US casualty levels are a function of the US ground strategy in the South; they are only distantly related to the bombing.

Yet as we address the prospect of a bombing cessation, it becomes apparent that, however tenuous the military linkage, a political linkage has been allowed to develop. This is usually expressed in some variant of the phrase that a bombing halt would force US troops "to fight with one arm tied behind their backs." For example, on January 15 the senior Marine officer in Vietnam told the press that "there is a direct relationship between the number of American troops killed and the bombing—there is no argument about that. When the bombing stops, more Americans are killed."

In my judgment we thus confront a linkage that is in large part a military fiction, but at the same time a palpable political fact. From this I draw the conclusion that, if the President is to accept the consequences of a bombing halt, he must take a corollary decision to alter the ground strategy in ways that will reduce US casualties; otherwise, the domestic political risks may be too high.

One can (I would say parenthetically) make a strong argument that a different ground strategy, less ambitious in purely military terms and more explicitly devoted to protecting the populated areas of South Vietnam, would improve the likelihood of the kind of untidy, unpleasant compromise which looks like being the best available means of our eventual extraction from the morass. It would give us a better chance to develop a definable geographical area of South Vietnamese political and economic stability; and by reducing the intensity of the war tempo, it could materially improve the prospect of our staying the course for an added number of grinding years without rending our own society. But it is not my purpose to advance that kind of argument here.

The point to be made here is simply that, given the political link between bombing in the North and US casualties in the South, an aggressive ground strategy that generates high casualties may prove to be an insuperable obstacle to a bombing halt, even if such a halt is judged by US officials to be in the national interest.

As you know, the President himself has contributed to this linkage on recent occasions—notably in his State of the Union message and in awarding the Medal of Honor to an Air Force officer. . . . I do not know what assessment of bombing effectiveness lies behind his words on these occasions, but several key journalists, some of them entirely sympathetic to his dilemmas, believe he is now attributing to the bombing an importance that is seriously at odds with the San Antonio formula. They see a contradiction, but have refrained from pointing it out up to now, out of a concern that this would endanger the San Antonio formula.

If I may summarize:

a. Bombing of the North is making only a marginal military contribution;
b. The San Antonio formula (as clarified by you) recognizes that we can accept the military consequences of a bombing cessation, while the VC continue "normal" hostile actions, provided this leads to prompt talks;
c. Our ground strategy of attrition generates significant US casualties. If the strategy goes unchanged, the casualties are likely to continue and may even rise. But if they rise this will not be properly attributable, as a matter of military fact, to a bombing halt. The casualty levels are primarily a function of the strategy of attrition;
d. Notwithstanding the tenuous military link between US casualties and a bombing halt, it exists as a political fact. Accordingly, if the President decides that a bombing halt is appropriate, it appears that a scaling-down of the ground war would be a necessary corollary decision, in order to make acceptable the domestic political risks of the bombing halt.

I look forward to your coming to the Pentagon, and to working with you on a range of consequential problems in a period of evident storm. You have my abiding respect, and warm wishes for success.

Sincerely
Tim

Appendix B
Memo from Townsend
Hoopes to Clark Clifford,
March 14, 1968

March 14, 1968

Memorandum for the Secretary of Defense

SUBJECT: The Infeasibility of Military Victory in Vietnam

As a contribution to current deliberations and to your own ongoing review of the situation, this memorandum argues the case that the idea of military victory in Vietnam is a dangerous illusion, at any price that would be compatible with US interests, the interests of the people of South Vietnam, or the cause of world peace. Secretary Brown agrees that it should be forwarded for your consideration.

Military victory—that is, the destruction or ejection of NVN forces and the reduction of VC guerrilla forces to impotence or at least to a level that is manageable by ARVN alone—has been the implicit (though not always clearly recognized) goal of US policy at least since the decision to build up

American manpower in 1965. It continues to be the unexamined assumption of General Westmoreland's strategy, of his request for additional forces, of the JCS support for his strategy and his requests, and of all other proposals for intensifying or enlarging our war effort in Vietnam.

Moreover, military victory (as defined above) appears to be a necessary precondition for the realization of a US political objective which defines "free choice" for the people of SVN as a process necessarily excluding NLF/VC from participation in either elections or government. Whether or not this definition reflects the true US intent, it is clearly the position of the GVN and has not been rejected by the USG. As is known, even non-communist politicians are now being jailed by the GVN out of fear that they will open a dialogue with the NLF. These facts suggest that if military victory is not feasible, the US political objective must be redefined.

One's assumption about the necessity or feasibility of military victory is therefore a critical fork in the road. Reaffirmation will lead in the direction of a larger and wider war effort aimed at destroying the NVN/VC forces. Refutation will lead to adoption of a far less ambitious strategy, aimed at protecting the people of South Vietnam, permitting a stabilization of the US resource commitment at tolerable levels, and followed by a prompt, utterly serious effort to achieve a compromise settlement of the war that reflects the enduring political and military realities in Vietnam. It is imperative, at this watershed in our Vietnam experience, to subject the assumption to the most searching re-examination. Our future ability to formulate rational policies for VN depends on this.

The history of our involvement in Vietnam, particularly since 1965, has been marked by repeated miscalculations as to the force and time required to "defeat the aggression," pacify the countryside, and make the GVN and the ARVN viable without massive US support. Each fresh increment of American power has been justified as the last one needed to do the job. Responsible political and military officials have consistently underestimated NVN/VC strength and tenacity, have promoted uncritical notions of what US military power can accomplish in the political and geographical environment of SEA, and have indulged in persistently wishful thinking as regards the present capacity and real potential of the GVN and the ARVN. It is important that these misjudgments be kept in mind as we weigh the alternatives that now lie before us.

The following points contain some material that may already have come to your attention. The purpose here is to combine all of the relevant arguments and bring them to focus on the root question of whether military victory is feasible.

The Political Factors

1. The GVN is a narrowly based military clique. While it is systematically corrupt, this fact does not particularly distinguish it from other military governments in Asia ▬▬▬▬▬▬▬* What does distinguish the GVN are its inefficiency, lack of popular support, and inability to protect or govern large areas of SVN. These deficiencies are interrelated and mutually reinforcing; they are also, of course, gravely aggravated by the powerful challenge of the NVN/VC on both the political and military levels. For better or worse, it is Ho Chi Minh and Hanoi who have harnessed nationalism to their cause and who have demonstrated superior determination, organization, and fighting qualities. To survive without permanent massive US support, the GVN must win broader allegiance and extend its effective authority. Yet its will and ability to do either of these things have never been in greater doubt.

2. About 80% of the people of SVN (13.7 of 17.2 million) live in the principal cities, the province and district capitals, and the adjacent countryside. The effectiveness and survival of any political system in SVN requires that it exercise primary influence in these areas. Prior to the Tet offensive our public position was that 67% of the people were under GVN control; in fact, however, all evaluators recognized that the "C category" hamlets (comprising 31% of the rural population) were subject to considerable VC influence. At the end of 1967, therefore, the GVN actually had dominant influence over only about 30% of the population; pacification was on a tenuous and fragile footing, and heavily dependent on US/GVN military presence, even though the pacification effort had been greatly expanded during the year.

3. Although our information is still gragmentary, it appears that the recent NVN/VC offensive has achieved the takeover of a large part of the populated countryside. ARVN forces have pulled back to defensive positions around towns and cities, and many of the RD cadres have similarly withdrawn (according to CIA, at least half of the RD teams have left the countryside together with 23 of 51 ARVN battalions directly earmarked for pacification support. On the other hand, Robert Komer has given his personal estimate that 75% of the RD cadres are still in place). The status of RF and PF posts outside of cities and towns is mostly unknown, but there are scattered reports of units withdrawing or being overrun. It is probable that, in those areas where the NVA/VC have regained access to populations formerly under GVN control, they will quickly destroy the GVN structure by eliminating those individuals identified as agents and servants of the GVN.

*The black bars indicate where material was deleted by censors when the memos were declassified.

4. Although again the information is inconclusive, reports indicate that ARVN and US forces in the towns and cities are now responding to mortar fire from nearby villages by the liberal use of artillery and air strikes. This response is causing wide-spread destruction and heavy civilian casualties—among people who were considered only a few weeks ago to be secure elements of the GVN constituency. If this evidence is confirmed, it will be another example of our conceptions of military necessity working to undermine our political objective.

5. The present mode and tempo of operations in SVN is already destroying cities, villages and crops, and is creating civilian casualties at an increasing rate. Recent statistics suggest that perhaps 5% of the people of SVN are now homeless refugees. While this is not of course deliberate, US and ARVN forces are contributing heavily to the destruction and dislocation, and the people of SVN are aware of this. We are progressively tearing the country apart in order to win "the hearts and minds" of its people. Unfortunately, the end and the means are mutually exclusive.

The Bombing Campaign

6. The bombing campaign against North Vietnam has now entered its fourth year. Since the beginning of the air strikes in 1965, the flow of men and material from NVN to SVN has definitely increased. The bombing has inflicted heavy damage on NVN's economy and society as a whole ($370 million of measurable damage and the diversion of up to 400,000 people from agriculture to road repair, transport and air defenses). But Russia and China have provided economic and military aid substantially in excess of the damage, and the cost of the manpower diversion may be quite small, owing to the considerable slack in NVN's underemployed agricultural labor force. In addition, the manpower situation is eased by the presence of an estimated 50,000 Chinese support troops. China is no doubt prepared to send more forces than NVN would find comfortable politically.

7. US bombing operations against the North did not notably hinder the recent NVN/VC attacks on the cities during the Tet offensive, nor have they prevented the current buildup of forces at Khe Sanh, Hue and other points in I Corps. The NVN regular army, the VC main forces, the VC local forces now have better equipment and more effective weapons than in 1965, and the Soviets could provide them with even more sophisticated weapons.

8. NVN has gone over to decentralized, dispersed and protected modes of producing and handling essential goods and safeguarding the people. It has made a durable adjustment to the bombing. On balance, NVN is a stronger military power today than before the bombing began.

9. The air war in the North (route packages V and VI), and over Hanoi and Haiphong in particular, seems increasingly a techno-electronic contest between the US and the Soviet Union with diminishing relevance to the struggle in the South.

10. It may be possible to reduce the present infiltration capability by concentrating a greater bombing effort south of the Red River, especially by augmenting the currently productive attack against trucks in Laos. New technology, new tactics, and particularly such systems as the AC-130 gunship show promise of producing measurable improvement. However, to cut off the required minimal supply flow (50–150 tons per day) to SVN, we would have to improve our present effectiveness by a factor of four or more. Such an improvement is possible in principle.

Relative Ground Force Strengths

11. NVN has about 1.2 million fit males in the prime military age groups (17–35) of which only about 20% have thus far been inducted into the armed forces. This pool is enriched each year by about 120,000 physically fit males turning 17.

12. North Vietnam has present military forces of about 460,000. CIA has estimated that Hanoi intends to hold 225,000 to defend against invasion. Not more than 85,000 have been committed to SVN. NVA/VC pre-Tet strength in SVN was estimated to be about 145,000; but when guerrilla, administrative, infrastructure and special assaults squads are added, the total insurgency base in SVN is believed to approximate 450,000 men. This estimate does not consider heavy enemy losses since the end of January, but neither does it include additions or potential additions to the VC forces through recruitment and impressment immediately prior to Tet or in the ensuing weeks. The winter-spring offensive has given the VC access to a substantially larger proportion of both the urban and rural population.

13. If we should decide to meet General Westmoreland's requests for additional manpower, in whole or in part, the probably NVN response would be to offset our advantage by adding proportionate forces from NVN. Based on the relative manpower ratios that have existed over the past three years (during which time the fighting has ebbed and flowed, but has remained inconclusive), it appears that NVN could neutralize a 206,000 US augmentation by adding less than 50,000 men (a ratio of about 1 to 4).

14. On the basis of the untapped manpower resources enumerated above, and in view of the newly gained access to a greater portion of the SVN population, it seems evident that NVN could go on making offsets of this kind for an indefinite period. Nor is there anything to suggest that Hanoi lacks the will. However, even if we assume that additional US measures (e.g., closing Haiphong) were to reduce the infiltration capability, NVN would retain the option of reverting to a lower scale of warfare, and could take additional casualty-limiting actions to preserve its political and military organization in SVN if that were necessary (there is however nothing in the present situation to indicate that Hanoi is worried about attrition).

15. Assuming we continue to pursue the present strategy of attrition, we

would have to expect that US casualties would increase in roughly direct proportion to the higher level of effort. This could mean 1300–1400 KIA per month. Yet it would soon be evident that the increase in casualties had not altered the fundamental condition of stalemate in SVN.

16. There is accordingly no foreseeable military resolution of the conflict at either the present level of US forces (plus ARVN and other friendly forces) or with a full 206,000-man augmentation as requested by General Westmoreland. Nothing that we know of Hanoi's determination, manpower reserves, and available weapons supply, and nothing in the past record, gives us any basis for a confident judgment that we could attrite the enemy, drive him from SVN, or destroy his will to fight as a result of fully meeting General Westmoreland's new requests. What is called into question by these facts is the US strategy of attrition in SVN—the strategy of attempting to wear down the enemy by inflicting more casualties than he can cumulatively bear. Recognizing not only NVN's available manpower resources, but also China's endless millions in the background, the question arises whether a US strategy of attrition in SVN was ever in touch with reality.

Impact of the Westmoreland Requests

17. The further augmentation of US forces as proposed by General Westmoreland would entail very substantial costs in South Vietnam, in the United States, and elsewhere in the world.

18. In *South Vietnam,* the presence of more than 700,000 US forces would add to the already crushing weight of the American presence on that small country. Worst of all, it would encourage the GVN to believe that the US was prepared to go on fighting its war without making enforceable demands for either administrative efficiency or economic and social reform. It would further relieve pressure on ARVN to achieve a viable effectiveness. It would definitely weaken US leverage on the political situation.

19. A decision to provide 206,000 additional men in the next 12 months would also have a profound impact in the *United States.* It would require mobilizing 250,000 reserves, increasing draft calls, and facing up to substantially increased costs (the annual cost of the VN war would rise from about $25 billion to about $35 billion). Our balance of payments situation would be considerably worsened, and the run on remaining US gold reserves might strain the international monetary system to the breaking point. There would be need for a larger tax increase and possibly wage and price controls.

20. The need for public and Congressional support (both authority and money) of this further force buildup would almost certainly require political rhetoric designed to create an atmosphere of national crisis; yet, barring further dramatic reverses in SVN, the crisis would look synthetic to both war critics and impartial observers (in the sense that the case for larger forces had to be justified by the existence of a situation decisively different from the

situation prevailing over the past three years). Extremists in Congress would probably demand, as the price of their support, elimination of all restrictions on bombing of the North, and some might advocate measures designed deliberately to provoke a US confrontation with China or the USSR. There would also be pressures to expand the war into Laos and Cambodia, which, if yielded to, would only serve to spread thinner the US forces in SVN.

21. At the present level the war is eroding the moral fibre of the nation, demoralizing its politics, and paralyzing its foreign policy. A further manpower commitment to SVN would intensify the domestic disaffection, which would be reflected in increased defiance of the draft and widespread unrest in the cities. Welfare programs on which our domestic tranquility might depend would be eliminated or deeply cut. It is possible that well-placed dissenters in Congress could paralyze the legislative process.

22. The Soviet and Chinese reactions would probably not be extreme, if our additional actions were confined to increasing ground forces and tactical air forces. But they would almost certainly step up their level of materiel support to NVN, as a means of helping Hanoi to offset our manpower increases. Soviet policy would also manifest a notable hardening toward US-USSR relations on a wide range of issues, including possibly the Nonproliferation Treaty. Moreover, if the Soviets believed that our world-wide posture had become seriously unbalanced by the heavy deployments to Vietnam, it is possible that they would test our will in Europe or at other points (e.g., new pressure on Berlin, or stimulation of the Syrians to aggravate the already uneasy Middle Eastern situation).

23. Our progressive diplomatic estrangement would continue. The Scandanavian countries, already visibly wavering, might adopt an open anti-US position. The Labor Government in the UK, which is paying an increasing domestic price for its support of US policy in Vietnam, might be less willing or able to go on paying it.

The Alternative of Intensified Bombing

24. As an independent alternative to ground force augmentation, we could greatly increase the bombing of North Vietnam. There is no doubt that an *area* bombing campaign, with emphasis on closing the ports of Haiphong, Hon Gai, and Cam Pha, and on attacking over-the-beach deliveries, dispersed storage facilities, and the northeast and northwest rail lines leading into China could impose further serious strains on the already overstressed NVN social and economic structure. The hopeful assumption is that North Vietnam would then be forced to decide on a priority of imports—war-making goods vs. life-supporting goods—and would choose the latter.

25. Imports into North Vietnam during 1967 averaged about 4500 tons per day (400 tons of munitions, 500 tons of POL, 600 tons of other war supporting materiel, 1500 tons of manufactured goods and miscellany, and

1500 tons of food). The uninterdicted capacity for imports is about 15,000 tons per day; the US interdiction effort to-date is estimated to have reduced this to about 8,000 tons.

26. Should we undertake an expanded bombing effort, the Soviets, Chinese, and North Vietnamese could be expected to devote more effort to the movement of supplies by truck from China along the northeast and northwest routes, and to over-the-beach operations. In the face of such efforts and in the light of our Korean war experience, we could probably cut the NVN import capability in half—to 4,000 tons a day; and it is remotely possible that it would fall to 2,000 tons. But NVN could still import the required munitions and other war-supporting materiel, most of the needed POL, and anywhere from very little (at 2,000 tons) to most (at 4,000 tons) of the needed manufactured goods and food. Living standards in NVN would fall, but this would not necessarily interfere with the capability to support actions in SVN. Household handicraft and family food plots would probably sustain them.

27. Only by a bombing campaign aimed at crop destruction does it appear that food import requirements could be increased to near the interdicted import capacity (if they increased from 10% to 50% of total rice needs, the requirement would rise from 1,000 to 5,000 tons per day). Only this kind of increased food requirement could seriously impact on the current level of military imports.

28. In military terms, an intensified area bombing campaign could limit NVN actions in SVN at or near the pre-Tet level, and below the level of February 1968. But such a campaign (unless it included widespread crop destruction) would be unlikely to reduce NVN capability in SVN substantially below the 1967 level. It is possible that a more drastic reduction could be effected, but given the long season of poor bombing weather (between November and May, the weather permits an average of 5 days per month of visual bombing), the NVN transportation system would begin to be reconstituted.

29. Notwithstanding its probable inconclusiveness, an intensified area bombing campaign could have far-reaching military and diplomatic repercussions. A major effort to close Haiphong would have to accept serious risks of hitting Soviet shipping; and if Soviet ships were struck, the USSR could not fail to react. Reaction could cover a wide range of possibilities from introducing minesweepers and naval escort vessels carrying anti-aircraft guns, to providing bomber aircraft and pilots to NVN, to creating a diversionary crisis in Europe or the Middle East. We could be sure only that it would be an utterly determined reaction.

30. If the bombing campaign included crop destruction through the use of herbicides, we would have to expect "germ warfare" and similar charges from both Russia and China. The propaganda campaigns would be broadgauged, intense, and shrill. Our moral image both abroad and at home would suffer further damage.

31. Even without attempted crop destruction, an area bombing campaign aimed at destroying dispersed stockpiles located in or near populated

areas would lead unavoidably to much heavier levels of destruction and civilian casualties. NATO as a whole would be severely strained by inner division on the issue. Public opinion in Scandanavia and the UK would very probably force their governments to denounce US policy in VN. This might also happen in Australia, New Zealand, and Japan.

The Alternative of Unlimited Manpower

32. It is conceivable (but no more than that) that we could drive out or totally defeat the North Vietnamese in SVN, destroy the Viet Cong and its infra-structure, and thus provide the remaining South Vietnamese with a "free choice"—if we were to *treble* the number of US forces in SVN. As earlier noted, the present tempo of operations in SVN is already destroying cities, villages and crops, and is creating civilian casualties at an increasing rate. While this is not deliberate, our forces are contributing heavily to the de-struction. The commitment of 1.5 million men (or any number approaching that magnitude) would inevitably produce a policy of scorched earth. Even assuming the battle could be contained without the intervention of Chinese ground forces or Soviet air forces, and without a serious Russian diversionary action in another part of the world, we could hardly avoid totally crushing the country and its people, leaving a wasteland. As was said of the Romans at Carthage, "You made a desert and called it peace."

33. A *trebling* of effort would probably raise the US cost of the Vietnam War to about $85–90 billion per year. It is difficult to believe the American people would accept such a burden or such a risk. Disaffection would be rampant and bitterly deep. Large segments of our society would be totally alienated, and the processes of orderly government might be seriously dis-rupted by both internal dissension and public demonstrations. It would be difficult, if not impossible, to convince critics that the USG had any interest in peace talks or in settlement, or that it was not simply destroying South Vietnam in order to "save" it.

34. If there were a serious prospect (as there would be) that the NVN/VC effort would be totally defeated, China might well enter the war with large-scale combat forces. The Soviets would almost surely increase the quantity and the level of sophistication of its material support; it might introduce Russian pilots and bomber aircraft; and it would more than likely create a serious diversion in another part of the world. World opinion would totally condemn the US for a Carthaginian policy.

Conclusion

35. Anything resembling a clear-cut military victory in Vietnam appears possible only at the price of literally destroying SVN, tearing apart the social and political fabric of our own country, alienating our European friends, and gravely weakening the whole free world structure of relations and alliances. Russian or Chinese military intervention on the side of NVN, or at another geographical point in the world, would be a serious risk if we greatly increased our own effort. They clearly have the capacity, and give every evidence of having the will, to prevent the outright defeat of NVN.

36. By any rational scale of values, a military victory in Vietnam is therefore infeasible at any price consistent with US interests.

A Revised Policy and Strategy

37. What follows inexorab from the foregoing conclusion is the need for a redefinition of our political objective in Vietnam, and a basic shift in military strategy. The objective should be an honorable political settlement of the war followed by the organization of an international agreement to guarantee the military neutralization of Vietnam, Laos, and Cambodia. Our military strategy should accordingly be adjusted to give maximum support to a negotiating posture.

38. A well-coordinated program of action will of course require the detailed attention of the USG. In particular, the State Department must seriously tackle the unpleasant realities of a genuine compromise settlement to be hammered out in negotiations with a weakened, but not a beaten foe. To-date the matter has been carefully avoided, avoidance being sustained by the tacit assumption that negotiations would involve little more than ratification of the other side's surrender, or that there would be no negotiations at all, but only a "fading away" of the Viet Cong. Negotiations will be painful and might be protracted, and they will inevitably involve severely disappointing the present GVN.

39. If, however, these unpleasant realities are faced, the essential actions required are apparent. They are a cessation of the bombing to get talks started, as soon as we have regained our military poise; a shift of our forces to protection of the population centers; willingness to talk to the NLF and to accept a coalition government; organization of the international community, including especially the Soviet Union, to guarantee the military neutralization of Vietnam, Laos, and Cambodia; and ultimately the phased withdrawal of US forces.

Townsend Hoopes

Appendix C
Memo from Walt Rostow to the President, March 19, 1970

Mr. President:

SUBJECT: Decision to Halt the Bombing

This memorandum traces the origins of the decision to halt most of the bombing of North Vietnam on March 31, 1968, with special reference to the roles of Secretaries Rusk and Clifford. It touches on other elements as well, which the President took into account; namely, evidence of some communist interest in negotiations, post-Tet; other proposals for a peace initiative; and the improving military and political position in Vietnam during March, which made a peace initiative more palatable in Saigon, possibly more appealing in Hanoi. It is based on the written record available to us.

Background.

The notion of a peace initiative involving some kind of bombing halt or reduction was widespread in official circles and, more important, in your mind through the fall of 1967 and up to March 31.

For example, the special Vietnam group that met regularly on Thursday afternoons in Under Secretary Katzenbach's office (Katzenbach, Rostow, Nitze, and others) discussed this matter on many occasions. The President was also getting opinions from those not directly involved in the Vietnam problem. For example, on October 27, 1967, Harry McPherson sent the President a memorandum in which he said he thought "we should give new consideration to bombing the area fifty or a hundred miles north of South Vietnam, and indefinitely postponing further bombing around Hanoi and Haiphong."

The most serious bombing halt proposal during that period came on November 1, 1967, from Secretary of Defense McNamara. He made three basic recommendations: 1) stabilize the U.S. ground effort at existing levels; 2) plan a bombing halt before the end of the year; 3) in the South, try to (a) reduce U.S. casualities; (b) turn over increasing responsibility to the South Vietnamese; (c) steps to reduce destruction of property and lives.

The President asked Rostow to get reactions to the proposal from a number of advisers and officials, without naming the author of the plan. The reactions were heavily negative, except for Secretary Rusk who thought it wise to cut back on bombing in the Hanoi-Haiphong area, and Katzenbach who favored a qualified pause. Reactions to the McNamara plan are summarized in the Table [not reprinted here]. Detailed reactions were as follows: Rusk; Bunker; Westmoreland; Katzenbach; Fortas; General Taylor; Bundy (before McNamara proposal but on same subject); Rostow; and Clifford.

On December 18, 1967, after studying carefully the proposal and the views of all his advisers, the President took the unusual step of writing a memorandum for the file setting forth his own views on the bombing pause and other proposals. He opposed a total bombing cessation at that time on grounds that it would be read both in Hanoi and at home as a sign of weakening will. He added, however, that: "I would not, of course, rule out playing our bombing card under circumstances where there is reason for confidence that it would move us toward peace."

During this period, October to December 1967, the President was getting a growing body of intelligence describing Hanoi's plans for an all-out Winter-Spring offensive. He became increasingly convinced that any peace gestures at that time would have no effect on Hanoi, except the negative effect of convincing them that the United States was weakening in its resolve as regards Vietnam. This was a major thought in his talks with the Australian Cabinet in Canberra. He stated that Hanoi would not be interested in talks until it came to recognize it could not win militarily in the South. In Rome on December 23, 1967, in his meeting with the Pope the President had said in an aide memoir that a bombing pause would not be effective then. He added: "I would not exclude the possibility that it may again appear wise at some point."

This strand of thought was strengthened by much evidence that the enemy intended to use the offensive to increase his bargaining leverage. As Westmoreland said on January 22, 1968, (a week before the Tet offensive): "Enemy documents increasingly talk of the possibility of negotiations and of a coalition government."

Meanwhile, discussions were going forward on this matter in a variety of circles. In the Katzenbach Group, mentioned earlier, the idea of a bombing pause once the Winter-Spring offensive had been defeated took definite shape. This accounts for memos written by Rostow on March 4, March 6, March 16, March 21, and March 25, in which he foresaw a possible bombing pause in May if we used the intervening time to strengthen our military position in the field. Nitze mentioned this possibility at the March 4, 1968 meeting with the President.

Role of Secretary Rusk

The first reference in the written record to Secretary Rusk's interest in a bombing halt is at a meeting of February 27, 1968. These notes, taken by Harry McPherson, have McNamara reporting on alternatives in Vietnam. He spoke of accelerated military and economic programs combined with a "new peace offensive" as one alternative. Rust at that point is quoted as saying:

"basis for peace in Southeast Asia: ending of Communist assaults in Laos, Thailand; we will stop bombing North of 20th parallel if NVN withdraws from Quang Tri province; or stop altogether in that event; or some other specific proposal."

In his report of this meeting to the Ranch on February 27, Rostow notes that the following, among other key questions, were raised: "What sort of peace proposals, if any, should be included in the Presidential statement?"

On March 4, 1968, at a meeting in the Cabinet Room on the Wheeler-Westmoreland proposal, the question of getting into negotiations was raised. Rusk said:

"We would stop the bombing during the rainy period in the North." The President replied: "Really get on your horses on that."

The next day, March 5, there was another meeting, the Tuesday Lunch group.

The President asked: "What about the suggestion of last night?"

Rusk said: "There is one idea which would throw additional responsibility on Hanoi."

He then read the following proposed statement that the President might use or that might be released:

"After consultation with our allies, the President has directed that U.S. bombing attacks on North Vietnam be limited to those areas which are integrally related with the battlefield. No normal person could expect us to fail to provide maximum support for our men in combat. Whether this stage can be a step toward peace is for Hanoi to determine. We shall watch the situation carefully."

At mid-March, Ambassador Goldberg wrote to the President suggesting a total bombing halt. That proposal was sent to the President at the Ranch on March 16.

At the President's instruction, Secretary Rusk went out to Saigon with an "Eyes Only" cable for Ambassador Bunker. In the message the Secretary asked for Bunker's estimate of likely South Vietnamese reaction to both his (Rusk's and Goldberg's proposal—a partial, or total, bombing pause.

Bunker answered Rusk on March 20. Bunker said the Goldberg plan "would create the greatest difficulties for us here." He said, "I recommend strongly that we not pursue this course. . . ."

The second plan (Rusk's) would have most of the negative effects, he thought, but "it would be easier to obtain GVN concurrence."

At a meeting with the President in the Cabinet Room on March 20, 1968, there was a length discussion of Vietnam and the President's speech.

Rusk is quoted as saying: "Major peace proposals aren't promising unless there is a cessation of bombing. There are serious political and military risks to a bombing halt. We have been exploring bombing limitations in the North, leaving open the bombing above the DMZ.

Rusk is also reported in the notes as reading a statement on bombing that he proposed the President make. The notes do not include the text of Rusk's statement, however.

At this meeting Clifford spoke of stopping bombing north of the 20th parallel "if the enemy would stop artillery, mortars and rockets in the DMZ area."

M. Bundy opposed the idea of making it a "trade." Rusk agreed with him. He said we should just do it and say: "Whether or not this is a step toward peace is up to Hanoi."

On October 23, Harry McPherson sent the President a memo on bombing limitation. The President asked immediately for comments from Rusk, Clifford and Rostow.

Rusk sent the President a memorandum in reply on March 25. He had been thinking along the same lines, of course. He included, again, a paragraph stating the case as he wanted to see it made. The language is very close to the proposal he made on March 5, almost identical. Rusk also set forth his comments on the proposed partial halt and how he thought it should be handled. He defined "related to the battlefield" as meaning "up to Vinh."

Rusk had long since made up his mind that a partial bombing halt was feasible *if* the President wished to make a peace offer. His position was consistent from February 27 right down to March 31.

At a meeting at State on March 28, Rusk, Clifford, Rostow, McPherson and Possibly Bill Bundy, discussed the latest draft of the proposed speech. Clifford pointed out that it still contained nothing on a bombing pause. Rusk then dictated proposed language along the same lines as his earlier memoranda. He also instructed Bundy to summarize all the proposals in the draft speech—including the limited bombing halt—for transmission to Bunker for Thieu. It was agreed that McPherson would incorporate the bombing halt proposal in a draft and get it to the President immediately. That was done by 6 p.m. and it was discussed with the President in the Cabinet Room from 6:37 to 7:27 p.m. that day. The President then cleared the draft for transmission to Bunker. It went out shortly after 8:00 p.m. Sec. Rusk left for the Wellington, New Zealand, meeting of SEATO.

After the meeting with the President, McPherson did a complete redraft of the full speech, including the bombing pause, at 9:00 p.m.

Sec. Rusk sent a cable to Ambassador Bunker outlining the proposal and asking him to get the approval of the South Vietnamese leaders. Bunker's affirmative reply went up to the President at 8:05 a.m. Sunday, March 30th. The President then instructed us to seek the agreement of other allied leaders.

The Role of Secretary Clifford

At the February 27, 1968, meeting Secretary-designate Clifford did not speak of any peace proposals or comment on Rusk's suggestion.

On March 4, in his report to you on the Wheeler-Westmoreland proposal, Clifford said flatly that there should be "no new peace initiative on Vietnam."

On March 20, at the meeting with Goldberg, Clifford vigorously opposed a total bombing pause. He did favor some kind of limited bombing halt but thought we should make it conditional on Hanoi's doing something in return. Rusk said that would not work.

There is nothing immediately available on Clifford's reaction to the McPherson memorandum of March 23.

As noted earlier, at the meeting of March 28 Clifford argued strongly for inclusion in the President's statement of a partial bombing halt as a peace overture. In other words, his earlier opposition to a peace initiative (March 4) and then his advocacy of a qualified bombing pause insisting on reciprocity, had shifted by March 28 to the position Rusk had taken four weeks earlier. Clifford agreed to Secretary Rusk's draft passage for the speech.

Analysis of the Various Drafts of the March 31 Speech.

The speech drafts run from February 5, 1968, to March 31.

They begin with the concept of reporting to the nation the Tet offensive, the Pueblo affair, and the Blue House attack; putting them into perspective; and steadying the nation. The February 5 draft has no reference to peace initiatives. It does put forward certain measures to strengthen our forces in Vietnam, but it is clear the President decided to send Wheeler to Saigon before making any such recommendations to Congress.

The February 25 draft reasserts San Antonio, but goes no further. There is, however, a peace passage.

The February 27 draft (with Wheeler about to return) is the same; but that is the day Sec. Rusk is first recorded in the post-Tet period as mentioning a bombing stoppage at the 20th parallel.

Speech-drafting obviously stopped on Wheeler's return. The review began on February 28 of the toop [sic] proposals.

Then follow: Rusk's suggestion of March 4; proposal of March 5; cable to Bunker of March 16 (after the Goldberg proposal which went to the Ranch the same day); the Bunker reply of March 20; meeting with the President after Bunker's reply.

The March 20 draft I has the first new proposals: to announce a bombing limitation specified distances from Hanoi to Haiphong and to assert a U.S. and South Vietnamese willingness to negotiate a ceasefire. (McPherson's notes of meeting he dates March 19, but should be March 20, are in his speech file: at the meeting where Goldberg's proposition was debated, Rusk and Mac Bundy argued for an unconditional limited bombing halt.)

The March 20 draft II has that passage removed and returns, in effect, to San Antonio.

March 21 draft is, in this respect, like March 20 draft II. (On March 22 Bill Bundy proposed an elaborate restatement of San Antonio.)

The March 25 draft sticks with San Antonio; but on that day, at the President's instruction, Rostow sent the McPherson memorandum of March 23 to Clifford (12:38 p.m.). Sec. Rusk must have received it earlier, because his response went to the President at 2:25 p.m. on the 25th. In the speech file of the March 25 draft is some language consistent with Sec. Rusk's memo and McPherson's. It is marked "from Clark Clifford"; but the draft of March 26 (12:30 a.m.) incorporating "Clark Clifford's redraft of the military section" does not contain the section; and the March 26 redraft stays with San Antonio. The copy of the March 26 redraft marked "from Clark Clifford" has no notations on the San Antonio passage. (From internal evidence documents left behind at speech-draft meetings were apparently marked by

Harry McPherson's secretary with the name of the man who left them; for example, a State Department cable drafted by Bill Bundy is also marked "from Clark Clifford.")

On March 28 at Sec. Rusk's office, Sec. Clifford expressed his dissatisfaction with the existing draft on, essentially, political grounds: "It offers nothing—neither hope nor plan for either military victory or negotiated settlement." With Sec. Rusk and Bill Bundy participating, Sec. Rusk's proposal of February 27, March 4, March 5, and March 25, was put into language for an alternative draft to be submitted to the President. By 9:00 p.m. March 28, Harry McPherson had redrafted the whole speech, with the peace proposal as the lead-off. (Rostow, who was present, recalls no serious debate or disagreement about submitting this now-familiar proposal in writing to the President.) At Sec. Rusk's instruction, Bill Bundy drafted a summary of the proposal (and other elements in the draft of the 28th) for Bunker's comment. It was despatched (obviously with the President's approval) March 29. The President's decision to move forward was almost certainly taken at a meeting on March 28 in the Cabinet Room at 6:37–7:37 p.m. Rostow had called Jim Jones at 2:45 p.m. stating that "Rusk, Clifford, Rostow, and McPherson have completed their discussions and Harry is now working on an alternate text. They would like to meet with the President for direction late this afternoon or early tonight." Harry had a draft by 6:00 p.m., and another at 9:00 p.m., after the session with the President.

Refinements of language were made on March 29 and March 30; but essentially the matter was settled on the evening of March 28.

Communist Interest in Negotiations, Post-Tet.

As noted earlier, the pre-Tet documents on the Winter-Spring offensive indicated, on balance, that it was designed to achieve a sufficient improvement in the military and political situation (the latter, via urban uprisings) to make viable a negotiation with the U.S. of a coalition government.

As early as February 4th and 8th, Bunker reported Thieu's view that the offensive was linked to an intent to negotiate.

On February 21, Goldberg, Clifford, Katzenbach, Harriman and W. Bundy went over with U Thant reports via the French in Hanoi and others that a bombing halt would lead to immediate talks and possibly mutual de-escalation if the bombing halt were officially notified to Hanoi. Confirmed in writing by U Thant on February 22, at U.S. request.

On February 26 ▬▬▬▬▬▬▬▬ report that a North Vietnamese official had said: "Ho is waiting, but has insisted that the bombing be stopped first."

On March 3 ▬▬▬▬▬▬▬ report of a Secretary of a VC District Committee, also member of a VC Province Committee, who indicated that negotiations between the NLF and the GVN might not be ruled out, while confirming that the Tet offensive might have a political objective.

██████████████ Sec. Rusk, on March 7th, asked that this item be called to the President's attention. Evidently it fitted his proposal of March 4 and 5th.

On March 8th we received two reports from Paris (French and Polish sources) that Hanoi was receding from its Tet political objective in view of actual results and might settle for less than a Communist-dominated coalition government.

████████████████

In short, the notion of negotiations in the aftermath of Tet was built into our understanding of the Winter-Spring offensive; and the possibility was repeatedly confirmed by post-Tet intelligence placed in the hands of the President. The evidence was *not* firm enough to give the President or others confidence that the March 31 proposal would lead to negotiations. It *was* sufficient to leave open the possibility that it *might* succeed.

Additional Peace Proposals, From In and Outside the Executive Branch.

While the Rusk and (then) Goldberg proposals were brought to the President's attention—discussed and debated—and while he was receiving word of various more or less forthcoming Communist hints, the President was being bombarded by a wide range of more or less pacific propositions from inside and outside the Executive Branch of the Government.

After the U Thant session, he went to Paris and the French issued a communique confirming their information from Hanoi that "an unconditional cessation of American bombardment of North Vietnam would be a necessary and sufficient condition for the opening of peace negotiations."

On February 29th the President received word via Bill Douglas from ████████████████ had received rather explicit and heartening responses to clarifying questions about negotiations.

As noted earlier, Rostow, starting on March 6, kept raising the possibility of a peace offensive about May 1, after we had weathered the Winter-Spring offensive and strengthened our hand, if necessary by additional military measures.

On March 4, Sec. Rusk, via a rare personal letter, called the President's attention ████████████████

On March 7, Gov. William Guy urged announcement of "our disengagement from offensive action in South Vietnam and against North Vietnam."

On March 9th, Max Taylor, in a memorandum to the President, states, at the end of an analysis of the military situation and options, "These considerations encourage the belief that an end—or at least the start of negotiations—may not be far off and we should place ourselves in the best possible position in anticipation of such a development."

On March 9 Rostow forwarded to the President a State Dept. document requested by the President at the previous Tuesday lunch. It was a massive compendium of "affirmative suggestions" for "Alternate Vietnam Policies by Key U.S. Public Figures and Organizations." It covered pre-Tet as well as post-Tet suggestions.

On March 11, ■■■■■■■■■■■■■ came in to see Rostow with a peace proposal for negotiations and "mutual de-escalation" to be initiated by a neutral country. Rostow referred ■■■■■■■■■■ Bunker was queried and responded on March 23d.

On March 11, Drew Pearson said he was leaving the President on Vietnam and filed a proposal for U.S. withdrawal to be negotiated by someone "the Russians like and trust, such as Justice William O. Douglas or Senator Bobby Kennedy." It suggested: "It may be necessary during the course of the negotiations to stop the bombing."

On March 12 Carl Marcy forwarded to Rostow a "late 1967 proposal, seen by Senator Fulbright, for total U.S. withdrawal from the Asian mainland over a period "not to exceed two years." It went to the President on March 14.

On March 14, Dean Acheson proposed a study leading to a policy "looking towards progressive disengagement over whatever period of time we judge appropriate."

Unknown to the President, on March 14 Bill Bundy, although opposed to a peace move "at the present time," which would above all "alarm Saigon extremely," said: "I *do* believe that your idea of a tactical cutback in the bombing justified for military reasons, is worth trying on Ambassador Bunker." This was done on March 16th, along with the Goldberg proposal.

On March 18 the President received Chet Bowles' proposal for a bombing cessation if various countries (including the USSR) "take responsibility" from that moment on to bring about "meaningful negotiations."

On March 21, Dick Bolling suggested we pick up from the Rockefeller camp the idea of "an Asian settlement."

On March 22, at the President's instruction, Rostow forwarded a bombing halt proposal to John Walsh to be included among "the alternatives" to be examined by the outside advisers.

On March 29, in a speech on China policy, Senator Mansfield proposed to make clear we are prepared at all times to discuss the Vietnam problem with Chinese representatives.

Improvement of Military and Political Situation in Vietnam.

The President's problem in March—with respect to troops (and, therefore, the budget and dollar)—and with respect to a negotiating initiative—was greatly eased by military and political progress beyond the expectations of the greatest immediate post-Tet optimists. This is reflected in the various reports the President received.

As a benchmark, there is Rostow's memo to the President of February 5, indicating the potentialities for "a shortening of the war" if: "the cities are cleared up and held against possible follow-on attacks; the GVN demonstrate effective political and relief capacity; we hold the Khe Sanh; we hold U.S. opinion steady on course."

On February 15 Bob Ginsburgh cited very tentative evidence to Rostow that North Vietnamese units might be moving *away* from Khe Sanh. This information was shared with the President in the Situation Room, the uncertain nature of the evidence being underlines.

In a summary of February 23, Rostow reported from Westy that "for the first time General Abrams was permitting himself to be somewhat encouraged." But he added: "I suspect Bus will report considerable anxiety in Saigon."

The President received Gen. Wheeler's assessment of February 27 the next morning. It is temperately optimistic; asserts 1968 is key year; but requests a "theater reserve" of 2 divisions for Westy as a matter of prudence.

On February 29 and March 1, Wheeler and Gen. Johnson suggested the daily post-Tet phone call to Westy could be shifted to once a week, as Wheeler notes progress in opening Route 1 and at Khe Sanh. President agrees.

On March 3, Westmoreland filed a report on our "offensive operations in Vietnam."

On March 4, Westmoreland filed a "rather heartening report" on state of U.S. and Vietnamese manpower in combat units.

On March 9, a report was forwarded to the President that enemy manpower around Khe Sanh "may have fallen to 6-8000," ▬▬▬▬▬▬▬

On March 13 Rostow reports: "In general, the battle is in a curious phase in Vietnam: no clear enemy attack plan discernible; clock ticking on good supply weather in Laos and poor weather at Khe Sanh; our side moving slowly over to the initiative in I Corps, III Corps, and IV Corps."

On March 14, "the first mildly hopeful report from the Delta," as General Thang takes over, where a great deal of post-Tet anxiety centered.

On March 14, Bunker's weekly reports progress with respect to Thieu's leadership, relief and reconstruction, movement back into the countryside, and military manpower. "Perhaps the most negative development this week has been the obvious tendency on the part of some Vietnamese leaders to return to politics as usual."

On March 15, Westmoreland reports his plan to go on the offensive in I Corps, about April 1.

On March 20, Bunker reports allied forces "have increasingly assumed the initiative" and that pacification damage "not nearly" as great "as we thought or the press still reports." Enemy being pushed away from cities. Large caches uncovered. Etc.

On March 22, the tough-minded ▬▬▬▬▬▬▬ in the Delta is increasingly optimistic.

The President was forwarded on March 25th a March 19 letter from

■■■■■■■■■■■■■■ with a vivid account of high post-Tet civilian moral in Saigon—an analysis subsequently vindicated by events.

On March 27th, the President received Dr. Phan Quang Dan's detailed, optimistic assessment of the Vietnamese people's reaction to the Tet offensive.

On March 28th, the President receives data on sharp increase in February 1968 over February 1967 Vietnamese draftees and volunteers (totals: 17,106 versus 7,930); and instructs the figures go to McPherson for insertion in speech draft.

On March 29th, Bunker's weekly cable shows progress on many fronts.

On April 3, Bunker reports: ". . . one immediate result of the speech is evidence of greater determination on the part of Vietnamese to shoulder the burdens of the war effort."

W. W. Rostow

Index

OF